Epigraphic Approaches to Indus Writing

Dedicated to Dave Kelley who got me started,
and to C. C. Lamberg-Karlovsky who would not let me quit

Epigraphic Approaches to Indus Writing

Bryan K. Wells

Oxbow Books
Oxford and Oakville

Published by Oxbow Books on behalf of the American School of Prehistoric Research.

ISBN 978-1-84217-994-9

Indus Seal H99-4064/8796-1 from Harappa Period 3C. Drawing courtesy of J. Mark Kenoyer and HARP (Harappa Archaeological Research Project). © HARP.

Fragment of an Indus seal from an early level of the Harappa phase at Harappa (Period 3A). H90-1600. © HARP.

Library of Congress Cataloging-in-Publication Data

Wells, Bryan K.
Epigraphic approaches to Indus writing / Bryan K. Wells.
    p. cm.
Includes bibliographical references and index.
ISBN 978-1-84217-994-9
    1. Indus script. I. Title.

PK119.5.W45 2011
491'.1--dc22   2010051319

TYPESET AND PRINTED IN THE UNITED STATES OF AMERICA

Contents

Preface

Bryan K. Wells

Introduction

The primary focus of this book is the Indus Script, a writing system employed from 2600 to 1900 BC in an area of what is today Pakistan and northwestern India. There is a long history of research into this ancient script, including many proposed decipherments (Possehl 1996). To date no decipherment has received widespread acceptance by the academic community and in my opinion the script remains undeciphered. This situation results from restrictive nature of Indus inscriptions (they are mostly short) and the fact that the Indus language is unknown.

This study examines the Indus script using an expansive database, detailed sign list and software specifically designed for this project - the Interactive Concordance of Indus Texts program (ICIT 5.2). The database contains information describing 3,835 inscribed artifacts, including ≈8,000 photographs and drawings, and 17,423 Indus signs. The sign data are represented by a replacement font (sign list) and are used by the ICIT 5.2 program in the analysis of Indus texts.

This book is organized into seven chapters as follows: Chapter 1 describes the database, its problems and the methods of data acquisition. Further, it describes the chronology and spatial distribution of Indus inscriptions, and defines the terms used in the rest of the book. Chapter 2 examines the phenomena of potters' marks using a wide range of geographic and temporal contexts. The question of whether the Indus script's sign inventory was derived in whole or in part (or not at all) from potters' marks is addressed. Chapter 3 examines the signs of the Indus script focusing on the mechanics of sign construction and the definition of the

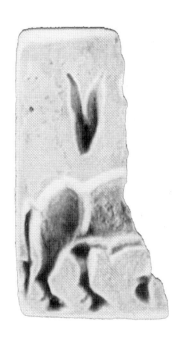

P.1 *Fragment of an Indus seal from an early level of the Harappa phase at Harappa (Period 3A). H90-1600.* © HARP.

graphemes. Sign distributions and their significance are also examined in detail. In Chapter 4 methods of decipherment in general, and the structure of the Indus texts are discussed. Additionally, a typology of Indus texts is suggested. In Chapter 5 the Indus number system is defined. Chapter 6 examines the evidence for the identity of the Indus language. Chapter 7 presents a set of observations regarding the Indus script that require further research or are of general interest in the study of the script.

The order of the chapters is not random. They are arranged so that arguments regarding the functions and uses of Indus signs, and the mechanics of writing can be elucidated from various perspectives. Based on these arguments the following arguments are made:

1) the Indus script developed autochthonically and drew upon the potters' marks of Baluchistan and northern Pakistan for inspiration;

2) the Indus script is logo-syllabic. That is, it uses both word signs and word building signs. Based on sign contexts it is possible to identify some signs as either logographs or syllables;

3) the method of combining signs into longer strings uses prefixing, infixing and suffixing;

4) sign order and the order sign clusters within texts are relatively consistent. This characteristic suggests syntax;

5) the mechanics of text construction eliminate Dravidian languages as root language candidates. Proto- and Para-Munda cannot be either eliminated nor verified as the Indus root language, and consequently remains a candidate in need of further research;

6) the Indus number system is complex and uses three basic systems supplemented by several special numerals. These systems count from 1 to 7 (Short Linear), 2 to 9 (Short Stacked) and 1 to 6 (Long Linear). Larger numbers are formed using strings of numerals; and,

7) the Indus Script may not be decipherable given the current situation, but the situation is such that the discovery of a continuous text of 50 or more signs could make decipherment possible.

The main purpose of this book is to dispel many of the misconceptions concerning the Indus script and to demonstrate that, given an adequate database and systematic treatment, real progress towards a deeper understanding of the Indus script is possible. Towards this end structural analysis was used in the definition of Indus signs and in the delineation of the syntax of Indus texts.

Contributor List

Bryan K. Wells
15A Oregon Road
Campbell River, British Columbia V9W 1H8
Canada
E-Mail: bdkj.wells@gmail.com

C. C. Lamberg-Karlovsky
Stephen Phillips Professor of Archaeology
Department of Anthropology
Harvard University
Peabody Museum
Cambridge, Massachusetts 02138
USA

Foreword

C. C. Lamberg-Karlovsky

> In the battle between truth and prejudice, waged in the field
> of history books, it must be confessed that the latter usually wins.
> - Stephen Runciman

Bryan Wells has spent the majority of his academic life puzzling over ancient scripts. Although he has contributed to the nature of the Maya script his academic career is spent puzzling over the Indus script. He came to Harvard as a graduate student intent on continuing his study of the Indus Civilization and its script. A study he began as an undergraduate. He was, and remains, committed to the idea that the Indus script represents writing and its decipherment will lead to an understanding of its texts and language. He did not think that at Harvard his dedication to this goal would meet with resistance. It did. This volume is a substantially revised edition of his doctoral dissertation.

Bryan's dissertation committee consisted of myself as Chair and Dr. Richard Meadow and Professor Michael Witzel. A near final draft of his dissertation was rejected by Meadow and Witzel. Bryan was required to return from Germany to confront and ostensibly correct and address its shortcomings. The basic problem was that Professor Witzel, influenced by Steve Farmer, had concluded that the Indus script was neither writing nor representative of a language.*

* See 'The Collapse of the Indus Script Thesis: The Myth of Literate Harappan Civilization' by Steve Farmer, Richard Sproat and Michael Witzel, 2004. "http://www.safarmer.com/downloads" http://www.safarmer.com/downloads. Steve Farmer believes the Indus signs to be magical symbols.

In light of Professor Witzel's strong commitment to the non-writing nature of the Indus script Bryan's effort was deemed spurious and unacceptable. Richard Meadow, less strident in his view as to the nature of the Indus script, nevertheless advised Bryan to "tone down" his view that the Indus represented 'writing'. Approximately six weeks were spent as Professor Witzel balked at any mention of the Indus being a script and having a logo-syllabic nature. He insisted that Bryan substitute the word 'marks' or symbols' for script. He was initially in opposition to the entire thesis. A Professor's opinion, which, in this case is a minority view within the profession, should never be used to impose or prevent an alternative hypothesis from being addressed by a Ph.D. candidate. It was not as if Bryan was addressing an untenable, absurd hypothesis. He was to spend weeks of uncertainty, anxiety, and, in a state of near depression he puzzled over what to do. The consternation endured and expenses incurred effected his entire family. He needed little encouragement from me to persist in his efforts and to maintain his approach of identifying the number of signs used in the Indus texts, their variations, and their logo-syllabic nature. With the passing of time and considerable discussion, and contrary to the quote from Stephen Runciman, the quest for truth was to prevail over prejudice. Perhaps, in the context of the confrontation between a contingent of a dissertation committee and a doctoral candidate one may recall the more positive optimism voiced by John Milton in *Areopagitica* (1644):

> Where there is much desire to learn, there of necessity will be much arguing, much writing, many opinions; for opinion in good men is knowledge in the making"

After several meetings of the dissertation committee, opinions gave way to reason. In response to Professor Witzel's demand that Bryan take into consideration the alternative views of Farmer, Sproat and Witzel, Bryan added the following two paragraphs, which accurately summarize the conclusion of the confrontation, and which appeared in his dissertation:

> Arguments have been made on the internet and in self-published e-journals that the Indus script is not writing but rather merely a symbol system not linked to a specific language (Farmer et. al. 2004). The argument is that the texts are too short, there are too many singly occurring signs (singletons) and too few high frequency signs, no commonly repeating signs, and no perishable or monumental texts.
>
> Many scholars currently working on the Indus script have dismissed this theory as highly unlikely and poorly conceived (personal communications from M. Coe, G. Possehl, A. Parpola, D. H. Kelly, S. Bonta and others). More importantly, many of the arguments and several of the issues raised by this theory are dealt with in this dissertation, with the data presented here refuting this theory, with regard to the Indus system of writing.'

Much is made in the Farmer, Sproat and Witzel thesis that the Indus is not writing and certainly cannot represent a language because there are too many single, non-recurring signs (singletons). This, as so much else in their thesis can be readily refuted. In fact, as Bryan readily documents the number of singletons in the Mesopotamian Proto-Cuneiform are almost identical to those in the Indus script while the Proto-Elamite script has more singletons than those in the Indus script. No-one has ever challenged the nature of Proto-Cuneiform or Proto-Elamite as scripts representative of a language.

Bryan has spent decades working on the Indus script. He makes NO claim of decipherment. His work has concentrated upon the development of a computer program that assists in identifying the number of signs, their variations, identifying specific signs that occur as nearest neighbors to other specific signs, identifying numerical systems, and offering the archaeological context in which the texts containing signs were discovered. Each and every one of these approaches are essential foundations upon which an eventual decipherment may become a reality. Bryan's approach has been quantitative, contextual, and empirical. It is based on the analysis of as large a corpus of Indus objects containing scripts as has ever been tackled. The completion of Bryan's dissertation unfolded as more of a trial than an open-minded quest for a better understanding of an intractable problem.

It is all too well known that the nature of the Indus script has been a volatile subject of debate for well over seventy-five years. Some scholars have offered full decipherments while others dismiss them out-of-hand as 'writing'. In each of the above cases opinions have been presented as facts. Some have championed decipherments in the interests of nationalism, 'proving' the texts to have Vedic, Aryan, and/or proto-Hindu content and iconography, others champion Dravidian, or even proto-Munda.

The Indus script has NOT been deciphered. In fact, there is not a single sign that can be said to have a specific 'reading'. Of the hundreds that have been involved in the study of the Indus script, Bryan Wells joins a relatively small number, most recently Asko Parpola, Walter Fairservis, and Iravatham Mahadevan, who have worked hard to make a meaningful contribution toward its understanding. In a recent manuscript submitted for publication, Bryan offers a compelling argument for the identification of numbers and a numbering system. Lastly, this book was sent out for peer-review to several distinguished scholars involved in the archaeology, history, and language of south Asia. We are grateful to them for their serious and constructive criticisms and for their unanimous support for the publication of this volume.

List of Figures and Tables

Figures

Tables

1

DATA COLLECTION AND RELIABILITY, CHRONOLOGY, AND THE TYPOLOGIES OF ARTIFACTS AND ICONOGRAPHY

Electronic corpus of Indus texts

The Indus script is an ancient south Asian script that remains undeciphered. It dates to between 2600 and 1700 BC and consists of more than 650 signs arranged in texts whose average length is five signs. This count of signs is likely close to the maximum number for the script, because when two sign cannot be combined with certainty they are kept separate. Indus texts are found almost exclusively on small artifacts and ceramics. The corpus consists of 3,833 texts with 17,427 signs.

It is necessary to create an electronic corpus of inscribed Indus artifacts for several reasons. First, there are many errors and omissions in the published Corpus of Indus Seals and Inscriptions [CIST] (Joshi and Parpola 1987; Shah and Parpola 1991). In fact, the CIST contains only about 56% of the extant Indus texts and does not give any archaeological information other than the site name and identification number tied to the publication or museum for any of the artifacts listed in it. Conversely, it is the only source for inscriptions from many Indus sites, and is therefore an important source in the construction of a more complete corpus. More complete listings of the Indus texts are available (Koskenniemi and Parpola 1979; Mahadevan 1977), but these rely heavily on sign fonts that have many problems. These problems are discussed in detail in Chapter 3. Additionally, neither of these sources give the details of archaeological contexts. An adequate corpus of Indus texts is further necessitated by the lack of other key details concerning the Indus script.

The Indus script has resisted decipherment for over 75 years and there are several good reasons for this:

1) no bilingual texts;
2) unknown language(s);
3) no long texts;
4) unknown type of script;
5) poor chronological control;
6) no adequate corpus; and,
7) no comprehensive sign list.

Some of these obstacles are a matter of luck (1 and 3) and this situation may change with further excavation. Additionally, some of these obstacles can be overcome through research (4, 5, 6, and 7). Point 2 is a more intractable problem and is dealt with in Chapter 6. As things stand, nothing can be said about the language(s) of the Indus people that is not tentative or speculative. To further complicate this issue the possibility exists that within the boundaries of the Indus Civilization (≈ 1 million square km) more than one language was spoken and written. It may be possible to discover the language(s) of the Indus people through a careful analysis of sign use and patterns of replacement, but this sort of detailed analysis is only possible with an adequate corpus and comprehensive sign list in hand. Finally, it was my intent from the beginning of this research to create an analytical computer program, Interactive Concordance of Indus Texts (ICIT). The data source for this analytical program is the Electronic Corpus of Indus Texts (ECIT).

The goals of the ECIT project were fourfold: 1) to assemble all available published information relating to inscribed Indus artifacts - to bring together the texts, artifact descriptions, and their archaeological contexts. The collection of these data is dependent on the availability of publications about the artifacts. Some sites have not been published (Kalibangan) and some are inadequately published (Lothal). Nevertheless, the information as it stands will enhance our ability to analyze the Indus Script; 2) to classify texts on the basis of artifact type, text type, and iconography using the photographs and drawings as available (Tables 1.1-1.2, and Figures 1.1-1.3); 3) to create a detailed sign list including variations; and, 4) to collect data for the ICIT program.

There are several sources of drawings and photographs of inscribed Indus artifacts. The most useful of these data sources are the site reports, especially from the period from 1937 to 1940. These reports are a major source of photographs, drawings and descriptive data for more than 3,000 inscribed artifacts from the two largest and best known Indus sites - Mohenjo-daro (Marshall 1931; Mackay 1938) and Harappa (Vats 1940). As stated earlier the CIST (Joshi and Parpola 1987; Shah and Parpola 1991) is of limited use because of its many omissions and errors. It is primarily useful as a source of photographs. To further complicate matters some inscribed artifacts are only published as journal articles.

This is especially true of the artifacts from outside the Indus Valley proper. Several edited volumes and popular books about the Indus Civilization have been published, and these form a minor but useful component of the literature dealing with Indus texts. How can all of this material be brought together to create a comprehensive listing of inscribed artifacts?

The strategy applied here is to deal with the early site reports first, as they are the richest sources of data. Next, the CIST can be used as a source of better quality photographs, and as a source for previously unpublished artifacts. These data can then be supplemented with information from journals and other publications. In the case of Harappa the interim reports of the Harappa Archaeological Research Project (HARP; Meadow and Kenoyer 1993; Meadow et al. 1994, 1995, 1996, 1997, 1998, 1999, 2001) added greatly to the inventory of artifacts. At the end of the ECIS project 5,643 artifacts from 58 sites were encoded into the database. With the sign entries, typological, and archaeological data combined, this resulted in the coding about 70,000 pieces of information describing inscribed Indus artifacts. Among these entries were sign numbers for 18,680 signs in the Indus Script.

Of the 5,643 artifacts 3,835 of these bare recognizable Indus texts and of these 2,289 were complete inscriptions. Items without signs - either because of damage or design - as well as potters' marks and drawings were omitted from the ICIT database. The 5,040 artifacts were inscribed with various iconographic elements, including scenes of the Indus people involved in various activities (n = 52), and various types of animals, plants and geometric symbols (Figures 1.1-1.3). While Indus signs are found inscribed on 32 different types of artifacts made from 21 different materials, but the vast majority are made of steatite (2,356) or ceramics (1,212). Seals (2,487) and miniature tablets (1,543) were the common artifact types in the ECIT database.

The data for the interactive concordance (ICIT) were extracted from the ECIT, resulting in 3,835 texts from 48 sites with at least one recognizable Indus sign. The first task in the analysis of ICIT texts is the comparison of sign contexts in order to further define graphemic boundaries. This process is discussed in detail in

Table 1.1 Typology of inscribed Indus artifacts

Abbreviation	Item	Description
TAB	Miniature tablets	
	B	Bas relief
	I	Incised
	C	Copper
POT	Pot sherds or ceramic vessels	
	T	Text
		s - Seal
		g - Graffiti
		p - Paint
	M	Potters' mark
	D	Drawing
SEAL	Intaglio carved seals	
S	Square	
	R	Rectangular
	C	Circular
	O	Oval
	CY	Cylinder
	L	Lenticular
	Ot	Other
TAG	Clay with impressions of intaglio seals	
	P	Palm sealing
	C	Cube sealing
	R	Pot rim sealing
	L	Sealing on textile or reed
	W	Wooden strips or poles
	B	Box
	Ot	Other
BNGL		Bangle
ROD		Cylindrical shaped, of any material
IMPL		Implement or tool
BEAD		Bead
MDLN		Medallion
MISC		All other artifacts not covered by the other categories

Table 1.2 Field symbols

a) Living Things
Bulls:

i:	*Bos* sp. (unicorn bull)	
i2:	*Bos* sp. with two horns	
	a.	Horns forming a "U"
	b.	Parallel forward facing horns
	Bull:i body markings:	
	M	= Mask
	I	
	II	
	O	
	Q	
	S	
	T	
	J	
	U	
	V	
	W	
	X	= Other
ii.	*Bos gaurus* (gaur)	
iii.	*Bubalus* sp. (Indian buffalo)	
iv.	*Bos indicus* (zebu)	
Capra - Goat:		
1		
2		
3		
4		
5		
6		
7		
8		
Elep	*Elephas maximus* (Indian elephant)	
Tigr	*Panthera tigris* (tiger)	
Htgr	Horned tiger	

Chapter 3. It is sufficient for the present to say that this resulted in the redefinition of the sign list and the assignment of final sign numbers to the sign font graphs. The final sign numbers were then integrated back into the ICIT. The completion of this phase of my research into the Indus script puts in place all of the data and software for the next step in the analysis of the texts (Chapter 4).

Factors influencing the reliability of the data

There are several important biases in the data collected for the ECIT. The first of these is a geographic bias. There are no texts from Cholistan, and only 21 from Dholavira in the ICIT. The reason for this is that this material has not been adequately published. The publication by Mughal (1997) of the Cholistan material includes only

Table 1.2 Field symbols (continued)

Rhin	*Rhinoceros unicornis* (Indian rhinoceros)
Gavi	*Gavialis gangeticus* (gavial)
Turt	Turtle
Comp	Composite animal
Scene	Pictorial representations of events
Anth	Anthropomorphic
Phyt	Phytomorphic
T-M-T	Tiger-Man-Tiger
Bird	Bird
Hare	Hare
Mult	Multiple field objects
None	There is clearly no field object
Othr	Items that do not fit into any of the above categories

b) Geometric Seals

Swas	Swastika
Cros	Cross
Maze	Maze
Box	Boxes
Bult	Bullet
Xdot	An "x" with dots around
Xhch	Crosshatched
T	Interlocking "T"s
Loop	Interlocking loops
Crs	An "X" with crosses
Hrls	Hourglass-shaped
Star	Asterisk-shaped
Beye	Bull's eye
Pipal	A pipal leaf
X	X-shaped
Fish	Like sign 220, etc.
Tri2	Two triangles
Tri3	Three triangles
Tri4	Four triangles
Misc	All others

very small photographs of inscribed potsherds most often without giving the sites of origin.

Another problem is the accuracy of the data given in the site reports from Harappa (Vats 1940) and Mohenjo-daro (Marshall 1931; Mackay 1938). The vast majority of the depth data is given to the nearest 6 inches. This means that detailed analysis of the relationship between artifacts is not possible. This problem is compounded by the fact that the planner provenience of artifacts is given at a very gross scale: at Harappa as a 20 yard-square grid, and at Mohenjo-daro to the section/area/block/house/room. The rooms of Mohenjo-daro vary greatly in size. To compensate for this Mackay (1938) gives find spots, and there can be several of these per room. The advantage of the Mohenjo-daro data is that the context of the data

Figure 1.1 Field symbols, Part 1: Living things and signs.

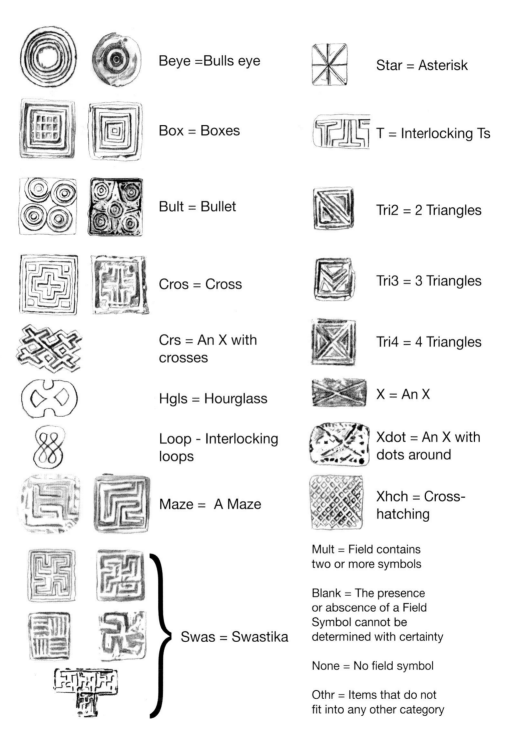

Beye = Bulls eye

Box = Boxes

Bult = Bullet

Cros = Cross

Crs = An X with crosses

Hgls = Hourglass

Loop - Interlocking loops

Maze = A Maze

Swas = Swastika

Star = Asterisk

T = Interlocking Ts

Tri2 = 2 Triangles

Tri3 = 3 Triangles

Tri4 = 4 Triangles

X = An X

Xdot = An X with dots around

Xhch = Cross-hatching

Mult = Field contains two or more symbols

Blank = The presence or abscence of a Field Symbol cannot be determined with certainty

None = No field symbol

Othr = Items that do not fit into any other category

Figure 1.2 Field symbols, Part 2: Geometric shapes.

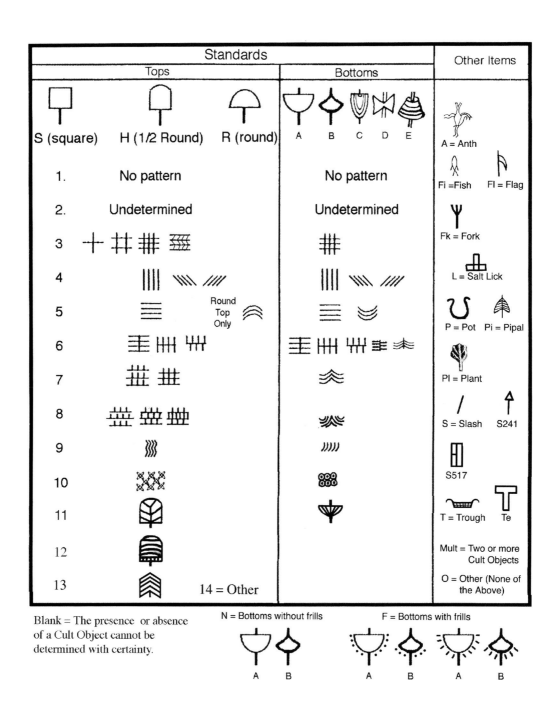

Figure 1.3 Cult objects: Shapes, components and fills.

imbedded in the coordinate system. For example, a seal found at DK.G, Block 1, House I, Room 1 gives us a good idea not only of its location but also its associated architecture. For the Mackay (1938) data the Period and Phase (Figure 1.4) can be worked out from the depth data and the descriptions in the text. The Marshall data is more problematic as it comes from more spatially discontinuous areas, and the descriptions of provenience are less clear than Mackay's (and depths are given below surface). There have been some efforts to improve the situation with the Marshall data (Jansen and Urban 1985). These improved data for inscribed artifacts is somewhat inaccessible, with all artifacts listed together and the electronic data files in a dated format. As it is not the goal of this book to resurrect Marshall's excavations, the Jensen and Urban's (1985) data are not used. Instead, spatial and temporal analysis uses the Mackay (1938) data focusing on the DK.G excavations.

The Vats (1940) data are very difficult to use as the grid coordinates are not particularly descriptive of the archaeological contexts, and the depth data (because the deposits of Harappa are in the form of mounds) are of little use. What Vats does give that can be used are stratum designations (I-VIII). While the correlation between mounds of these strata is tentative at best (Figure 1.4), they are adequate to allow the seriation of the artifacts within mounds. This allows the temporal analysis of texts within mounds and the comparison of these distributions between mounds. The correlation between the strata of the various mounds are uncertain, based entirely on Vats (1940), and is unlikely to be completely accurate. Nevertheless, the results of the within mound analysis give us an idea of the variations over time in sign usage.

To further complicate the interpretation of the data from these early site reports, the lowest levels were excavated in only a few isolated areas of the sites (often referred to as "Deep Soundings") and at Mohenjo-daro these excavations quickly filled with ground water. The overall reliability of these data are also negatively impacted by the primitive excavation techniques employed in the first five decades of the 20th century. It seems likely that many of the smaller artifacts could have been missed and simply ended up in the back dirt. One final problem worth considering here is the fact that many of the "minor finds" were not reported nor published. This is especially a problem at Harappa (Vats 1940) and Lothal (Rao 1973).

The recent excavations from Harappa (Meadow and Kenoyer 1993; Meadow et al. 1994, 1995, 1996, 1997, 1998, 1999, 2001) have done little to rectify the problems described above. Chronological information, which is rarely given, always takes the form of Period 1 through Period 5 (Figure 1.4). For example, H99-3961 is a bas relief tablet for which the chronological data Period 3B(?) and 3C is given. That is, sometime between 2450 and 1900 BC a span of 550 years. The planner data for this artifact is given as Mound AB, Trench 39N (gully) - again not very useful.

The main problem with the published data from Harappa is that photographs of the artifacts are seldom published, and we must rely on drawings for the details of artifact design. The drawings are very artistically rendered, but contain errors in the depictions of some of the sign graphs. I am only aware of this problem because I had access to photocopies of unpublished HARP photographs for comparison (thanks to Dr. Richard Meadow). These photographs are not currently available and will be published in the forthcoming volume (III) of the CIST. Therefore, I do not use them here, nor in the database. However, the database entries and the

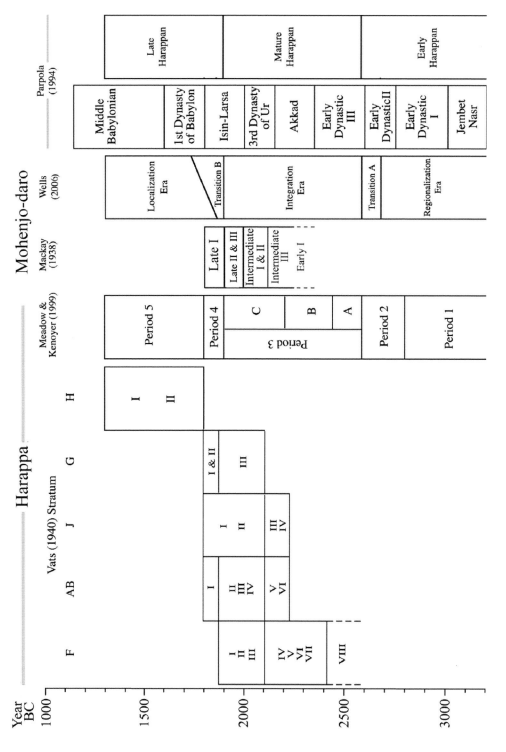

Figure 1.4 Chronological chart comparing Indus sites and suggested chronological divisions.

ICIT reflect the photography not the drawings. Other problems with the HARP data include: artifacts being published in more than one (sometimes several) interim reports, which causes some confusion, duplicate accession numbers, and in some cases important data not included (especially artifact color and chronological data). If a data entry was uncertain it was omitted from the ECIT. This results in blank fields in the ECIT and ICIT databases.

Terminology

It is useful to define just what writing is. For the purposes of this book writing is: the systematic encoding of information using a specific set of symbols such that the information can be retrieved verbatim by someone other than the writer without loss of information. Further, the structure of the symbolic system will reflect the structure of the underlying language and its syntax. This cognitive frame of reference allows the language and its writing to be linked.

The issue of what terminology is appropriate for referencing the 'Indus' or 'Harappan' Civilization has been reviewed by Possehl (1984:27-28). He concludes that both Harappan and Indus, as well as civilization, are all problematic terms. This problem of terminology begins with naming the archaeological culture and extends to the naming of artifacts (miniature tablets), time period (Pre- vs. Proto- vs. Early-Harappan), and sites (Dholavira or Kotada). My own belief is that the terminology applied is irrelevant as long as the terms of reference are clearly defined at the outset and used systematically. To this end I will define some important terms that are used in the rest of this book.

The terms Indus and Harappan Civilization both have problems. Neither recognizes the vast extent of this archaeological phenomenon (>1 million km^2), and both imply homogeneity of material culture that does not exist. There is considerable inter-site variation on all levels. Having said that, there is something recognizably 'Harappan' or 'Indus' about the material remains of this culture. Recently Hyper-Nationalists in India (Gupta 1995; Jha and Rajaram 2000, and others) have further complicated the literature by adopting the term Sarasvati-Sindhu Civilization (ca. 3200 to 1500 B.C.), positing an unbroken continuity between the Indus and Vedic peoples, and claim the whole of Indus culture for India. The application of the term Sarasvati has the purpose of claiming the archaeological record for a resinous and political agenda. This follows in an archaeological tradition (Hall and Neal 1902) that relies on nationalism for its inspiration. This practice has happily fallen out of use in mainstream archaeology.

I prefer the terms Indus Civilization and Indus Writing, regardless of their problems, and these terms are used here. Possehl (1984:29) says about the term civilization: "... civilization can be said to relate to the cultural aspects of life and to historically long-lived cultural traditions." He goes on to point out that "... the concept has a long and chequered history which, to some, conjures notions good and evil, legitimate and illegitimate and a typology of cultures implying vaguely stated notions of progress as postulated by Lewis Henry Morgan (1907)" (Possehl 1984:29). By civilization I mean: a unified and complex socio-cultural entity that supports craft specialization, a stratified social structure with distinct social institutions (economic, religious, political, legal, etc.), in which there is a differential access to power, and that is (at least in part) focused in an Urban settlement pattern. These systems of organization have many interdependent and interlinked institutions that function as the conduits of centralized control. Centralized decision-making results in a recognizably uniform infrastructure, and is likewise expressed in a uniformity in certain aspects of material culture - certain types of ceramics, weights and measures, some forms of public architecture, and other items that are mandated by the controlling institutions to facilitate the maintenance and replication of the system. Underlying the similarities there is a great deal of variability. As for the names of artifact types, I use the typology given in Table 1.1, but none of the type names are meant to imply artifact function. Rather, these names are meant to differentiate artifacts on the basis of the form.

Chronology

The Indus Civilization was a Bronze Age culture extant over Pakistan and much of northwest India from 2600 BC to 1900 BC. The details of its archaeological remains suggest that it was a complex, urban-focused social formation with highly standardized material culture, but with distinct regional variations. The origin and demise of the Indus Civilization are not known with certainty. Several models have been suggested (Konishi 1984; Possehl 2002).

The developmental model, which reaches its final elaborated form in Kenoyer (1991), is given in Figure 1.4. It proposes four general Eras for the Indus Tradition. It is important to emphasize that "Eras do not have fixed boundaries in time and space and more than one Era may co-exist within a Tradition" (Kenoyer 1991:3). The Era boundaries given in Figure 1.4 are meant to be guidelines and not intended as dates of events.

The first of these Eras is a postulated Early Food Producing Era (6500 BC to 5000 BC) although no sites from this period have yet been found within the Indus valley (Kenoyer 1991:84). It is postulated on the basis of the excavations at Mehrgarh (Jarrige et al. 1995) in the Kachi District of Baluchistan. This is the period when village farming and the domestication of the plants and animals that would later support the Indus civilization were developed. This period is often referred to as the Neolithic.

The next period is the Regionalization Era (Early Harappan Phase), 5000 BC to 2600 BC (Kenoyer 1991:25). In brief this is the period leading up to urbanization, when "numerous crafts were invented... Distinct artifact styles evolved in specific regions, and different regions were connected by trade networks" (Kenoyer 1998:25). This period sees the regional cultures come to the brink of urbanization. In other formulations the period from 5000 BC to 2600 BC is divided into two Stages (Possehl 2002:29). The first of these Stages (Two) consists of three Phases (Togau Phase 4300-3800 BC, Kechi Beg Phase 3800-3200 BC, and Hakra Wares Phase 3800-3200 BC) that are essentially defined based on distinct ceramic traditions. "Three themes characterize this age: growth, continuity, and geographic expansion" (Possehl 2002:34). Stage Three (Early Harappan) consists of four roughly contemporaneous archaeological phases; the most well known of these is the Kot Diji Phase. During Stage Three "There is a minimum of technological change, and the paradigm already established for the subsistence regime was expanded rather than modified" (Possehl 2002:40).

In Kenoyer's (1998:25) third Era, the Integration Era (2600 BC to 1900 BC), material cultures of the specific regions of the Greater Indus Valley merge into a homogeneous cultural entity, often referred to as Mature Harappan Phase or Indus civilization. The shift from the non-urban settlement pattern of the Regionalization Era to the urban-based settlement pattern of the Integration Era is accompanied by an increase in the complexity of Indus social structure on all levels. According to Kenoyer (1998) complex long distance trade relations, urban planning, a bureaucracy, large-scale food production, craft specialization, and writing become a part of the new social order. The transition is relatively rapid, taking 100 years or less (2600 BC to 2500 BC), and is a dramatic shift from the previous Era in all aspects of culture. Possehl (2002:55) tells us: "The immense differences between the Indus Civilization, as compared to the Early Harappan, can be seen as a replacement of the older Early Harappan symbolic system with a new order and way of life. The Indus people turned their backs on their own past...". There is also a shift in the location of Indus sites. It is only during the Integration Era (Mature Harappan) that writing was used by the Indus people. Texts are found inscribed on a variety of small objects including seals, mold made tokens, ceramic vessels and copper wafers, but no books, monuments, or clay tablets like those found in Mesopotamia or Egypt survive.

During the final era of the Indus Tradition, the Localization Era (1900 BC to 1300 BC) there is a shift away from the homogeneity of material culture which was so prevalent in the previous era, to less connected and regionally more diverse material cultures. This period is often referred to as the Late Harappan Phase (Parpola 1994:19). There is a shift to a smaller scale in both the settlements and regional connectivity. The transition is not uniform in the Greater Indus Valley and occurs between 1900 BC and 1700 BC.

The main problem with this model is that it oversimplifies the relationships between the various eras and overemphasizes the degree of continuity within eras. Because of the nature of the archaeological data, a detailed analysis leading to a more precise understanding of variations in material culture over time is not possible. However, there are at least two additional periods that can be added to the chronology of the

Indus Tradition. These are transitional periods at the beginning and end of the Integration Era. The first of these is Transition A (2600 to 2500 BC) proposed by Possehl (2002:29) and meant to represent a period of transition in the Greater Indus Valley from a non-urban (Regionalization Era) to an urban-based (Integration Era) settlement pattern. The second transition (B) occurs from 1900 BC to 1700 BC and was proposed by Meadow et al. (1998). This is a period of de-urbanization and marks the transition to the Localization Era of the Indus Tradition. Figure 1.4 brings together several chronological schemata for comparison.

Typology of artifacts

The use of a variety of chronological terms does not change the fact that between 2600 and 1900 BC there was an urban, Bronze Age culture centered in the Indus and Ghaggar-Hakra drainages of what is today northwest India and Pakistan. This culture had well-developed trade networks (with standard measures) that left remnants of their material culture from Syria to the Ganges and from the Oxus River to Arabia. Their system of writing was an important part of their system of exchange and production, and comes to us in the form of short texts on a variety of small artifacts and on ceramic vessels.

The need for terms describing the various inscribed artifacts led to the early (1920s–1950s) adoption of the terminology used in Mesopotamia and Egypt. Some of these terms (sealing, amulet, and tablet) imply a specific function in cases where the exact function is either unknown or demonstrably unrelated to the function this nomenclature implies. Further, the categorization of artifacts is not consistent in the various sources and this has led to a great deal of confusion. There is no attempt here to create a definitive typology of Indus artifacts, nor to craft categories that are linked to function but free of the traditional or implied meanings. My purpose is rather to create categories that group artifacts of generally the same form and function, but to do so in such a way as to have category frequencies sufficiently high to allow meaningful inter-group analysis. Classification must address the fundamental differences between artifacts without becoming mired in the endless details of their difference. For this reason a two level approach is used here.

In the typology of inscribed artifacts (Table 1.1), artifacts are categorized into 10 broad categories. These categories are not necessarily linked to artifact function. For example, the term SEAL (n = 2,457) identifies objects that are carved in intaglio and are designed to be used to make impressions. These artifacts are further subdivided into seven subcategories based on their planer form. Their forms may or may not be linked to differences in function. The term TAG (n = 161) is used to identify items bearing the impressions made by seals, and these are further subdivided based on what they were attached to. Analysis of the tags and their archaeological contexts leads to the conclusion that seals have several functions not related to their form, and seals of the same form can have several different uses. For example, several tags bearing square seals (SEAL:S, n = 1,974) with Bull:i iconography have the impression of reeds or textiles on their reverse. Seals (SEAL:S) with geometric designs are also found on tags, as are rectangular seals (SEAL:R, n = 360) with no iconography. Tags of these types were used in sealing shipments of goods, some found as far away as Umma (Figure 1.5). Other tags with SEAL:S impressions and Bull:i iconography have been found sealing jars used in the glazing of stoneware bangles (Jensen and Urban 1983:82). Within the typology used here tags take eight forms. We can conclude from the archaeological

contexts of tags that square seals with Bull:i (n = 1,354) iconography had several uses within the Indus economic system not restricted to trade practices. This functional virtuosity may extend to all seals. What is unknown is whether specific iconography or texts are linked to specific uses, or if the same seal could have several uses in its life. These radically different functions of near identical artifacts point to one of the fundamental problems with classifying inscribed Indus artifacts - different types of seals can have identical uses, while nearly identical seals can have very different uses.

Rectangular seals (SEAL:R, n = 357) are another common seal type. While less common than square seals, this type is found at all major Indus sites, and throughout most of the deposits at both Harappa and Mohenjo-daro (Figure 1.6). From Harappa they are most common in later deposits (Vats 1940, Mound F: Stratum IV). Recent excavations at Harappa suggest that these SEAL:R artifacts are a more recent development at that site (Kenoyer and Meadow 1996:5). At Mohenjo-daro they are found in every level of the deposits (Early I - Late Ia). These seals lack an iconographic element, bearing only signs. Impressions of these seals are found on tags.

Another problematic artifact type are the so called miniature tablets, which are not tablets at all. Tablets (TAB, n = 1,543) are objects, either in bas relief (B = 731), incised (I = 560), or scratched on copper (C = 252); hereafter referred to as copper tablets, and not to be confused with the bas relief tables from Harappa that can be molded in copper. Different forms may have had identical uses, but their exact function is unknown. While incised (TAB:I, Harappa = 556, Mohenjo-daro = 4) and bas relief tablets (TAB:B, Harappa = 611, Mohenjo-daro = 109) are common at Harappa, they are relatively rare elsewhere. Copper tablets (TAB:C, Harappa = 1,

Mohenjo-daro = 251) are found in significant numbers only at Mohenjo-daro. These distributions suggest that they had site-specific uses. The most interesting feature shared by all types of tablets is that they are not necessarily unique. The bas relief forms are mold made and therefore many identical artifacts of this class exist. Incised tablets (both TAB:I and TAB:C) also have many repeated texts, despite the fact that they had to have been incised one at a time. This may be a clue to their function, and suggests to me that they are tokens of some sort.

Ceramic vessels (POT, n = 1,266), or at least their remaining fragments, can be subdivided into three varieties: potters' marks (M = 428), drawings (D = 25), and texts (T = 581). Texts can be subdivided further into graffiti (g = 501), seal impressions (s = 73), and painted (p = 7). This is the only case of a third level of classification. In the literature there is a great deal of variety in the classification of inscribed ceramic vessels, and there are a considerable number of examples of ceramic markings that are very difficult to classify with confidence.

In the ECIT there are 232 items that could not be differentiated beyond the first level of classification (POT). This is normally because of their fragmentary state. Potters' marks are alleged by some to be the precursors of Indus writing (Lal 1962, 1975; Potts 1981, 1982). This theory is dealt with in detail in Chapter 2. These four categories (SEAL, TAB, TAG, and POT) account for the vast majority (97%) of artifacts in the ECIT.

Typology of iconography

The iconography of the inscribed artifacts presents an interesting challenge. The endless variety of graphic images leads one towards a typology with many divisions but low category frequencies, but for meaningful analysis to be possible category frequencies need to be sufficiently large.

The typology offered here begins by dividing all iconographic elements into two broad categories: Field Symbols and Cult objects (after Marshall 1931). In the typology used here (Figures 1.1-1.3) Cult Objects and Field Symbols are defined below.

Cult Object

A Cult Object is any element that is found immediately in front of a depiction of an animal on a seal (Figure 1.3). Cult Objects are further subdivided into Standards (n = 1,094) and Other Items (n = 256). Standards are a special kind of cult object. They consist of three elements: Tops, bottoms, and frills. Tops can take one of three shapes and have one of 14 internal patterns. Bottoms can take one of five shapes and have one of 11 internal patterns. Additionally, bottoms either have frills or not. The vast majority of standards have square or round tops and have Type A or B bottoms. There are 14 different elements in the 'Other Items' category. These are iconographic elements that occur in the same position as standards, but are not standards in design. Cult objects almost always occur paired with Field Symbols, the only exception being the mold-made model standards and a small number of TAB:B artifacts from Harappa.

Field Symbol

The term Field Symbol identifies not only those animals associated with standards, but includes all iconography that is not identifiably a cult object (Figures 1.1-1.2, and Table 1.2). Field symbols are further subdivided into two categories: Living Things and Signs (Figure 1.1), and Geometric shapes (Figure 1.2). It is worth pointing out that 2,544 artifacts (45%) have no field symbols and 599 artifacts have field symbols that could not be specifically identified. This leaves 2,499 artifacts with field symbols

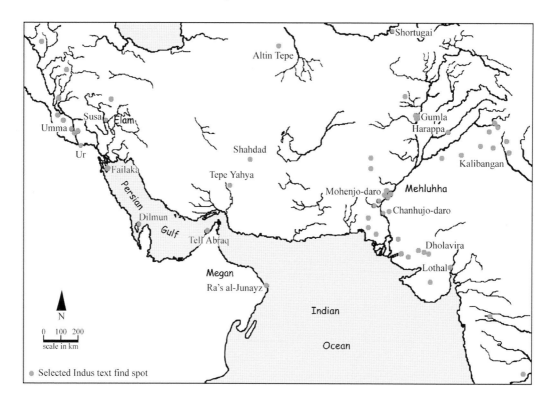

Figure 1.5 Sites with Indus seals and other inscribed artifacts.

that are classified into 56 separate categories. Of these categories 12 are different markings on Bull:i (n = 1,354) field symbols. A similar typology has been proposed for Standards (Rissman 1989).

It is common for Field Symbols and cult objects to be paired, especially on SEAL:S artifacts. There are 28 Field Symbols that commonly combine with 15 "Other Item" and 12 varieties of standards (ignoring the internal designs of standards for now). This results in 756 possible combinations of Field Symbols and Cult Objects. This results in some very small frequencies of combinations, including a large number of null combinations. What is surprising is that there are many high frequency combinations and 334 (44%) of the combinations are not used at all.

This is particularly noticeable for combinations of standards (12 types) and Bull:i:I, II, J, S, and W (the five most common) Field Symbols (Figure 1.7). In total there are 810 examples tabulated in Figure 1.7, and they come from more than 20 sites. The most obvious feature of this table is that three types of Cult Objects are not used at all (HBN, SAB and SBF). Just as obvious is that some cult Cult Objects are very commonly used (SAN, SAF, RAN, and RAF). The first conclusion that can be made from the distributions in Figure 1.7 is that these combinations are not random. Therefore, they must either be the result of: a) local carving traditions and would be geographically distinct, being restricted to one site; or b) culturally based (religious, economic, or familial, etc.) and would have an uneven but Pan-Indus distribution. The most

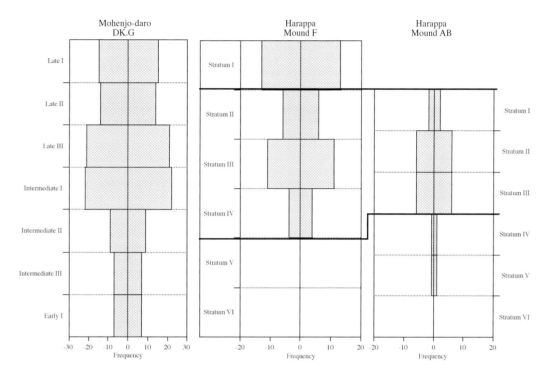

Figure 1.6 Type SEAL:R artifacts by stratum from Mohenjo-daro and Harappa
(negative numbers mirror positive numbers and are not interpreted).

frequent type of standard in Figure 1.7 is SAN (Square top, Type A bottom, and No frills). The geographic distribution of SAN standards, both by itself and in combination with the Bull:i markings in Figure 1.7, are given in Figure 1.8 for the fiv largest sites in the ECIT. This figure maps the percentage that combinations comprise of the total examples from each site. SAN standards comprise about 60-80% of standards from all sites but Kalibangan where SAN standards comprise about 25% of all standards. Additionally, SAN standards have an uneven, but Pan-Indus, distribution.

Figure 1.8b maps the distribution of SAN and Bull:i:I combinations. While the percentages are low, there is a definite north (6-7%) vs. south (4-5%) polarization. Figure 1.8c has the inverse distribution (north = <4%, south = 8-16%). This

pattern is repeated in Figure 1.8d, and to a lesser degree in Figure 1.8e. The final map is Figure 1.8f maps the most common pairing (SAN and Bull:i:W), and again there is a distinct distribution with Harappa (57%) having the largest proportion, Lothal (12.5%) the smallest, and Mohenjo-daro in between (27%). These distributions confirm the cultural nature of the Field Symbols and Cult Objects. The distributions are not random, are Pan-Indus and, while they have distinct regional variations, they are not completely restricted geographically. Another aspect of Standards that adds to this discussion is the internal design patterns of Tops and Bottoms (Figure 1.3). There are 14 patterns that can combine with three types of Tops giving 42 pairings. The situation with bottoms is more complex, but for the moment we

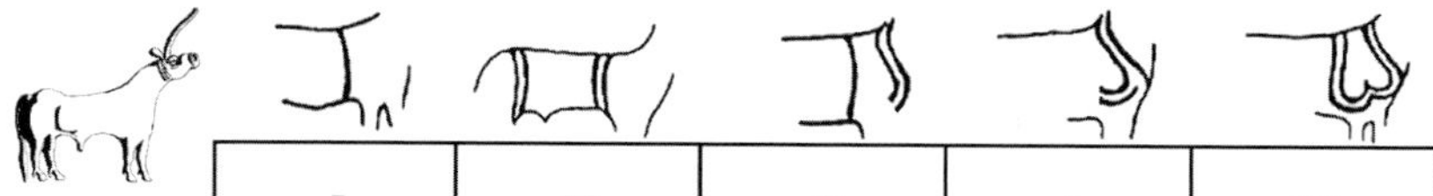

	I	II	S	J	W	CO %
HAN	0.12		0.12	0.12	0.25	0.62
HBN	✕	✕	✕	✕	✕	✕
HAF				0.49	0.37	0.86
HBF	0.25			0.12	0.37	0.74
RAN	1.11	0.74	1.73	2.84	1.73	8.15
RBN	0.37		0.12	0.37		0.86
RAF	0.62	0.12	0.86	3.46	0.99	6.05
RBF	0.25		0.25	1.23	0.37	2.10
SAN	4.44	6.30	13.95	12.10	29.51	66.30
SBN	✕	✕	✕	✕	✕	✕
SAF	0.37	0.49	1.11	1.11	11.23	14.32
SBF	✕	✕	✕	✕	✕	✕
FS %	7.53	7.65	18.15	21.85	44.81	

Figure 1.7 Percentage of total frequency of Bull:i sub-types by Standard sub-types (n = 810).

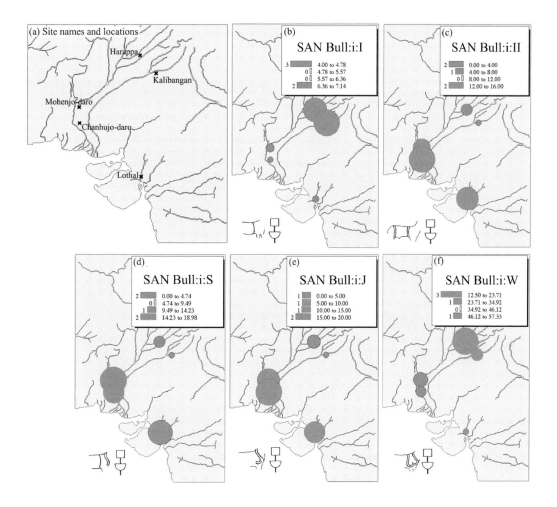

Figure 1.8 SAN Type standards and Bull:i markings for the five largest Indus sites.

can restrict our analysis to Type A and B bottoms (C-E are very low frequency special cases), which can take 11 different designs, giving 22 varieties. Additionally, bottoms can have frills or not, effectively doubling the number of bottom varieties to 44. This gives 1,848 possible combinations of Tops and Bottoms, with or without frills. Yet only 195 (10.5%) of these combinations are used. Some combinations – S8:A5:N (4%), S6:A6:N (1.6%) and S3:A10:N (1.6%) – form significant clusters. Most of the internal patterns are formed using combinations of straight or curved lines. It is possible that the variations in pattern usage could be stylistic.

This is not true for Type 10 tops and Type 10 bottoms (Table 1.3). There is only one example of a Type 10 top and it combines with a Type 10 bottom and so it is part of this larger group. Type 10 bottoms have a pattern of multiple 'doughnut' shaped markings, and are distinct from all other patterns. This makes them ideal subjects for the study of non-stylistic variations in the internal patterning of standard tops and bottoms. There are 69 examples of Type 10 bottoms and they come from four sites (Mohenjo-daro, Harappa, Lothal and Chanhujo-daro). They have a Pan-Indus but uneven distribution, and there are several interesting characteristics of Type 10 bottoms and their pairings with tops and with Bull:i markings. First, the proportions of Type 10 bottoms with or without frills are very close to those of the entire inventory of standards – Type 10s have 19.5% with and 80.5% without frills, departing from the overall dataset by only 0.38%. In other words, frills are not combining more frequently with Type 10 bottoms. Second, there is a higher than average pairing of Type 10 bottoms with Square tops (all standards = 85.5%; Type 10 bottoms = 98.5%). Third, the pairing of Type 10 bottoms with Bull:i:W is very high (95%) compared with all standards (45%). There

seems to be a strong preference for Type 10 bottoms to pair with square tops and Bull:i:W DS. These results support the idea that pairings of standards and Bull:i markings are not simply random variations, but are linked to unknown cultural practices.

The geographic distribution of all standards compared with Type 10 standards supports this conclusion. Standards are found at the following sites in these proportions of the total number of standards: Mohenjo-daro 65%, Harappa 23%, Lothal 4%, Chanhujo-daro 3%, Kalibangan 2%, and all other sites 3%. Standards with Type 10 bottoms occur in the following proportions: Mohenjo-daro 65% (as expected), Harappa 30.5% (7.5% more), Lothal 3% (1% less), Chanhujo-daro 1.5% (1.5% less), Kalibangan 0% (2% less). The number of Type 10 bottoms from Harappa is higher than expected, while Mohenjo-daro is exactly what is expected. The smaller sites seem to have less than the expected number of Type 10 bottoms.

Some individual items are much more common at specific sites (for example, goats at Banawali, geometric seals and bullet iconography at Harappa, and troughs at Mohenjo-daro), while other items are rare at major sites (Frilled standards at Harappa).

It is not my purpose here to supply a complete analysis of these iconographic elements nor of artifact types, as the Indus script is the main focus of this study. Any comprehensive study of the script must however consider the artifacts and their iconography, especially the relationship between these various elements and the texts with which they are associated. This brief overview serves to demonstrate that the simple typologies used in this study adequately classifies the artifacts and their iconography, allowing meaningful analysis. Further, it has demonstrated that the graphic elements

Table 1.3 Cult object combinations by site (frequency at left, percentage at right)

Frequency	Mohenjo-daro	Chanhujo-daro	Harappa	Lothal	Total	Percentage	Mohenjo-daro	Chanhujo-daro	Harappa	Lothal	Total
H3:A10N	-	1	-	-	1	H3:A10N	-	1.4	-	-	1.4
S2:A10:F	-	-	1	-	1	S2:A10:F	-	-	1.4	-	1.4
S2:A10:N	1	-	-	-	1	S2:A10:N	1.4	-	-	-	1.4
S3:A10:F	2	-	2	-	4	S3:A10:F	2.9	-	2.9	-	5.8
S3:A10:N	15	-	13	1	29	S3:A10:N	21.7	-	18.8	1.4	41.9
S4:A10:F	1	-	-	-	1	S4:A10:F	1.4	-	-	-	1.4
S4:A10:N	6	-	-	-	6	S4:A10:N	8.7	-	-	-	8.7
S5:A10:F	-	-	-	-		S5:A10:F	-	-	-	-	-
S5:A10:N	-	-	-	-		S5:A10:N	-	-	-	-	-
S6:A10:F	3	-	-	-	3	S6:A10:F	4.3	-	-	-	4.3
S6:A10:N	5	-	-	-	5	S6:A10:N	7.2	-	-	-	7.2
S7:A10:F	-	-	1	1	2	S7:A10:F	-	-	1.4	1.4	2.8
S7:A10:N	3	-	1	-	4	S7:A10:N	4.3	-	1.4	-	5.7
S8:A10:F	1	-	1	-	2	S8:A10:F	1.4	-	1.4	-	2.8
S8:A10:N	5	-	1	-	6	S8:A10:N	7.2	-	1.4	-	8.6
S9:A10:F	-	-	-	-		S9:A10:F	-	-	-	-	
S9:A10:F	2	-	-	-	2	S9:A10:F	2.9	-	-	-	2.9
S10:A10:F	-	-	-	-		S10:A10:F	-	-	-	-	
S10:A10:N	1	-	-	-	1	S10:A10:N	1.4	-	-	-	1.4
S14:A10:N	-	-	1	-	1	S14:A10:N	-	-	1.4	-	1.4
Total	45	1	21	2	69	Totals	65.2	1.4	30.5	2.9	-

have culturally based meanings, rather than being randomly based or simply variations in carving traditions. The likelihood that the connections between the pairings of Cult Object and Field Symbols are economic or political is supported by archaeological contexts of the seal impressions. The combinations of the various standards and Field Symbols suggest a complexity of social formation that we may never fully understand. Geographic variations in the combination of Cult Objects and Field Symbols suggest a complex of many small groups configured in various of ways. We can assume that Cult Objects and Field Symbols represent different classes of groups (for example, political vs. economic vs. religious) therefore the system is one where social groupings are defined based on multiple criteria. There is no noticeable connection between iconography and Indus texts. Specific signs are not associated consistently or exclusively with specific iconographic elements.

POTTERS' MARKS
AND THE ORIGINS OF THE INDUS SCRIPT

This chapter examines the relationships between the various systems of south and southwest Asian potters' marks for the purpose of determining if they were part of a geographically larger system of related markings. Further, this chapter addresses the question of whether the Proto-Elamite and Indus scripts arose directly from this system of marking, were influenced by them, or developed independently. Finally, the existence of 'graphic universals' is explored. In this chapter I argue that:

1) relationships between systems of pottery markings suggest that they are not part of an integrated system spanning all of south and southwest Asia during the Bronze Age, but rather different local traditions of markings employed in similar cultural contexts. The strongest evidence for this can be seen in the chronological disjunction between these systems evident in Figure 2.1, and the existence of regional number systems;

2) similarities between the potters' marks from various south and southwest Asian sites can be explained in part by the existence of graphic universals and in part by geographic proximity and the exchange of ceramics through trade;

3) the similarities between south and southwest Asian potters' marks and the linear scripts of south and southwest Asia (the Indus and Proto-Elamite scripts) are systematic, but can be accounted for in the greatest part by the existence of graphic universals, and in part by borrowings into the system of potters' marks from Proto-Elamite;

4) the idea of using potters' marks is widespread geographically (from Neolithic China to the Vinca culture), but the specific inventories of marks (other than graphic universals) seem to be geographically and temporally limited; and,

5) the Indus script and the Proto-Elamite script are not related in a systematic way. An autochthonic developmental model can be applied to both scripts.

Before beginning this examination of potters' marks there are several aspects of these data that must be considered. First, there has been no sourcing of the ceramics bearing the potters' marks in the literature, nor is there any discussion of the origins of the ceramics based on stylistic considerations. Consequently, it is difficult to be absolutely certain that the sites at which the ceramics are found are their sites of origin. This factor is especially important when analyzing the inter-site similarities of potters' marks, particularly at Shahdad because burials often contain prestigious trade wares. Second, chronological control is not very precise, nor can all site chronologies be linked with confidence. Third, descriptive information concerning the numbers of examples of each sign, their chronological distribution, ceramic type, placement on the ceramic, and associated archaeological contexts are often not given. Finally, because photographs are rarely published, sign lists of potters' marks cannot be verified. The net result of these factors is that sources of minor variations in the distributions of potters' marks cannot be identified with confidence. Regardless of these problems, an examination of potters' marks is necessary to understand the relationship of the Indus script to these symbolic systems.

Defining potters' marks

Potters' marks are markings found in many locations on ceramic vessels (see Figure 2.3). This chapter focuses on the potters' marks of south and southwest Asia (Figure 2.2), but also call upon comparative data from further afield. In this study potters' marks are defined as: pre- or post-firing markings (usually 1 or 2 symbols) that are found on all parts of ceramic vessels.

Other class of markings found on ceramics are: 1) pseudo-writing - linear strings or clusters of signs that do not seem to be actual writing; 2) script - texts in a recognizable script; and, 3) drawings - pictorial representation of recognizable objects.

When potters' marks occur more than two at a time they are referred to here as pseudo-writing or pseudo-texts. There are many gray areas between all of these categories. For example, some potters' marks (especially from Shahdad) look very much like texts, while some texts on ceramics from Mohenjo-daro could be mistaken for potters' marks. Further, some researchers (Quivron 1997) refer to all post-firing marks as graffiti, while others (Lal 1962) differentiate graffiti from potters' marks based on the nature of the symbols involved. This situation is further complicated by the fact that many of the site reports and articles do not specify if the marks were made pre- or post-firing, so it is not practical to use this aspect of potters' marks as a definition. Future research may show this to be an important feature of potters' marks.

The existence of examples, which are not easily categorized, raises the question of how we know potters' marks are not script. The difference being two fold, the first is visual - scripts and writing are arranged in patterned sequences, and second, they express language (they are read). Conversely, marks and drawings convey information that is not necessarily linked to a specific language. For example, two potter's may have the same name but different marks (if this was indeed one of the functions of potters' marks).

The chronology of four south and southwest Asian sites that contain the majority of the potters' marks used in this paper is given in Figure 2.1. The most obvious feature of this table is that periods of intensive use of potters' varies from site to site (the denser the shading, the more common potters' marks were). Equally clear is that the use of potters' marks overlaps between sites. This temporal distribution does not argue for a unified, regional system of potters' marks. As is seen in the following discussion, the temporal distribution is relevant to the assessment of the function of potters' marks. In most cases potters' marks are coeval or post-date the writing systems of southwest Asia. In some cases these are the writing system they are supposed to have given rise to (especially Proto-Elamite).

Potters' marks can occur in virtually any location on a vessel with preference for certain locations depending on the site of origin (Figure 2.3 and Table 2.1). Unfortunately most publications give few details about the placement of potters' marks. If this information is given it is usually vague or generalized. While Figure 2.3 gives eight possible placements of potters' marks, the following table (Table 2.1) uses only four. Further, the frequency of placement can only be expressed in comparative rather than quantitative terms. Nevertheless, these data point to important differences in the placement of marks between sites.

What is obvious is that the south and southwest Asia potters' marks fall into two distinct groups based on placement. In one group (Tepe Yahya, Shahdad, and Rehman-dheri) marks are

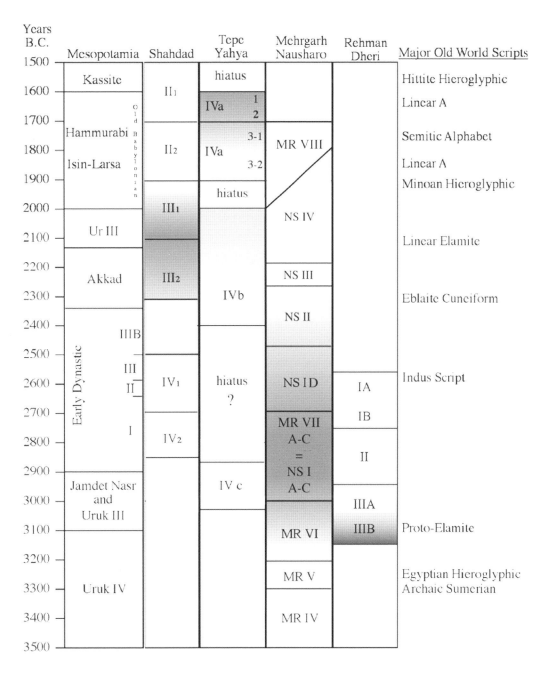

Figure 2.1 Chronology chart of south and southwest Asian potters' marks

(shading indicated density of potters' marks over time).

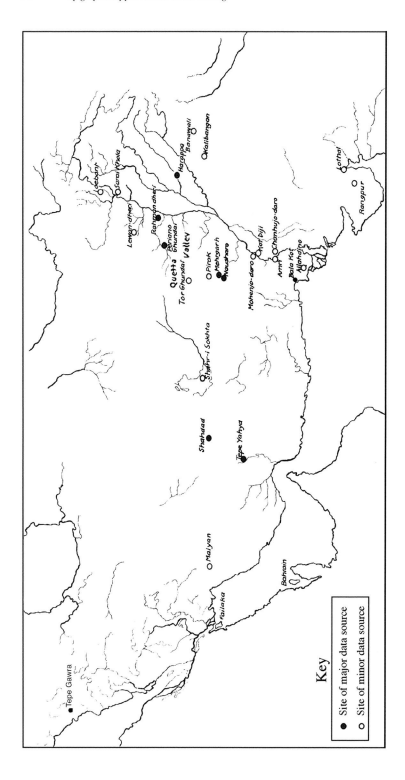

Figure 2.2 Location of sites with non-control group potters' marks used in the this study.

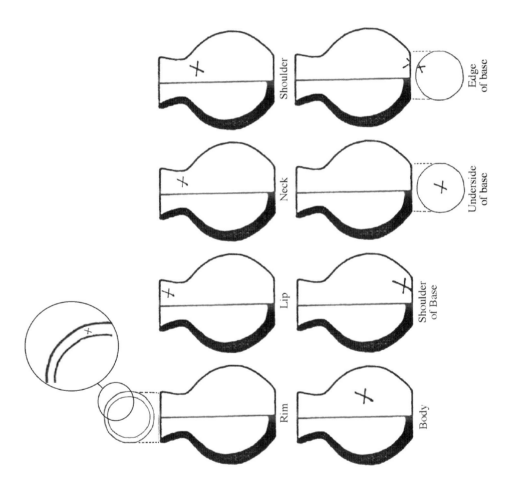

Figure 2.3 Location of potters' marks on ceramics.

Table 2.1 Placement of potters' marks on vessels by site

Site	Source	Rim	Body	Base Shoulder	Base
Tepe Yahya	Potts (1981)	Never	Less Frequent	Most Frequent	Less Frequent
Shahdad	Hakemi (1997)	Rare	Less Frequent	Most Frequent	Less Frequent
Rehman-dheri	Durrani et al. (1995)	Rare	Seldom	Very Frequent	Seldom
Merhrgarh/ Nausharo	Quivron (1997)	Never	Seldom	Less Frequent	Most Frequent
Quetta Valley	Fairservis (1956, 1959)	Never	Less Frequent	Less Frequent	Most Frequent

most frequently found on the shoulder of the base, while in the second group (Merhrgarh/ Nausharo and the Quetta Valley sites) marks are most frequently found on the base. These various preferences are not absolute, but rather demonstrate that certain placements of marks are more common at certain sites than others. At all sites potters' marks are placed in more than one position on pots. The location of potters' marks on the vessel might be a clue as to how the marks were used or how the pot was made.

The function of potters' marks

The exact function of potters' marks is unknown, but several suggestions have been made (Quivron 1997:52):

1) they represent goods that might be contained in the vessels;

2) they represent the capacity of the vessel (volume);

3) they are the identifying marks of the potter;

4) they are tallies of the number of pots in a firing; and,

5) the marks function as organizational aids in the cycle of production.

Quivron (1997:52-54) gives very good reasons why most of these suggestions are improbable. The first suggestion is unlikely because there is no correlation between marks and vessel types. That is, plates, goblets, and storage jars all contain the same inventory of marks. For the second, there is no correlation between marks and vessel volumes and therefore it is not possible for the marks to be measuring the volumes of the vessels. Even when groups of vessels were found in a storage context at Mehrgarh, there is no correlation between volumes of the ceramics and the marks they bear. The third suggested interpretation seems unlikely because there is no spatial or temporal clustering of specific marks. So it seems they are not connected to the makers of the pottery. The fourth suggestion is difficult to assess, but the issue of numerals and their uses are returned to later in this chapter. The final suggestion is addressed by Quivron in detail. Quivron (1997:53) tells us of a find from Period VII ($\approx$3000 to 2700 BC) at Mehrgarh:

> ...more than 100 pots were found on the floor of room CXVIII, and one third of them were incised with marks showing 16 different sign types. Among the various forms of vases, miniature pots, small globular painted pots or small jars in wet ware, none of these were incised with marks. On the other hand 60% of the goblets and 66% of the plates were found with marks.

This was not an isolated occurrence and the same pattern is repeated in other finds from the same period at Mehrgarh. Quivron concludes that potters' marks "most probably represent a system of intelligible symbols" (Quivron

1997:45), whose "...purpose was probably fulfilled during the manufacturing cycle before the pots were finished and stored" (Quivron 1997:53-54). A supporting piece of evidence is that at Merhrgarh/Nausharo pre-fired potters' marks disappear with the beginnings of the influence of Mature Harappan culture, and the disappearance of Greyware. The disappearance of pre-firing potters' marks at Merhrgarh/Nausharo correlates to a shift in ceramic types and changes in firing technology (the introduction of the Indus style kiln). Pre-firing potters' marks are an earlier phenomenon at the sites closer to the Indus Valley, and their decline coincides with the spread of the influence of Indus civilization and Indus technology.

Part of the problem with Quivron's (1997) analysis is that it looks for a single function for potters' marks. This ignores the possibility that, while marks had a function within the process of producing ceramics, they may have had several different functions within the overall process of ceramic production. Quivron (1997:53) suggests that some of the marks might have been used to identify firing containers or saggers, but never takes the next step in suggesting multiple uses for marks. One reason for this is that there is little uniformity in the manner in which these pots are marked (Figure 2.4).

Nine out of the 24 marks given in Figure 2.4 consist of three strokes (37.5%). Other than this there is little similarity in the markings. These are not from a single context and Quivron (1997) does not control for temporal variations in their distribution. It is not possible to analyze these marks as a related set, although they all come from similar artifacts (saggers). The large number of stroke signs (numerals) suggests something is being counted or measured.

There is some evidence to support the suggestion that potters' marks had more than one

Figure 2.4. Potters' marks found on firing containers from Mehrgarh (after Quivron 1997:54).

function in the form of multiple markings on pots. In several cases these markings are located in different positions on the vessel. On a plain buffware pot from Grave 021 at Shahdad two marks are found on the shoulder of the base, and an additional mark was placed on the base (Hakemi 1997). This placement implies that there are different functions for marks in different positions on the vessel. While it is possible that these marks were meant to be understood as a single mark, it is far more likely, that they would be given together as is a common practice at Shahdad (pseudo-texts). In fact this potters' mark is given in the Shahdad catalog as number 177 with the two element occupying different surfaces, and therefore should be considered as two separate marks. This raises the question of how many of the pseudo-texts from Shahdad are really multiple markings removed from their original positions.

Additionally, one might question how representative the drawings are of the potters' marks. This is a major problem when drawings are published instead of photographs.

If potters' marks had multiple functions, this would make the analysis of their distribution difficult. A situation could arise where a pot is marked to identify the maker, its position within the kiln, as a firing container, and/or firing tallies. Some pots might bear one or other of these, and some might bear all of them, depending on the exact function of potters' marks at that specific time and place. So clearly the uses of the potters' marks are complex and not necessarily uniform. It is un necessary for the potters' marks to have the same function at every site or for these functions to be static over time.

Another interesting phenomenon at Shahdad is the mixing of potters' marks and seal impressions (Figure 2.5). The use of stamps seals may have been introduced for a number of reasons:

1) when the component of the potters' marks they replace became more formalized or standardized. That is, there are fewer different marks thereby justifying the manufacture of a seal. For example, if instead of marking for each individual potter it became necessary only to mark to which group the potter belonged. This would account for why the seals are unrelated in design to the potters' marks;

2) when an additional layer of control over ceramic production was introduced. For example, the introduction of appointed production overseers or master potters, who needed to add their identifying symbol to the potters' marks system already in use; and,

3) in order to eliminate possible confusion created by multiple markings. That is, the seals replace one set of signs previously used during ceramic production in order to clarify the meaning of the symbols.

At Shahdad, seal impressions and potters' marks can occur independently or together. There are 327 different incised potters' marks, 275 different impressed marks (including seals), and 274 mixed incised and impressed marks from Shahdad. Unfortunately, there is little information about the placement of these marks, or about the numbers of pots with multiple marks. The chronological control at Shahdad is nonexistent, and it is impossible to determine what

came first the seals or potters' marks. Nor is it possible to seriate the marks or group them into chronologically related units.

At Rehman-dheri the vast majority of the potters' marks are on the shoulder of the base. Most of the marks found on the base of pots are identical with those found on the shoulder of the base, suggesting an integrated system of marking, and that exact placement is not a critical feature of the use of potters' marks. If the pre-firing marks were applied while the pots were stacked for drying, then the exact placement of marks may be opportunistic. Marks found on the body of pots at Rehman-dheri, with one exception (Figure 2.5.5:8) are not incised in other positions on pots. The body marks are not repeated, that is they are all unique designs. This would suggest a second and unrelated set of marks more like drawings. There are at least three examples of pots with marks in two positions, all with one mark on the base and one mark on the shoulder of the base.

I agree with Quivron (1997:45) that potters' marks seem to be part of a well-organized system of marking related to ceramic production and their significance and function are not clearly understood. Nevertheless, there is some interesting research that can be pursued with regards to the relationship between systems of potters' marks, although it is restricted to the grossest level of chronological control (Figure 2.1).

Graphic universals and the relationships between systems of marking

Is there a set of signs so rudimentary that they become part of any system of marking whenever these systems arise? In the following discussion I argue that such signs do exist, and I refer to them as graphic universals. The definition of graphic universals is not straightforward. This concept should not be confused with the linguistic concept of language-independent universal

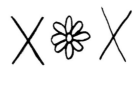

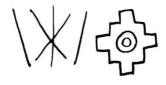

Figure 2.5 Mixed seal impressions and potters'
marks from Shahdad (after Hakemi 1997).

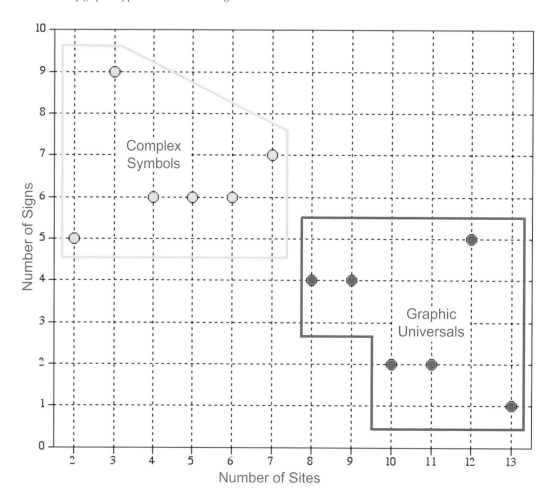

Figure 2.6 Potters' marks listed in rank order of number of sites of occurrence.

characters (Coulmas 2003:33). Graphic universals are simple marks that seem to have a very wide spatial and temporal distribution such that the transmission of these signs between systems was not possible. This study does not offer a definitive final list of universal markings. This is because, for reasons of sample size and chronological control, there are many symbols that cannot be fully analyzed. Nevertheless, the definition of a large number of graphic universals can be achieved with some confidence. This is an important step in the process of comparing inventories of potters' marks from various sites and for assessing the relationship between potters' marks and writing. Graphic universals, because they occur more or less everywhere, have the effect of making unrelated systems appear related. By way of a definition of graphic universals, the following four attributes are most important: 1) they are simple in design and easy to execute; 2) they have wide cross cultural and geographic distributions; 3) they are not associated with a specific archaeological culture; and, 4) they do not convey an implicit semantic value as do pictographic signs (for example, = man, = fish, or = bird), but in some cases may be numbers.

The meaning of graphic universals likely varies from system to system. Universals are still part of individual systems, but relationships between systems cannot be defined in terms of their presence or absence. Non-universals with specific regional and temporal distributions have a greater likelihood of being part of a related system of annotation, whether they are potters' marks or signs in a script. The conundrum is that if marks have a broad geographic distribution they become defined as graphic universals. To avoid this problem control groups must be used. Here the control groups are from Neolithic China, Roman period Egypt, and the Vinca Culture of southeast Europe. These three examples are far removed in time and space from the potters' marks of southwest Asia and are therefore unrelated systems that can be used to help identify graphic universals.

It is possible that the proposed systematic relationships between systems of annotation including scripts (Hunter 1934; Lal 1962, 1975; Fairservis 1971, 1976; Dales 1979; Potts 1981) can be explained wholly in terms of graphic universals. This is an important point because several researchers have pointed to these similarities as evidence for potters' marks being the source of both the Indus script (Lal 1962, 1975; Fairservis 1971; Dales 1979; Potts 1981) and of the Proto-Elamite script (especially Brice 1970). One goal of this chapter is to examine these relationships and compare them to the list of symbols defined as graphic universals.

In order to generate a list of graphic universals it is first necessary to collect inventories of potters' marks from the 11 locations for which data is available in southwest Asia, in addition to

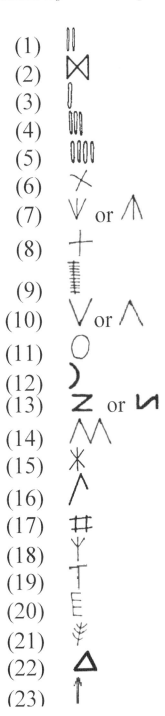

Figure 2.7 Comparison of graphic universals and complex signs.

sign lists for the Indus and Proto-Elamite scripts. Marks were included in the list if they occurred at two sites or more. This resulted in 57 entries (marks/signs) for the 14 sign inventories. The south and southwest Asia potters' marks, those from Tepe Yahya (Potts 1981), Shahdad (Hakemi 1997), the Quetta Valley (Fairservis 1956), Rehman-dheri (Durrani 1995a), and Mehrgarh (Quivron 1997), are the most numerous. Mature Harappan, chalcolithic and megalithic potters marks were also considered (Lal 1962; Meadow and Kenoyer 1993; Meadow et al. 1994, 1995, 1996, 1998, 1999, 2001). Because of the temporal and geographic characteristics of these data they are used here for comparison only. Additional comparative sets of potters' marks come from Vinca culture (Winn 1981), Neolithic China (Cheung Kwong-Yue 1983), and Abadiyeh (Petrie 1901). Comparative material for the Indus script (Wells 1999) and Elamite (Scheil 1923; Damerow and Englund 1989) were also considered.

The suggestion made here is that the most frequent signs are be graphic universals. The absolute order for sets of marks with the same frequency is arbitrary. The 23 highest loading symbols are given in Figure 2.6. All of these symbols occur in all three of the control groups, or in two of the control groups and ≥ 8 study groups. These symbols are the most likely to be graphic universals. This does not mean that other symbols in this table are not graphic universals, only that the further down the list a symbol is found the less likely it is to be a universal. There are categories that are mixtures of universals and complex symbols. If we count the number of times that symbols are found at a given number of sites, and look at the frequency of each score, they are not uniform. For example, only two signs occur at 13 sites (Figure 2.6:1 and 2) while five signs occur at 12 sites (Figure 2.6:3-7). What can be

seen clearly in Figure 2.7 is that these sign graphs can be divided into two clusters. Graphic universals occur at many sites while complex symbols occur at fewer sites.

The next step in this analysis is to look at the five south and southwest Asian sites for which there is usable information about a relatively large sample of potters' marks (Tepe Yahya, Shahdad, the Quetta Valley, Rehman-dheri, and Mehrgarh.). The list of marks can be sorted by their frequency at these five sites. An examination of the number of symbols that occur at these sites create a somewhat different sequence than the overall ordering, but the basic inventory remains the same.

The shift in the distribution of the sequence of marks indicates that the core set of potters' marks from southwest Asia are not just universals, but rather a mix of graphic universals and complex signs. This shared set consists of 29 marks that occur in at least three of the five sites for which there is data. Seven marks occur at all five sites (Figure 2.6:1-4 and 6-8), and five marks occur at four sites (Figure 2.6, 11, 13, 22). The system of southwest Asia potters' marks can be seen to consist mainly of graphic universals, with the exception of four symbols (Figure 2.6). As this table shows, three out of four of these signs come from Shahdad, Quetta, and Rehman-dheri. Four signs are about 14% of the total marks.

Relationships between south and southwest Asian sites

The comparison of potters' marks has been made before (Potts 1982:517; Fairservis 1971:46-49; Quivron 1997; Lal 1962:4-5). Of these comparisons Potts (1982) was the broadest and most detailed. His comparisons were based on a table (Potts 1982: his Figure 4) that listed 11 locations and compared 27 symbols. This table had two major problems. First, it was incomplete in terms of the presence or absence of some signs occurring at the listed sites. Second, the signs as defined by Potts were both redundant in some cases, and not detailed enough in other cases (Figure 2.8). For example, while Potts (1982) differentiates between variations of Figure 2.6:10 (which I do not) he lists Figure 2.6:7 left while ignoring Figure 2.6:7 right. It is my opinion that, because the orientation of the symbols on the pots varies indiscriminately, orientation is not an important factor in identifying discrete symbols. Additionally, in the Shahdad site report (Hakemi 1997) signs are reoriented unsystematically when added to the sign list. Further, the orientation of symbols on the bases of pots cannot be known with certainty, because it depends on the orientation of the pot at the time of marking. This makes considerations of orientation doubly useless in the process of symbol identification. Potts also treats Figure 2.6:7 and 2.6:23 as the same sign, while they are differentiated in this study.

While Potts (1981) does not use the same inventory of locations, a comparison of the sign frequencies is informative. Potts's reworked table (Figure 2.8B) contains 23 symbols and 15 locations. Fourteen symbols from this table are on the list of likely graphic universals, and nine are not. If we eliminate the five symbols not used here and graphic universals, this leaves six symbols unaccounted for (Figure 2.a, at right). These occur at 5, 5, 3, 3, 4, and 5 sites, respectively, in Figure 2.8b. Do these similarities suggest a connection between the sites in Potts's Figure 4?

We still cannot be certain of the answer to this question. I would point out that the overlap is 4.8% of the total symbols from Tepe Yahya. Additionally, Figure 2.b may be graphic universals and Figure 2.c could be a variety of Figure 2.d as they fall into the gray area between universal and complex symbols. This would leave an overlap of 2.4% of the signs from Tepe Yahya. This is not a very convincing result, and may or may not be due to coincidence.

It is obvious from the foregoing discussion that relationships between symbols are complex and difficult to define. Rather than focusing on a limited set of symbols shared by sites, it may be useful to look at the overlap in terms of the number of sites that a symbol occurs at. In the following table (Table 2.2) relationships between sites are expressed as the percentage of overlap of the 57 marks used here.

Only the columns are interpreted in Table 2.2. For example, 24 of the 57 marks used here are found at Tepe Yahya, and 17 of these 24 (or 70.83%) are also found at Shahdad. This is a strong relationship. These relationships need not be reciprocal. Notice that the 17 symbols shared by Shahdad and Tepe Yahya represent only 47.22% of the 35 symbols used at Shahdad. These relationships indicate that there is a strong relationship

廾, #, ♯, Ψ, 人, and ✳
2.a

#, 人, ✳   2.b

Ψ   2.c

Υ   2.d

A. Potts (1981) Figure 4

B. Potts (1981) Figure 4 revised

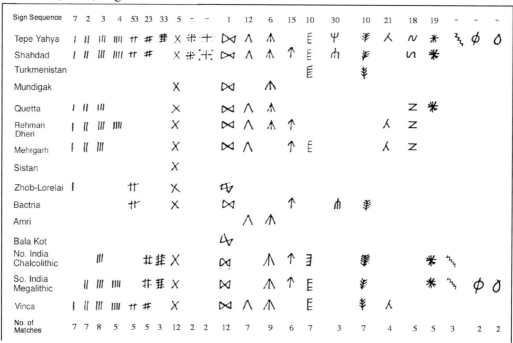

Figure 2.8 Graphic universals and connections between sites (after Potts 1981).

Table 2.2 Percentage of potters' Marks shared by sites

Site	Tepe Yahya	Shahdad	Quetta	Rehman-dheri	Mehrgarh
Tepe Yahya	X	47.22	28.57	31.43	63.64
Shahdad	70.83	X	60.71	60	72.73
Quetta	33.33	47.22	X	60	54.55
Rehman-dheri	45.83	58.33	75	X	77.27
Mehrgarh	58.33	44.44	42.86	48.57	X

between the Tepe Yahya and Shahdad marks (but less so with Mehrgarh/Nausharo). The relationship between the marks from Tepe Yahya and both Rehman-dheri and Quetta is weak.

From Table 2.2 it is clear that Quetta, Rehman-dheri, and Mehrgarh are closely related. This is an expected result because of the geographic proximity of these sites. What is somewhat unexpected is that Shahdad shared more of its inventory of marks with Rehman-dheri than with Tepe Yahya, which is also true of Figure 2.6. Shahdad and Rehman-dheri are represented by much larger samples of potters' marks, and this may have an influence on the degree of overlap.

Numerals

Table 2.2 measures the degree of the connection between sites without regard for the nature of these relationships. For example, Potts (1982:his Figure 4) points to near identical marks from Shahdad and Tepe Yahya. These sorts of exact matches are rare in southwest Asia, but systematic similarities are common between the potters' marks from these two sites. One way to assess the qualitative relationship between the potters' marks from Shahdad and Tepe Yahya, and the other sites, is to compare the marks that appear to have thematic similarities. One such set are the stroke and dot marks that may have a numeric function (numerals). The reasoning behind this choice is that we can reasonably expect that even if numeral symbols are graphic universals, systems of counting will combine these symbols in

different ways (Figure 2.9). Minimally 12 different sets of related symbols can be differentiated and tentatively identified as numerals. Set a consists of combinations of one to eight linear strokes. Symbols of one to four strokes have already been identified as graphic universals. It is of little surprise to see they occur at every site. Set b consists of one to four arc shaped symbols. One of these has likewise been identified as a graphic universal and is a common sign in the Indus script. All the rest of the symbols are complex signs. Figure 2.9 is arranged so that Tepe Yahya, Shahdad and Shar-i Sokhta (Iranian Plateau) are on the left, and Quetta Valley, Mehrgarh and Rehman-dheri on the right. The numerals of the Indus Script are at the extreme right of Figure 2.9. This figure arranges the numerals in a more or less west to east geographic order.

Numerals from Set a are found at all sites in Figure 2.9, but values greater than four are found only at Shahdad and Tepe Yahya. Set b numerals are also found everywhere, but they are least common at Rehman-dheri, Shahdad and Tepe Yahya (i.e. both geographic extremes). Set b numerals are most numerous at Mehrgarh and the Quetta Valley. Set c numerals are found only at Shahdad (and possibly rarely at Tepe Yahya). The top half of Figure 2.9 shows a general but not absolute trend in which geographically closer sites are more similar to each other than to sites further away – forming three groups: Shar-i Sokhta, Mehrgarh and the Quetta Valley in the first, Shahdad and Tepe Yahya in the second, and Rehman-dheri in the third.

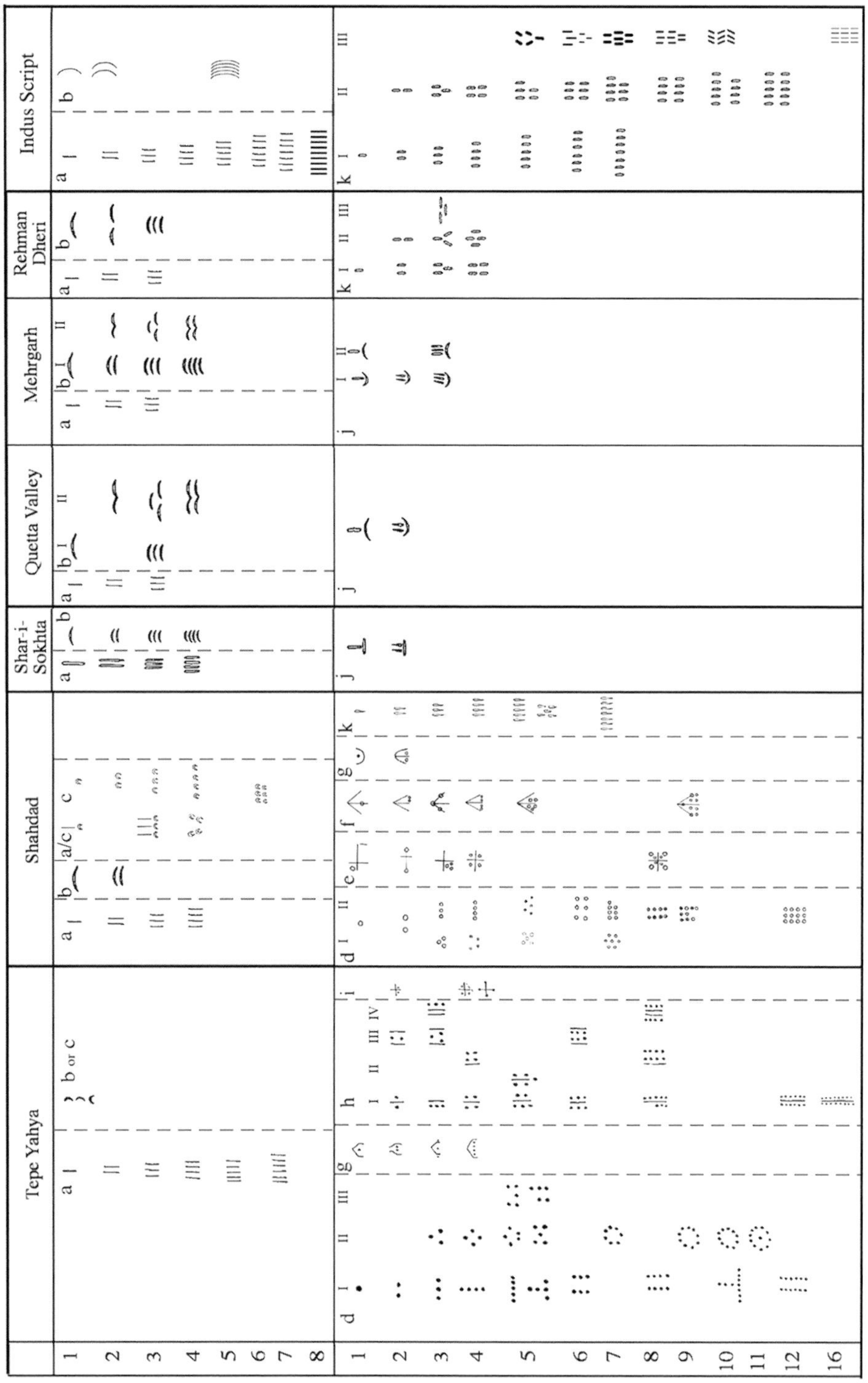

Figure 2.9 Systems of numerals from southwest Asian potters' marks.

This pattern is reinforced by the data presented in the bottom half of Figure 2.9. It is clear from the distribution of these symbols that the three groups of sites have different inventories of numerals. First, Rehman-dheri has its own unique set of numerals (k), while Shar-i Sokhta, Mehrgarh and the Quetta Valley are the only sites with Set j numerals. There are many specific and general similarities between the numerals of Shahdad and Tepe Yahya. Most striking are the similarities of the symbols in Set d. These two sets of symbols seem to be a related system of notation, which is more elaborate at Tepe Yahya. At Shahdad the Set a/c and c systems are unique. Regardless of differences in detail Shahdad and Tepe Yahya have far more complex systems than any of the other sites analyzed in Figure 2.9, and much of this complexity is shared.

It seems unlikely that there is a degree of similarity between some sites in Table 2.2 that cannot be accounted for by graphic universals. As can be seen in Figure 2.1, there is little chronological overlap between Rehman-dheri and Shahdad. Conversely, Shahdad and Tepe Yahya were in contact throughout the Bronze Age and were part of a system of trade stretching from Susa to the Indus valley and from the Persian Gulf (Bandar Abbas) to Shahdad and beyond. Bampur, Shahr-i Sokhta, Mundigak, the Quetta valley, and Mehrgarh/Nausaro were all part of this inland trading complex (Ratnagar 1981:26-42). The connectivity varied over time, but the routes were maintained from at least 3000 B.C. The relationships between systems of notation given in Figure 2.9 are surely tied to the greater or lesser integration of these sites into the trade networks of south and southwest Asia.

I would suggest that the within group sites are more related because: 1) they are in more intimate contact through trade and therefore: a) share an integrated system of common notation;

b) are likely to have been trading ceramics; 2) they are culture areas with similar or identical traditions of numeration; 3) they use potters' marks in similar ways; and, 4) they are in contact and this leads to the spread of general ideas about the proper method of notation, but with specific regional differences.

Suggestion 1 (a and b), 2 and 3 seems possible for Mehrgarh and the Quetta Valley system. They are both very close geographically and share related material cultures. Further the systems of notation are nearly identical. Shar-i Sokhta has a subset of the inventory of Set b marks, and has a unique way of rendering the Set j marks. This case seems more like suggestions 1b and 4. Rehman-dheri has even fewer of the Set b marks, and a unique system of its own (Set k). Again this seems like suggestion 4 but with a weaker connection to Mehrgarh and the Quetta Valley. The comparison of Shahdad and Tepe Yahya is more complicated, both because the systems of numeration are more complex and because the potters' marks at Shahdad are poorly recorded. If we take the data at face value we seem to have three shared systems (Sets a, d and g). Additionally, Shahdad has at least two other systems of unique markings, and Tepe Yahya has two unique sets as well.

The method of analysis offered here for the numerals has proven to be a useful tool for examining the similarities and differences between the potters' marks of the sites in question. The suggestions for why these relationships exist are highly speculative, but nevertheless are a positive first step towards a more complete analysis of the archaeological relationship between sites.

There is one additional point about numerals that is worth mention - namely the relationships between sets of numerals and the possible sequence of numerals in Sets a and b. An interesting feature of Set a numerals is that in the west of

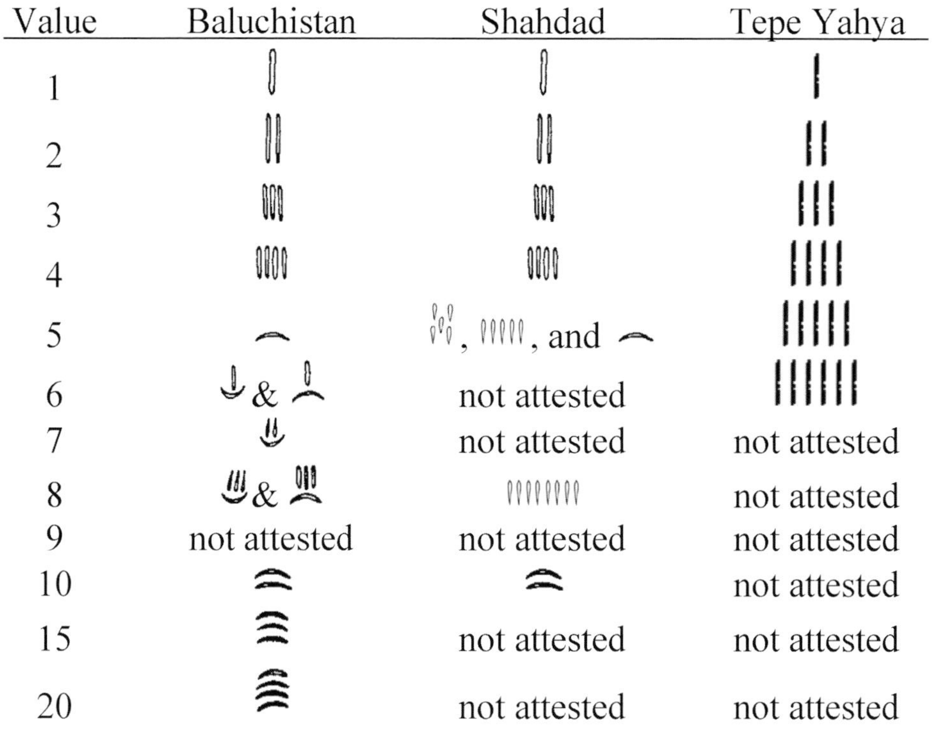

Value	Baluchistan	Shahdad	Tepe Yahya
1	〰	〰	ꟾ
2	‖	‖	‖
3	ꟾꟾꟾ	ꟾꟾꟾ	ꟾꟾꟾ
4	ꟾꟾꟾꟾ	ꟾꟾꟾꟾ	ꟾꟾꟾꟾ
5	⌒	⁙, ꟾꟾꟾꟾꟾ, and ⌒	ꟾꟾꟾꟾꟾ
6	↓ & ⌢	not attested	ꟾꟾꟾꟾꟾꟾ
7	↓↓	not attested	not attested
8	⫶ & ⫶	ꟾꟾꟾꟾꟾꟾꟾꟾ	not attested
9	not attested	not attested	not attested
10	≈	≈	not attested
15	≋	not attested	not attested
20	≋	not attested	not attested

Figure 2.10 A partial reconstruction of the south and southwestern Asian a and j number systems.

the study area they consist of one to eight strokes, in the central one to four and east one to three. In the central and east there is a j system that is absent in the west. From other research into the system of numerals in the Indus Script (Wells 2002) there is evidence for Figure 2.6:12 having a value of 5. A similar potters' mark is the basis for the Set b system. It is interesting that both potters' marks and Indus signs combine with short strokes and Figure 2.6:12 to list only the most obvious parallels from Mehrgarh and the Indus script. A value of five makes some sense for the potters' mark Figure 2.6:12. It would allow the whole system to be reconstructed (Figure 2.10).

It seems from this table that these two systems are related (Sets j and a), but one system uses five

and the other does not. It would be interesting to know if the ceramics from Shahdad with Set b numerals are trade wares or locally made. There is also one example (i.e. 1 sherd) with a Set b numeral from Tepe Yahya (9c from the IVa 3-2 Period ≈1800-1900 BC). Potts (1981) gives no other details about this specific item. Again the question arises: Is it trade ware or locally made?

If more attention was paid to the recording and adequate publication of potters' marks, much more could be done in the analysis of this material. For example, how many of the Set b numerals from Shahdad occur on traded wares? What are their frequencies? Is there some pattern to the burials, or other ceramics marked with Set b numerals? Of the 68 burials with potters' marks

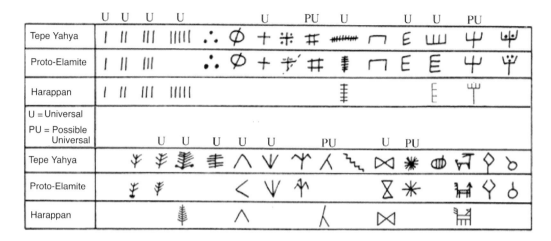

Figure 2.11 Tepe Yahya potters' marks compared to similar signs in the Proto-Elamite
and Indus scripts (after Potts 1981:117).

from Shahdad for which details are given, there is one that may have a Set b numeral (Grave 038, Object 0318, Plain Redware). Unfortunately, the photograph is not very clear, but it may bear the following mark: (12?). Its form is unsure and it does not appear in the Shahdad sign list, for these reasons it is omitted from Figure 2.9.

Potters' marks and the origins of south and southwest Asian linear scripts

As outlined earlier in this paper, there have been some suggestions that the Indus script, the Proto-Elamite script, or both were derived from potters' marks (Lal 1962, 1975; Fairservis 1971; Dales 1979a; Potts 1981; Brice 1970). Additionally, It has been suggested that the two scripts were related in a systematic way (Hunter 1932; Lal 1962, 1975; Brice 1907; Fairservis 1971, 1976; Dales 1979a; Potts 1981). Potts (1981:117) has tried to construct a table of signs shared by the Tepe Yahya potters' marks, and the Proto-Elamite, and Indus scripts (Figure 2.11).

I have modified Potts' original figure by replacing the Indus (Harappan) signs because of the many errors in their representation. Symbols are marked with U for Universals and PU for Possible Universals. It can be seen from Figure 2.11 that 67% of the symbols are Universals or Possible Universals. All but one of the symbols that overlaps with the Indus script are Universals or Possible Universals, and these signs are similar at only the grossest level.

The similarities between the Proto-Elamite script and the Tepe Yahya marks seem more convincing. This is not unexpected as the Proto-Elamite script came into use about 3100 BC, and the potters' marks about 3000 BC, but potters' marks do not come into common use at Tepe Yahya until after 2350 BC. At Shahdad potters' marks are also late (2600 BC). It would seem unlikely that Proto-Elamite developed out of potters' marks. In fact the inverse may be true; potters' marks from Tepe Yahya and Shahdad were profoundly influenced by Proto-Elamite, with some symbols being adopted directly.

In the Indus valley the situation is much different. The tradition of potters' marks begins 300 to 600 years earlier than the earliest evidence for the Indus script. There are 23 signs shared by the Indus script and the Baluchistan potters' marks. Of these 13 are universals, two are possible universals, and eight are complex symbols. These two systems seem highly related in comparison to the magnitude of the number of related signs shared by potters' marks of the Iranian Plateau and the Proto-Elamite script. We can construct a cross-matrix similar to Table 2.2 for south Asia (Table 2.3). The percentages in this table are calculated using the total number of symbols from each site. As in Figure 2.6, only the columns are interpreted.

For example there are 166 potters' marks from northwestern Pakistan, and of these 15.66% are shared with the Indus Script. The Indus Script has 620 signs, and of these 4.19% are found in northwestern Pakistan sites. There is a clear relationship between these two sets of symbols, as they both score the highest in relation to each other. The Indus script is twice as highly related to the northwestern Pakistan potters' marks as it is to Mature Harappan potters' marks. As can be seen in Figure 2.10, the highest scores in each column are in the northwestern Pakistan row. One possible interpretation of this is that all of these systems are derived from the chronologically earlier northwestern Pakistan potters' marks. It is also possible that, as Potts (1991:116) puts it, "...the potters' mark tradition provided, in some sense, a symbolic sub-stratum upon which, in part, the Harappan [Indus] script was built". Potts was referring to the work of Lal (1962, 1975) with the potters' marks of India, but the concept is even more appropriately applied to the much more highly related northwestern Pakistan potters' marks. The reason for the major difference between the Mature Harappan potters' marks and the signs of the Indus script might be purposeful in order to avoid confusion.

As for the relationship of the Proto-Elamite and Indus Scripts there are some problems with the idea that they are related. First, the sign inventories are very different. For example, in the Indus sign inventory there are 50 anthropomorphic signs (8%), there are none in Proto-Elamite (Scheil 1923). Zoomorphic signs are likewise common in the Indus script and much rarer in the Proto-Elamite. There are also a whole set of signs in Proto-Elamite based on triangular shaped basic signs (Figure 2.e) that have no counter part in the Indus script. The same can be said for other shapes in the Proto-Elamite script: (Figure 2.f). In terms of the symbols used in this study the Indus and Proto-Elamite scripts share 13 signs of which seven are universals and six are complex (no possible universals). This means the meaningful overlap (six signs) is about 0.97% of the Indus sign

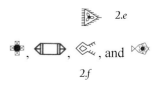

2.e

2.f

Table 2.3 Symbol overlap expressed as a percentage of total symbols from a site

	Northwestern Pakistan	Mature Harappan	Indian Megalithic	Indian Chalcolithic	Indus Script
Northwestern Pakistan	X	56.52	37.25	48.65	4.19
Mature Harappan	7.83	X	25.49	29.73	1.94
Indian Megalithic	11.45	56.52	X	43.24	2.1
Indian Chalcolithic	10.84	47.83	31.37	X	1.45
Indus Script	15.66	52.17	25.49	24.32	X

inventory and about 0.42% for the Proto-Elamite. From this I conclude that the Indus and Proto-Elamite scripts are not highly related, nor do they share a symbolic sub-strata.

Returning to Figure 2.9, a systematic similarity can be seen between the system of numerals in the Indus script and those of the various systems of potters' marks, especially those of Rehman-dheri. As expected Set a numerals are everywhere, and the Set b numerals are found at all sites but Tepe Yahya. It is the combination of Set a and b numerals combined with Set k numerals (shared by Shahdad, Rehman-dheri and the Indus script) that seems the most convincing connection. The Indus system looks very much like an elaborate form of the systems used at Shahdad and Rehman-dheri.

Conclusion

This chapter has examined the relationships between the various systems of south and southwest Asian potters' marks. The purpose of this research was to determine if these symbols formed a geographically and temporally related system of markings. The suggestion of a developmental relationship between the Proto-Elamite and Indus scripts, and whether they arose directly from potters' marks was also a major focus of this chapter. What was found is that potters' marks were related on a regional level with major differences in sign inventories occurring between sites (Figure 2.9). Most similarities between local systems could be attributed to a shared inventory

of graphic universals, or geographic proximity to other systems. The influences of trade could not be assessed, but this factor could account for significant inter-site similarities.

The similarities between south and southwest Asian Potters' Marks and the linear scripts of south and southwest Asia are systematic in several ways. First, the potters' marks from Tepe Yahya and Shahdad are related in detailed ways to Proto-Elamite signs. They share complex symbols and numerals. Second, the placement of potters' marks also varies with regionally recognizable patterns. The potters' marks from Tepe Yahya and Shahdad are most often found on the shoulder of the base of ceramics. Third, during the period of Elamite influence, signs from the Proto-Elamite script found their way into the inventory of potters' marks at both sites, and this, along with a shared inventory of universals, accounts for the similarity between potters' marks from Tepe Yahya and Shahdad, and the Proto-Elamite script.

The Merhrgarh/Nausharo and Quetta Valley potters' marks are related in the same way as the ones from Tepe Yahya and Shahdad. They share an inventory of symbols (Figure 2.9) and are most frequently found on the base of ceramics, but they lack any similarity to the Proto-Elamite script that cannot be explained in terms of graphic universals. Instead there is a weak but noticeable relationship between the Merhrgarh/Nausharo and Quetta Valley potters' marks and the Indus Script. As the initial use of potters' marks in this area predates the earliest evidence for the Indus script by several hundred years, it is possible that the potters' marks from Baluchistan had an influence in the signs chosen for the Indus script. One interesting point about potters' marks from Rehman-dheri is that, despite its close proximity to Merhrgarh/ Nausharo and the Quetta Valley, there does not seem to be any strong relationship between the symbols from these two areas (Table 2.4 and Figure 2.9). Nevertheless, there is a strong relationship between the potters' marks of Rehman-dheri and the signs of the Indus Script (77.78% overlap) and this is particularly true of numeral signs. The Rehman-dheri potters' marks predate the Indus script by several centuries, it seems possible that during the initial development of the Indus script its authors drew upon symbols from potters' marks of Kodiji, Rehman-dheri and Harappa. This makes sense in terms of trade relations and the movement of people and ideas. What is striking about the analysis offered in this chapter is the lack of any strong relationship between Mature Harappan potters' marks and the Indus script, despite the fact that they are geographically and temporally coincident. This may be a case of purposeful avoidance to eliminate potential confusion because both sets of marks are used on ceramics, but for different purposes.

Harappan period potters' marks are relatively rare within the Indus Valley as early excavators did collect pot sherds with potters' marks. They are often confused with inscribed ceramic texts in the Indus script and subsumed under the rubric of "graffiti", which includes all post-firing marks on ceramics. Of the 1,269 markings on ceramics listed in the ECIT, 426 (33.57%) are potters marks and 321 of these come from Harappa (75.35%). This obvious bias should be factored into any consideration of the analysis of these

marks. One way in which the Indus potters' marks differ from the other potters' marks studied here is that there is less variety of numeral marks. Only five different numerals are used: one to three long strokes, and two and three short strokes. This compares favorably to the potters' marks published from Harappa for the late Regionalization Phase (3300 BC to 2600 BC; Meadow et al 2000: his Figure 37). It may be that the numeric function of Mature Harappan potters' marks were supplanted by the Indus script.

The relationship between the Indus and Proto-Elamite scripts has already been discussed. It is only necessary to add that the degree of overlap between these scripts is significantly weaker than their relationships to the potters' marks from their respective regions. This, added to the large number of differences in sign inventories, leads to the conclusion that they are not related in a developmental sense. Rather, they developed along autochthonic trajectories, drawing on the local symbolic traditions for inspiration. It is unfortunate that the impact of trade on these relationships could not be assessed, as this information could significantly improve our understanding of the origins, development, and influences of potters' marks in the Bronze Age of south and southwest Asia.

Potters' marks are not the only concern with regard to the origin of the Indus script. Shendge (1997:7-17) goes into considerable detail concerning the absence of cultural continuity between the Early Harappan and the Mature Harappan periods. At many sites there is a clear break at this point in the chronology, with the possible exception of Harappa. We may have to look to Cholistan and the Hakra-Ghaggar drainage for the origins of the Indus civilization and the earliest forms of Indus writing.

This whole issue needs to be revisited with future fieldwork.

3

DEFINING AN
INDUS SIGN LIST

Once an adequate corpus of Indus texts is in place, the next logical step towards a decipherment is the creation of a comprehensive sign list. This strategy has been employed by most serious attempts at decipherment (Parpola 1970; Knorozov 1970; Mahadevan 1970). In retrospect, these sign lists were too generalized. With sign inventories ranging from 250 to 450 signs, they conflate many signs that can be demonstrated to have separate graphemic values, and many more that cannot be demonstrated to have the same value. This approach results in a flawed analysis that looses or confuses some sign relationships, and sometimes creates sign relationships that do not exist (Wells 1999:52-57, and Example 6 below). The definition of an Indus sign list is not straightforward, and there is great variety in the results offered in the literature.

The number of signs employed in a script can tell us what type of script it is - alphabetic, syllabic, logographic, etc. All of these have been suggested, as sign lists vary from 52 (Rao 1984) to more than 600 (Wells 1999). This in part depends on how you define the term sign. Rao (1984) looks for the basic elements that comprise Indus signs and differentiates deconstructable signs from 'picture' signs. Using this approach he defines 62 signs for the 'early' Indus script (40 cursive signs and 12 picture signs) and 24 signs (all cursive) for the 'late' Indus script. Unfortunately, Rao's basic premise is untrue. Picture signs do not fall out of use in the later levels at any site, including Lothal. In fact quite the opposite is true. Picture signs are absent or very rare in the earliest levels and become more frequent over time and then decrease slightly in the latest levels at all major Indus sites for which chronological data is available.

This does not imply that Rao's (1984) ideas are entirely uninformed. On the contrary the concept of basic, compound, and picture signs is taken up and elaborated on in this chapter (see Figure 3.7 and the discussion of components).

With the exception of one seal (Meadow and Kenoyer 2001: their Figure 4:1) and some potters' marks from Harappa there is little evidence of early examples of Indus writing. One basic assumption made here is that the vast majority of Indus texts available for study at present are from the part of the Integration Era dating to 2300 BC to 1900 BC, and likely represent a synchronic set of inscriptions with some development over the 400 year period for which there is data.

Defining Indus signs

The process of defining the sign list is a multiple step process. The first step (after a corpus is in place) is to examine the texts in as much detail as possible. My first sign list had more that 900 signs and included many graphic variations. It quickly became obvious, because of the overlapping contexts of graphic variations, that signs such as (sign 740) had a good deal of allographic variation and could be represented by a standard sign without risk of combining graphemes (see Figure 3.15). After a careful study of sign contexts (Wells 1999) using the CIST (Joshi and Parpola 1987; Shah and Parpola 1991) the sign list was compressed to 610 signs. Through the process of entering the ECIT data (adding 1,299 text not in the CIST) the sign list grew again to 762 signs. The availability of a comprehensive corpus and the ICIT program (v1.4) allowed a detailed analysis of sign contexts in a way that was previously impossible. There are still some sign definitions that are questionable - primarily with signs that have low frequencies of occurrence, but the vast majority of the signs offered in the current sign list are well understood through the analysis of their contexts, temporal distributions, and components. The sign list currently consists of 676 signs grouped into 71 sets. Signs are assigned to Sets based on their graph design. For example, all fish signs are assigned to Set 11. The number of signs given here (676) is likely an overestimate of the actual number of graphemes as there are many examples of sign graphs that have minor variations that cannot be clearly defined as either independent graphemes or as variants. In these cases signs are kept separate in the absence of clear proof that they are variants of the same signs. Note that the vast majority of Indus texts read right to left, and in the following sections and in the ICIT database, texts are standardized to read in this order whenever possible.

The following example demonstrates how sign varieties can be defined as either graphemes or graphic variants.

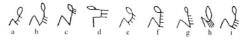

Example 1. Figure 3.a.

Example 1

This sign (Figure 3.a) has nine varieties, which are initially identified by their graphic similarities: (Figure 3.a). They all share identical distributions, and sign variants all inter-grade stylistically. Intergrading is a term applied to sign variants where the major design elements vary in such a way that all variations between extremes are attested in similar or identical contexts. On the basis of these features they can be defined as variations of a single grapheme, that can then be represented by a single sign (176) and assigned a temporary sign number (in this example 078). After the completion of the analysis a permanent sign number (176) was assigned. The same can be done for signs 177, 175, 180, 179, 178, and (Figure 3.o). The analysis of signs (Figure 3.o) and 175 results in the identification of sign (Figure 3.o) as a single occurrence of sign 175 in a text that reads left to right. Therefore,

3.o

175

176

177

178

179

180

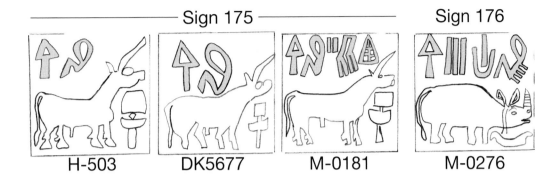

Figure 3.1 Comparison of texts containing sign 175 and 176.

sign 175 can represent them both. Signs 178, 179, and 180 are single occurrence signs, and the analysis of their contexts is inconclusive; therefore they remain as separate graphemes. The analysis of signs 176 and 177 identifies many left to right texts, but not all occurrences of 177 can be explained in this way. Signs 176 and 177 remain separate graphemes, but the left to right texts are subsumed under sign 176. The final comparison is between 176 and 175 and asks the question: are variations in the attachments on the right hand side of 176 merely stylistic or do they change the value of the sign? Contextual analysis of these signs yields two lines of evidence indicating they are separate graphemes: 1) there are seven clear mutually exclusive contexts - three where 175 occurs but not 176 and four where 176 occurs and not 175. These contexts occur in several texts each. The most compelling of these are the complete absences of sign 001 and sign 060 in texts containing 175. Additionally, when there are similarities between the sign inventories they have very different forms in 175 and 176 texts (Figure 3.1). In this example there are four of 18 sign 175 texts containing sign 520, but only one of 193 sign 176 texts contain 520, and in a very different context (i.e. non-adjacent); and, 2) they occur in the same texts in three cases (H99-3811, H-742, M-023). Based on this analysis 175 and 176 remain separate graphemes.

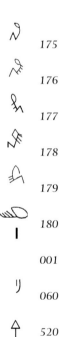

	175
	176
	177
	178
	179
	180
	001
	060
	520

The process of analysis

It can be seen from Example 1 that the analysis that leads to the differentiation of graphemes and allographs is a five-step process as follows:

    1) graphically similar signs are grouped into a single analytical set;

    2) if two similar signs occur in the same text, it is most likely that they

are separate graphemes. Stylistic variations are unlikely to occur within a single text, carved by one person;

3) the direction of reading must be considered (the left/right effect). If one of the signs is the mirror image of a second sign, and all non-coincidental contexts are found in texts read from left to right, then the two signs in question can be considered a variation of the same grapheme;

4) the effect of TAB artifact texts that repeat several times must also be controlled for. They can create the illusion of a large number of identical contexts, but these cannot be used to define graphemes, nor should they influence consideration of contexts. For the purposes of sign analysis they should be considered a single text; and,

5) if two signs with similar graphs are found in mutually exclusive contexts, even if they share some contexts, they are most likely different graphemes. Conversely, two signs that intermix freely in all contexts are most likely graphic variations.

As with all analysis, multiple lines of evidence reinforce these identifications, and some lines of evidence are stronger then others. Not all five steps are productive in every case, and the order of analysis is not fixed. In the following examples this process is applied to five sets of common Indus signs.

Example 2. Figure 3.b. Sign 353.

Example 2

350

353

3.c

3.d

3.p

Signs 353 (Figure 3.b) and 350 were initially defined on the basis of graphic similarity, but a careful analysis of their contexts had some surprising results. First, signs 350 and 353c occur in the same text (SD1911): Figure 3.c. Second, while the contexts of 353b and 353c are completely different from 350, the contexts of 353a and 350 cannot be distinguished on the basis of their context and sometimes occur in the same context, but never in the same text. Third, the graphs of 353a and 350 entirely inter-grade (Figure 3.2). What these lines of evidence indicate is that signs 353 and 350 need to be reorganized as follows: (Figure 3.d) = 353, and S350 (Figure 3.p) = 350. All varieties of sign 353 are represented by 353, and sign 350 varieties by 350. These signs are symmetrical, and so the R/L effect is not relevant.

VS1558

DK.H 31

Figure 3.2 Examples of the intergrading of sign graphs for signs 353a and 350.

DK8254

DK6713

920   921   *Example 3. Signs 920 and 921.*

Example 3

The system of dividing texts into fields was proposed more than five years ago (Wells 1999), and is now somewhat dated. This system is replaced in Chapter 4 by a more detailed one, but as the new system takes a good deal of detailed explanation, the old system is maintained for this discussion as it is adequate for this purpose.

This example illustrates the necessity of not assuming all mirror signs are resulting from the L/R effect. The contexts of signs 920 and 921 are summarized in Figure 3.3. This is not a list of all contexts but rather a list of the most telling contexts. Sign 921 (top of table) is found in several single contexts, but Figure 3.3 lists the most common mutually exclusive context with sign 920. The bottom half of the table lists four contexts of sign 920 that are not shared by sign 921. The first of these (A and B) is in the same structural (syntactic?) position as the 921 contexts (Field IV), but there is no overlap in the signs that they are adjacent to either left or right. Further, Figure 3.3c contains a very common context for sign 920 that is completely lacking in sign 921 contexts.

920

921

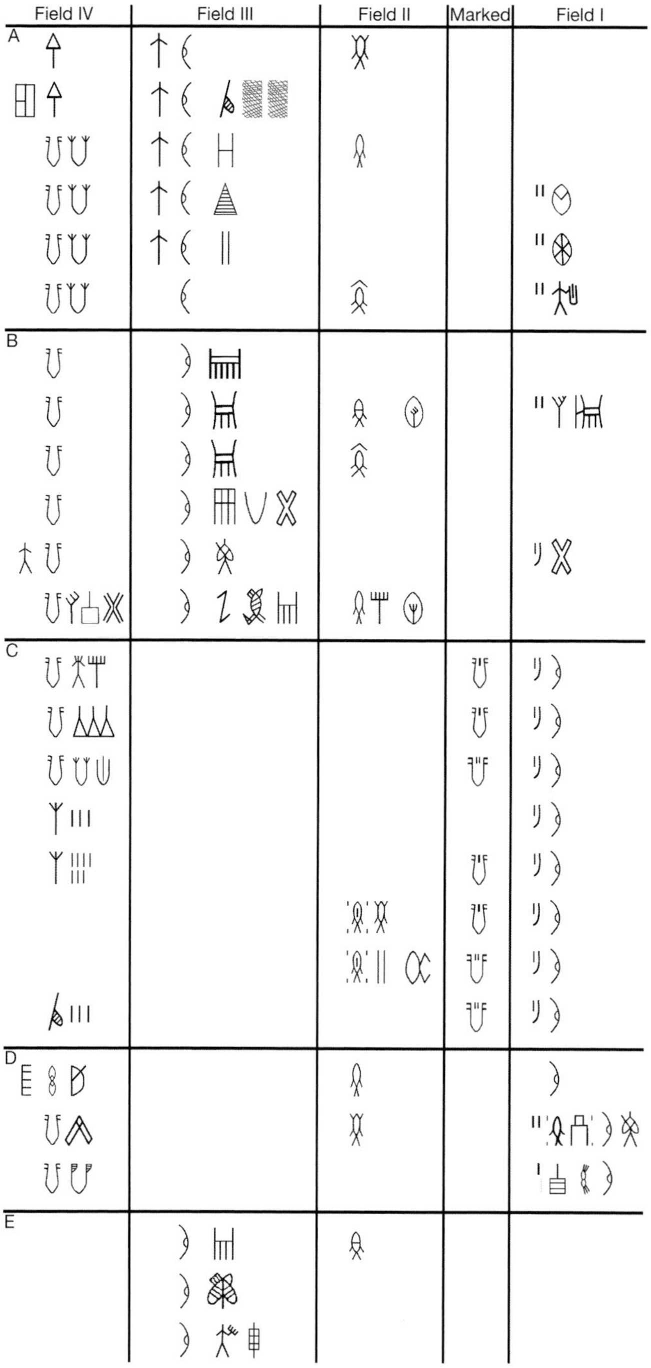
Field IV
Field III
Field II
Marked
Field I
A
B
C
D
E

Figure 3.3 Comparison of signs 921 and 920.

Example 4. Figure 3.e. Signs 527, 525, and 526.

This is also true for the less common, but very distinctive, contexts of Figure 3.3d and 3.3e. As there are very few texts with a left to right reading, this plays almost no role in the analysis of these two signs; they are two distinct graphemes.

Example 4

Signs 527 (Figure 3.e), 525 and, 526 are graphically similar, with the 525 having no internal markings, and the 526 being the mirror image of 527. From Example 3 we can reasonably expect 527 and 526 to be distinct graphemes and the many varieties of 527 to be allographs. A close examination of the varieties of 527 does verify that they are all variants of the same sign (now represented by the standard graph 527, but the distinction between 527 and 526 is less clear. Figure 3.4 lists 14 texts containing both 527 and 526, but this is a relatively small sample (27) of the total number of texts containing these signs (76).

This sample is composed of selected texts that also contain fish signs (Field II), and the syntax is somewhat different than that of Figure 3.3 in that there is no Field III. In these texts 527 and 526 intermix with no pattern. These contexts suggest that there is no preference for either sign regardless of circumstances. This can be said for all texts as far as adjacent signs are concerned. However, the ICIT program allows the texts to be sorted by their initial signs, and this has lead to a somewhat different result (Figure 3.5a).

The top of this table has the texts that also contain the sign sequence 002, 817, and these texts collocate exclusively with sign 527. This is curious in that, as the bottom of the table shows, no other texts with an introductory sign followed by 002 used either 527 or 526 exclusively. The texts using 527 come from Harappa (2) and Mohenjo-daro (6), and the uniformity of this context cannot be attributed to the effect of tablets. The same is true for the texts in Figure 3.5b. As in the top portion of Figure 3.5a, Figure 3.5b presents a limited example of a systematic preference for sign 527 in a specific context. The texts in Figure 3.5b are all of the texts with both 527 and 798, so the relationship here is absolute. These two contexts indicate that signs 527 and 526 could, in fact, be different signs. This can be contrasted by the large number of contexts in which these signs seem to intermix randomly (Figure 3.4).

525

526

527

002

817

526

527

798

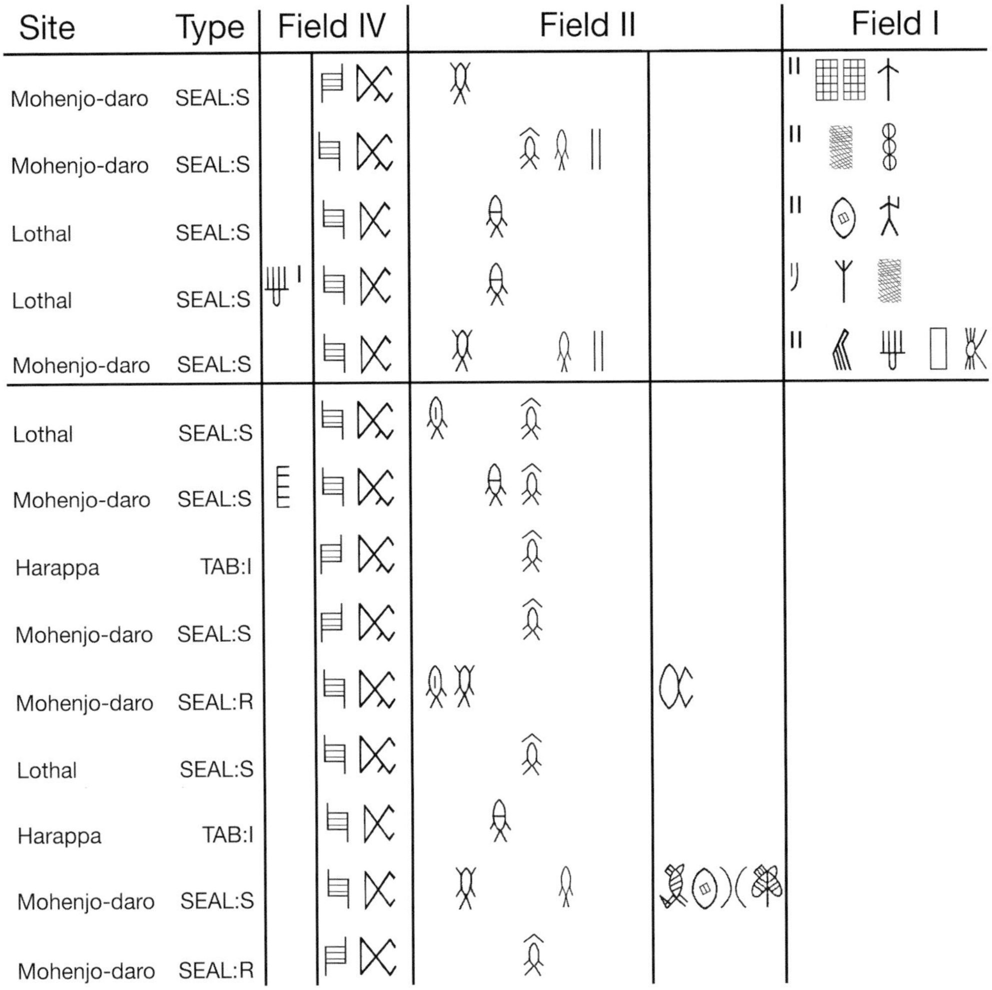

Site	Type	Field IV		Field II			Field I			

Figure 3.4 *Comparison of text with signs 494 and 618, and fish signs.*

This case is not clear-cut, and the evidence for variations being meaningful is not based on adjacent signs but rather on signs several syntactic units removed from these subject signs (527 and 526). There are two problems with the data supporting these signs as being separate graphemes: 1) sign 527 (n = 55) is much more common than 526 (n = 22); and, 2) the number of texts in this table is small (n = 8, n = 5).

Taken together these problems raise the possibility that these contexts are statistical aberrations on the boundaries of the expectations raised by probability.

There are no other contexts for which these signs have a preferential distribution. That is, in all other contexts they seem to intermix without pattern. While there is a small chance that 527 and 526 are separate graphemes, it is also

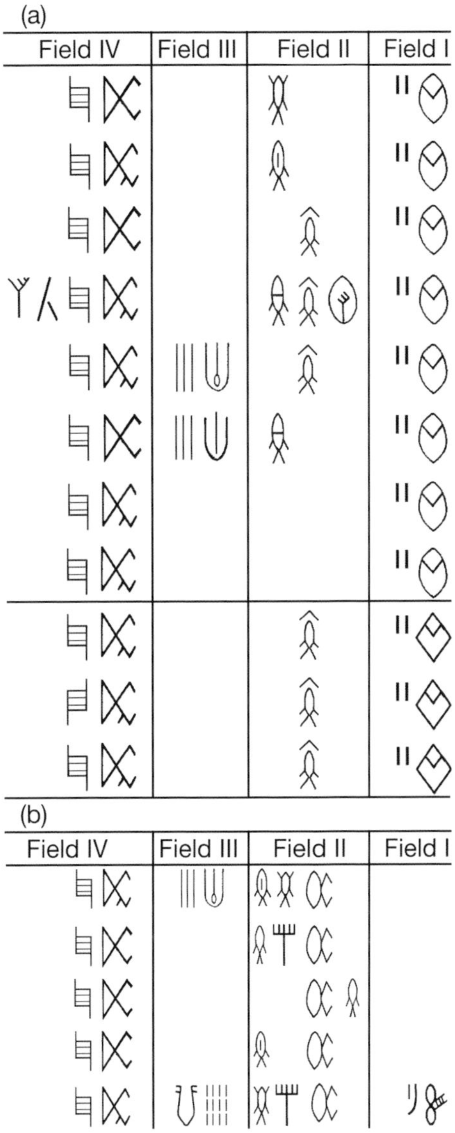

Figure 3.5 Sign 527 contexts.

likely that they are graphic variations of the same grapheme. As this issue cannot be clearly resolved, a policy of caution must be followed. Therefore, signs 527 and 526 will remain separate graphemes. As for sign 525 it does not seem to have exclusive contexts, but again the frequency of examples is low (n = 5). It cannot be subsumed under sign 527 and also must remain a separate grapheme awaiting further analysis.

Example 5. Figures 3.f, 3.g, and 3.h. Signs 705, 706, and 704.

Example 5

In this example the signs are symmetrical and therefore mirroring is not an issue. Instead, minor design elements are the focus of this analysis. Signs 705 (Figure 3.f), 706 (Figure 3.g), and 704 (Figure 3.h) are a set of graphically similar signs. They are differentiated by the design of their internal elements. Setting aside sign 704 for now, analysis can focus on signs 705 and 706. Within each set, sign varieties are demonstrated to be graphic variants as there is no pattern to their contexts. Consequently, varieties of sign 705 are represented by the sign graph 705, and sign 706 by 706. Signs 705 and 706 share several contexts including many examples of 520, 706, 033, and 520, 705, 033. In many of these contexts 705 and 706 intermix without pattern. Conversely, 705 occurs in six contexts exclusively and 706 occurs in two. What these distributions indicate is that 705 and 706 are mutually exclusive contexts and are therefore different graphemes.

These examples have demonstrated the methods used to define the graphemes of the Indus script. Not all signs can be analyzed in this way because of the low frequency of occurrence of many signs. There are no hard and fast rules about how many examples of a specific sign are necessary before it can be fully analyzed. Instead it is a matter of circumstances. In Example 4 relatively common signs could not be fully analyzed, while in Example 2 the relatively low frequency sign 353 could be analyzed as a separate grapheme with a high degree of confidence. It depends on how explicit the contexts are, and if the sign in question is being compared to a substantial set of texts. The purpose of this approach is to maintain the detail of the texts as far as is possible, and to avoid combining different graphemes, which has the effect of confusing the analysis of the more completely understood signs. This problem is common in the analysis offered in many of the proposed decipherments (Parpola 1970, 1975, 1994; Koskenniemi and Parpola 1979, 1980, 1982; Mahadevan 1986; Knorozov 1968). This effect is highlighted by the following example.

704

705

706

520

033

353

Example 6. Figures 3.i and 3.j.

Example 6

There are good reasons not to compress two signs when there is some doubt if they are separate graphemes. First, subsequent research that might

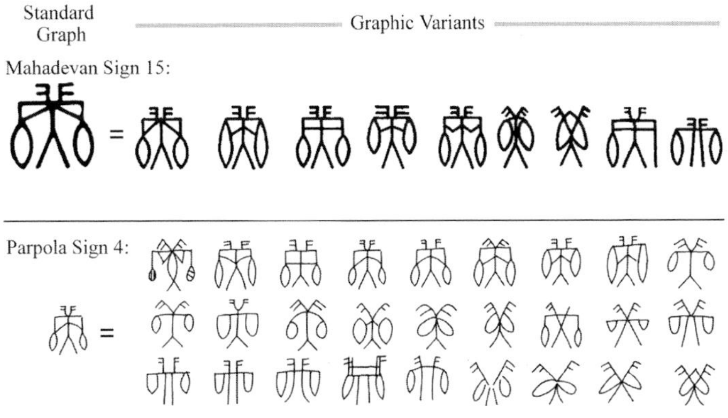

Standard
Graph ————————————— Graphic Variants ——————————

Mahadevan Sign 15:

Parpola Sign 4:

Figure 3.6 Variations in signs 155, 156, and 159.

reveal their true relationship cannot occur if they are reduced to a single grapheme. Second, if through some chance these signs are identified as separate graphemes separating them from one another becomes difficult. Nevertheless, several would-be decipherers have systematical compressed different graphemes resulting in sign lists with about 400 to 450 signs. This would mean that they are conflating as many as 250 to 300 signs. This creates confusion as signs that have no relationship are assigned the same graph to represent them.

Mahadevan's (1977) sign 15 can be described as the ligature of three graphic elements: (Figure 3.i) depicting a bearer using a yoke to carry some load represented by the two ellipses. The first two are common Indus signs, while (Figure 3.j) never occurs as an individual sign (see Example 6). Mahadevan lists nine varieties for his sign 15 and Parpola (1994) lists 27 varieties in his sign 4 as shown in Figure 3.6.

Some of these signs are obviously separate graphemes. Through the analysis of their contexts the remaining examples can be grouped into four separate graphemes: Sign 156 - those with arms and a carrying pole; Sign 155 - those with no arms, but which have a carrying pole; and sign 158 - those with neither arms nor carrying pole. Completely unique varieties (Parpola's sign 153 and Mahadevan's sign 157 can be divided into a separate analytical group. Sign 153 is a separate grapheme despite Parpola's list.

Sign 156 has six unique contexts including adjacency to sign 142 and sign 176. Signs 158 and 155 share some contexts, as do signs 156 and 155, but signs 156 and 158 share no contexts.

The context most relevant to these signs (155, 156 and 158) is the sequence: signs 155, 806, 468 that occurs five times at Mohenjo-daro and

	142
	153
	155
	156
	157
	158
	176

	155
	156
	157
	158
	390
	407
	468
	803
	806

17 times at Harappa, with signs 155 and 158 co-varying, and signs 467 and 468 occurring in most cases. Sign 156 never occurs in this context. The most constant element in this sign cluster is the middle sign 806. Sign 806 is never replaced by sign 803 and therefore signs 806 and 803 are not allographs as Parpola (1994:17) suggests. Likewise signs 390 and 407 must be separate graphemes, as their ligature forms are separate graphemes.

Sign 156, sign 155, and sign 158 are commonly represented by the sign 156 graph, and in Parpola's (1994) sign list sign 806 and sign 803 are also represented by the sign 803 graph. This results in (Figure 3.r) being represented by (Figure 3.s) in Parpola's system. The relationship between sign 155 and sign 806 is lost, and a relationship between sign 156 and sign 803 is fabricated where none exists. This cautionary tale demonstrates the folly of defining graphemes based on graphic similarity alone. Further, to separate these signs after they have been conflated is no simple task. The lesson then is to maintain separate signs until it is certain that they are allographs. This example also demonstrates how a single context can be used to identify several graphemes.

The mechanics of sign construction

	031
	063
	090
	381
	400
	415
	480
	510
	520
	590

Figure 3.7 lists the variations in the mechanics of sign construction that are applied to basic signs. In this study a basic sign is a sign with a simple graph. These signs are the basic units used to create the various more elaborate signs using one of the mechanisms described in Figure 3.7. An exact inventory of basic Indus signs is not possible with certainty because it is impossible to know where to draw the line between basic and compound signs. For example, is sign 415 a basic sign or is it a compound sign composed of two basic signs sign 0400 and sign 031? The same question can be asked of many Indus signs including: sign 510, sign 520, sign 381, sign 590 and others. Even the so-called 'man' sign sign 090 can be analyzed as a compound sign: sign 063 + sign 480, or as sign 480 + sign 031 + sign 480. Depending on where you draw the line there can be between 30 and ≈120 basic signs. My count is about 145 signs, 30 of these being the basic number system. It is tempting to equate basic signs with syllables and conclude that the Indus script is heavily syllabic with a small inventory of logographs, but (as is always the case with the Indus script) it is not that simple. Syllabic signs should appear compounded, and alone in every position in texts. Signs that have restricted contexts (fish signs and several of the basic signs) are most likely logographs because of their fixed syntactic positions. Further, syllabic and determinative signs will be regularly associated with logographs, which can give the impression that they have fixed contexts. The work on

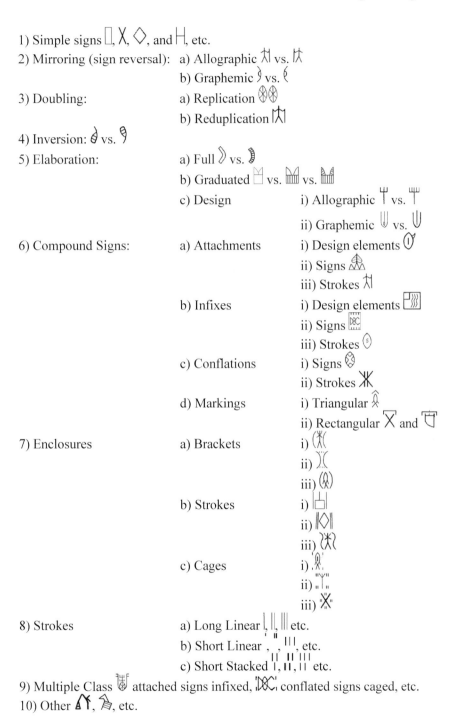

1) Simple signs ⬚, ⋎, ◇, and ⊢, etc.
2) Mirroring (sign reversal):   a) Allographic ⼦ vs. ⼫
                                 b) Graphemic ⼁ vs. ⼂
3) Doubling: a) Replication ⼀⼀
                                 b) Reduplication ⼧
4) Inversion: ⼁ vs. ⼁
5) Elaboration: a) Full ⼁ vs. ⼁
                                 b) Graduated ⼙ vs. ⼙ vs. ⼙
                                 c) Design   i) Allographic ⼁ vs. ⼁
                                                ii) Graphemic ⼁ vs. ⼁
6) Compound Signs: a) Attachments i) Design elements ⼁
                                                 ii) Signs ⼁
                                                 iii) Strokes ⼁
                                 b) Infixes   i) Design elements ⼁
                                                 ii) Signs ⼁
                                                 iii) Strokes ⼁
                                 c) Conflations i) Signs ⼁
                                                 ii) Strokes ⼁
                                 d) Markings   i) Triangular ⼁
                                                 ii) Rectangular ⼁ and ⼁
7) Enclosures   a) Brackets   i) ⼁
                                                 ii) ⼁
                                                 iii) ⼁
                                 b) Strokes   i) ⼁
                                                 ii) ⼁
                                                 iii) ⼁
                                 c) Cages   i) ⼁
                                                 ii) ⼁
                                                 iii) ⼁
8) Strokes   a) Long Linear ⼁, ⼁, ⼁ etc.
                                 b) Short Linear ⼁, ⼁, ⼁, etc.
                                 c) Short Stacked ⼁, ⼁, ⼁ etc.
9) Multiple Class ⼁ attached signs infixed, ⼁ conflated signs caged, etc.
10) Other ⼁, ⼁, etc.

Figure 3.7 Strategies used in Indus sign construction.

the Proto-Elamite sign list (Dahl 2005) demonstrated that many of the complex and compounded signs in that script are the combination of logographs with other logographs and numbers.

Compound signs

If we examine the contexts of some compound signs and their components we find that there is little agreement between them. For example, sign 142 can be analyzed as either 090 + 031 or 095 + 031. Yet, neither of these pairs occurs together as separate sign pairs in an inscription. It seems unlikely that there would be no examples of these signs as pairs when they occur together in a compound sign so frequently. This is also true of most of the other compound signs. Exceptions might be any or all of sign 136 (sign 090 + sign 400), sign 130 (sign 090 + sign 400; or sign 090 + sign 415), or sign 132 (sign 090 + sign 400; or sign 090 + sign 407), depending on how you deconstruct the compound signs. This highlights another problems with the deconstruction approach - the exact constituents of compound signs are often difficult to determine. Further, the analysis of compound signs in this way assumes that they are meant to be deconstructed and understood as separate elements.

Why then bother to conflate them in the first place? One possible reason is that this would save space in the crowded format of the Indus artifacts. There is some evidence supporting the idea that the conservation of space is a concern to the Indus scribes. One clear example of this need to conserve space is the variation of sign 460 (Figure 3.k), where the shifts in orientation are always linked to a lack of space. There is no evidence that compounding of signs occurred to save space. The most likely reasons for compounding of signs is that the combination is a fixed spelling (for example a diphthong or common word), or that the combination is a new sign with its own value (either logographic or syllabic).

As Figure 3.8 demonstrates the contexts of sign 130 do not support the idea that these compound signs result from compression due to lack of space. Instead they seem to indicate a completely separate context for sign 090 + sign 400, especially as sign 130 and sign 400 occur in the same text. The first text would seem to be the replacement set of sign 400 + sign 090 for sign 130, but this does not account for sign 740. As for the sign 090 + sign 415 possibility these signs never occur in the same texts. What then is the purpose of compounding signs? Given the data at hand, a linguistic explanation seems the most probable, but it is not simple syllabic spelling because of the sign 400 + sign 130 combination. It is important to realize that sign 400 + sign 090 + sign 740 is a relatively common combination of signs (n = 10). There are no examples of sign 090 + sign 415 nor do the 10

	031
	090
	095
	130
	132
	136
	142
	400
	407
	415
	460
	3.k
	740

contexts of sign 090 + sign 400 suggest any connection to either sign 136 or sign 130. There is likewise no connection between the contexts of either sign 136 or sign 130 that would suggest they are allographs of the same sign. These compound signs are likely to have separate and unique semantic values.

In the Indus script one sign dominates the compound and gives it its form. For example, sign 090 compounds with 22 other signs, but in all circumstances sign 090 dominates the pairing. For example, one never finds Figure 3.z1, nor Figure 3.z2. If we look to Proto-Cuneiform for how signs compound, we find two clear examples that are analogous to what happens in the Indus script: mouth (ka, inim) + bread (nig, sha) = food (ku), and mouth (ka, inim) + water (a) = drink (nag). In both cases the head sign (mouth) dominates the conflation (conflation is any time two signs are joined in such a way as to overlap and appear as on sign), but the resulting signs have unique phonetic and semantic values.

Some elements - sign 390, sign 407, and sign 405 - are commonly found as minor elements in compound signs. For example, sign 130, sign 045, sign 046, sign 571, sign 570, sign 404, sign 394, sign 806 and sign 803 to list just a few. In addition to two sign compounds, there are three sign compounds (sign 585 and sign 115), four sign compounds (sign 153 and sign 823), and five sign compounds (sign 778). Some compounds seem to form sequences: sign 090 - sign 152 - sign 153 - sign 156, or related set: sign 712, sign 753, and sign 751. The signs most often used as subsidiary signs in compounds are sign 390, sign 407, sign 031, sign 001, sign 002, and sign 003. Not all relationships between compounds and constituent elements of compounds are as transparent as those discussed above. Compound signs are found in all parts of Indus texts, and once compounded the distributions of these signs are no longer related to those of their constituent signs. Compounding signals a shift in semantic values of the constituent signs.

Markings

Marking in the Indus script consists of three varieties. Triangular markings (13 signs) are relatively rare in the Indus script being about 1.4% of all Indus signs. They are, however, an important analytical set in that they represent a relatively large number of texts (n = 257). This large number of texts is mostly sign 235, which accounts for 229 of these texts. This method of marking has often been separated from other types of compounding and, along with rectangular markings, treated as a special class of sign. But is this special treatment warranted? Within the Indus system of compounding they are not unusual, in that elements and signs are

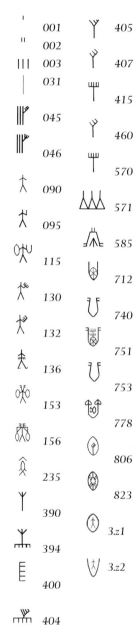

added in a way in which all members of the compounded sign are distinct and legible. A brief survey of the triangularly marked signs reveals that infixing or conflating the triangular element (sign 480) is not possible for reasons of aesthetics, clarity, or space. In short, the compounding of sign 480 with other signs is just another form of compounding, but has been given a special status because of subconscious analogies made to diacritic markings used in familiar alphabetic systems.

Rectangular marking is relatively rare, both in terms of the number of signs (n = 9) and the number of texts involved (n = 34). The most common sign in this group is sign 679. This rectangular element can be found compounded with two other signs - 094 and 150. These signs are found in very different contexts, implying the placement of this element affects its meaning. The placement of markings above the sign may also have a separate value. Note that the compound (Figure 3.l) is not attested in the Indus script, and therefore has no meaning in the Indus system.

Doubled signs

There are two types of doubling evident in the Indus script - replication and reduplication. The process of replication is one in which a sign is duplicated in whole and becomes part of a fixed pair (sign 821). This sign has a distribution unrelated to the single version of the sign. There are 18 examples of replicated signs and they occur in 199 texts. Reduplicated signs are signs in which some element of a sign is doubled and added to a new compound sign (sign 143). There are 24 reduplicated signs. Again, the distributions of the resulting signs are not related to the distributions of the original compounded signs. An interesting feature of doubled signs is their tendency to occur in texts with other doubled signs in many examples (S. Bonta pers. comm. 2004). Bonta (pers. comm. 2004) has suggested that this tendency may be linked to the necessity for elements within a sentence to agree, perhaps in number. In Shang Chinese writing, the symbol for 'tree' is doubled to create the symbol for 'wood' and tripled to create the symbol for 'forest' (Bottero 2004:256). There is no evidence as to the function of doubling in Indus texts, but if Bonta (pers. comm. 2004) is right it may be marking pluralization.

Elaboration

Signs with identical shapes can have different types of internal markings. This internal elaboration can take two forms: a) none vs. full, sign 923 vs. sign 924; or, b) graduated, sign 335 vs. sign 336 vs. sign 337. Differences are particularly clear for sign 335 and sign 337, where there are many distinct contexts. Both of these forms of elaboration result in a change of sign distributions when compared with the unfilled form. The most difficult obstacle to full analysis of these signs is the often low frequency of their various forms. For example, the definition of sign 336 as a separate grapheme is less clear because of limited comparative contexts available for analysis.

Design element elaboration is very common in the Indus script. It can be either stylistic (with no effect on sign behavior), or graphemic (there is a noticeable effect on sign behavior). Both sign 400 and sign 415 are particularly good examples of signs with many varieties of design element elaboration. The tines in the comb elements of these signs vary considerably without any noticeable effect on sign distributions. Conversely, minor variations in sign design can have a remarkable effect on sign behavior. For example, the addition of a minor design element in the sign sign 704, creates sign 705 which have both identical distributions and their own unique distributions. This may be indicating a minor variation in semantic value. The example of Mahadevan's sign 15 given above is a more dramatic example of minor design elements (arms) being important in differentiating graphemes with otherwise identical graphs.

Enclosures

There are three types of enclosures: Brackets, Strokes, and Cages (64 signs in total). Each of these has three subtypes depending on the details of usage. Enclosures have a somewhat unclear function but often change the behavior of the enclosed sign so that unique contexts of the enclosed sign occurs. The detail of enclosed signs is dealt with in Chapter 4. It is sufficient here to point out that enclosures do not affect sign behavior universally. When enclosure (especially cage marks) shift sign position within the text, it is likely changing the syntactic value of the sign and may be analogous to circumfixes used in some languages (i.e. German, Bahasa Indonesia and Guaraní).

Stroke signs

Stroke signs are very common in the Indus texts (37 signs). There is some hesitation to identify them as numerals per se in all instances, and there are several good reasons for this. First, in some ancient scripts numerals have homophonic syllabic values (Dahl 2005:6). Some of the long linear strokes, especially sign 031, sign 032, and sign 033, seem to function in this way. Second, in some cases numerals mark sign 231 or compound sign 145 with other signs (n = 35). Third, two of the short stroke signs (sign 001 and sign 002) have at least four identifiable functions (see Chapter 4). They are sometimes Initial Cluster Terminators, word dividers, numerical signs, and in rare cases are used as syllabic signs. As is demonstrated in Chapter 5, stroke signs, in the majority of contexts, functions as numerals and are part

	335
	336
	337
	400
	415
	704
	705
	001
	002
	003
	031
	032
	033
	145
	231

of a highly patterned system of numerical notation that includes positional notation among other features.

The Indus sign list

By my current count the Indus script is composed of 676 signs that can be
classified into one of 34 types (Figure 3.7). These types are based on the various strategies applied in sign construction. Figure 3.7 shows that Indus
signs are part of an organized system that utilizes definable mechanics in
the construction of signs. The count of total signs (676) is in the range of
logo-syllabic scripts, but the count of unique signs is actually closer to 145
with 30 of these being the basic number system. Sign numbers range from
001 to 958 with many unused numbers interspersed between sets. This
allows for the expansion of the sign list as necessary. Signs are further classified by their graphic similarity to each other (Set). This results in Set numbers from 1 to 71 (Set 26 is not used), with Set 71 containing all of the signs
that do not fit in any other Set. The complete sign list is given in Figure 3.8.

This sign list is the result of more than 10 years of research. The process
of creating a sign list is one that begins with collecting as much detailed
information about signs as possible (Wells 1999). This process leads to
a very large sign list with many graphic variants listed separately.
For example, sign 740 (formerly sign 288) began as (Figure 3.m), is now
represented by a single sign graph sign 740. The same is true of most signs
with a frequency of greater than one. The differentiation of graphemes and
the compression (i.e. subsuming them under a single sign number) of graphic variants cannot begin until a detailed listing of all variants is made. The
compression of graphic variants in Figure 3.8 is based entirely on contextual
analysis using the ICIT program (v1.58) and the methodology outlined
above. The resulting sign list is not a definitive listing of Indus graphemes,
as there are many groups of signs that cannot be compressed with confidence, either because of their low frequency or because they are part of a
group of signs that graphically related (for example, sign 298 + and the
majority of Set 17). These may all be allographic variants of a single
grapheme, but the variety of forms is complex and patterned in a way that
suggests some purpose. Compressing these signs into a single grapheme
would effectively remove detail from the sign list that cannot be easily recov-
ered. Additionally, compression precludes further analysis of these details
that may turn out to be graphemic in the light of new additions to the corpus. This sign list attempts to strike the balance between the extremes of
Rao (1984) and recording every graphic variant as a separate sign. Too many
signs that are actually graphic variants complicates analysis, too compressed
of a sign list looses important details (Example 6 above).

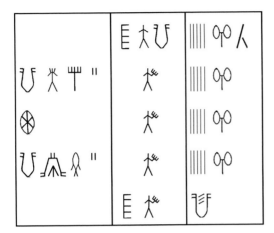

*Figure 3.8 Some important
contexts of sign 130.*

A properly constructed sign list is critical to the next phase of analysis –
the counting of signs, their positions in the texts and relationships to one
another. For this purpose a set of counting programs have been written that
count all signs in the ICIT database, their position in the texts (initial, medial,
or terminal), which signs occur together, and which signs occur with numeral signs (see Chapter 5). These tallies are counted by site and by artifact type.

The Figure 3.2 sign list and corrected ICIT database combine as a pow-
erful tool with the newest version of the ICIT program (v1.58). The analysis offered in the following chapters is based on the results of the counting
programs and ICIT program. The ICIT program allows the collection, dis-
play, and sorting of texts containing any number of signs. This means that
sign 298 and all of Set 17 can be analyzed together, in subsets, or individually. The following sign list is based on the methodology described above,
and can be verified using the ICIT program.   298

The use of computer-based analysis has in the past been somewhat robot-
ic. The expectation has been that the computer will supply the answer, or
some insight into the question. The approach used here places the emphasis
on the computer as a tool aiding of human analysis. Computers are useful in
the management of data, but it is the individual human interpretation of the
data that will lead to an improved understanding of the Indus script.

Analysis of the Indus script sign list
Constructing a detailed sign list of Indus signs is not the final goal of this
chapter, but rather a necessary initial step in the analysis of the character
and behavior of Indus signs. Having the sign list in hand makes it possible to answer several important questions. First, the frequency of Indus
signs can be compared to other ancient scripts in order to examine the
relatedness of these systems – as can the search for matching signs.

Second, inter-site comparisons of sign inventories can be analyzed for indications of multilingualism in the Indus texts. Third, sign inventories can be used to define differences in subject matter between sites, and between artifact types, both for a specific site and between sites. Fourth, comparison of sign inventories can isolate signs that locate preferentially at a site or on a certain type of artifact. Fifth, the analysis of some of the chronological aspects of sign distributions can lead to the identification of changes in the system over time. The following discussion focuses on these aspects of the sign list and database.

The nature of Indus signs

The inventory of Indus signs makes several aspects of sign construction clear (Figure 3.7). One method commonly used to create Indus signs is compounding. Two signs are conflated to create a third sign that has its own characteristic distributions. This is the most common method of creating new signs. Signs can also be modified with a variety of enclosing marks. The resulting signs have distinct distributions from the unmarked varieties. There are also design elements that can be added to signs to create more elaborate forms of basic signs. Up to six different signs, enclosures and elements can be combined to create a single sign. For example, sign 751 is composed of sign 031 + sign 400 + sign 400 + sign 790 + internal elaboration (to form sign 820) + sign 740. Some signs with complex graphs are not divisible into separate signs or elements. These signs are called complex signs in this discussion. For example, sign 157 and sign 363 have complicated sign graphs that do not consist of other known signs, enclosures or elements.

Many signs belong to groups of graphically similar signs, and it is uncertain whether these signs are intended as one sign or if minor graphic variations are meant to differentiate signs. For example: (Figure 3.n) - is this one sign or 17 signs? Seven of these signs are singletons, and seven occur twice. Fifty-eight signs in the sign list (Figure 3.2) belong to such allographic sets.

Singletons (1×) in Figure 3.10 are most commonly constructions of several sign components, or members of one of the allograph sets. The most frequent signs (n > 29) are most often-single component (basic) signs. Of the signs that occur more than 100 times none consist of more than three components. Given these distributions one could postulate that the high frequency, single component signs are good candidates for

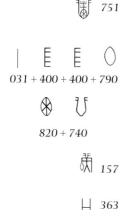

751

| 031 + 400 + 400 + 790

820 + 740

157

363

289 290 291 292 293 294 295 296 297 299 300 301 302 303 304 305 306

3.n.

Figure 3.9 An Indus sign list by sign number (continued on the following two pages).

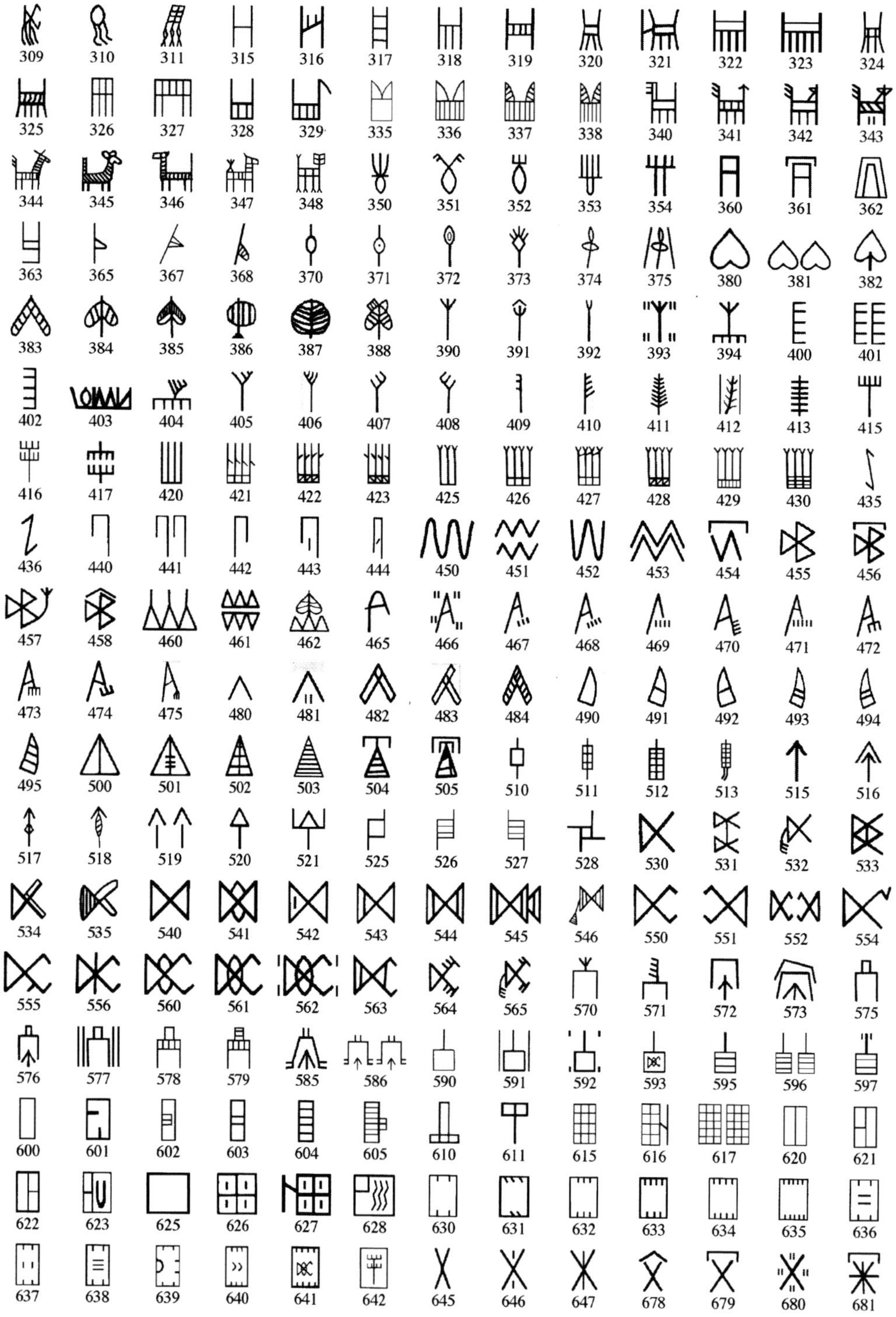
309 310 311 315 316 317 318 319 320 321 322 323 324
325 326 327 328 329 335 336 337 338 340 341 342 343
344 345 346 347 348 350 351 352 353 354 360 361 362
363 365 367 368 370 371 372 373 374 375 380 381 382
383 384 385 386 387 388 390 391 392 393 394 400 401
402 403 404 405 406 407 408 409 410 411 412 413 415
416 417 420 421 422 423 425 426 427 428 429 430 435
436 440 441 442 443 444 450 451 452 453 454 455 456
457 458 460 461 462 465 466 467 468 469 470 471 472
473 474 475 480 481 482 483 484 490 491 492 493 494
495 500 501 502 503 504 505 510 511 512 513 515 516
517 518 519 520 521 525 526 527 528 530 531 532 533
534 535 540 541 542 543 544 545 546 550 551 552 554
555 556 560 561 562 563 564 565 570 571 572 573 575
576 577 578 579 585 586 590 591 592 593 595 596 597
600 601 602 603 604 605 610 611 615 616 617 620 621
622 623 625 626 627 628 630 631 632 633 634 635 636
637 638 639 640 641 642 645 646 647 678 679 680 681

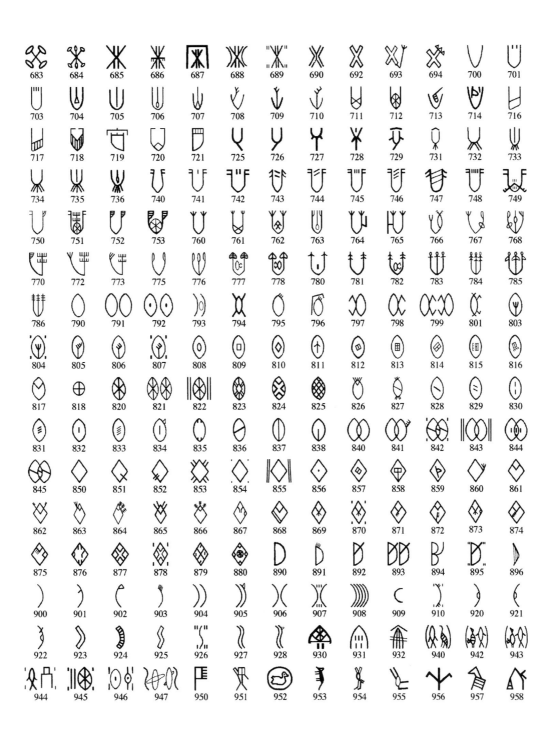

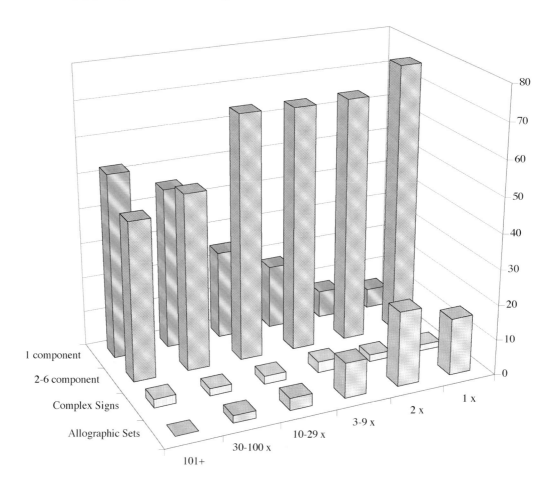

Figure 3.10 Number of sign components by sign frequency.

syllabic signs. Clusters of these signs may be syllabic spellings. This postulation is tested in Chapter 4.

The comparison of sign frequencies from related scripts

There are two striking features of the frequency distribution of Indus signs - the large numbers of signs that occur only once (singletons) and the small number of signs that occur extremely frequently. This sort of distribution is not unusual in sign lists from evolving ancient scripts. In southwest Asia it is very common, as Figure 3.11 shows.

The most obvious feature of this graph is that the Proto-Elamite script has many more singletons than either of the other two scripts. It can also be seen that the Indus script is most similar to proto-cuneiform. The reason for the large number of singletons and large numbers of allographic variants is that these scripts had not yet been standardized (Damerow 1989). This is exactly what happens with the Indus script. There are sets of signs that are graphically related

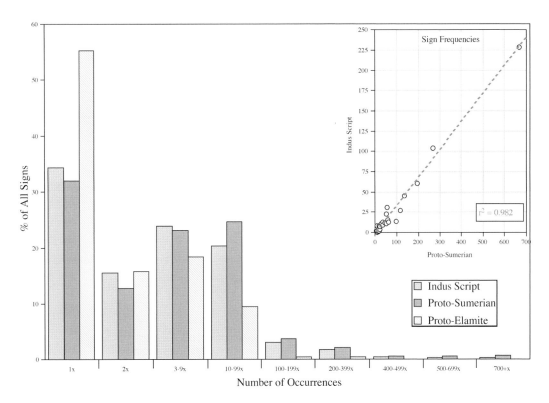

Figure 3.11 Comparison of sign frequencies from three ancient scripts (Proto-Sumerian, Demerow 1989; Proto-Elamite, Dahl 2005; and Indus Script 2006).

but with minor variations in the design of their graphs (allographic sets). In the case of the Indus script this lack of standardization may be linked to some cultural feature. It has long been noted that, despite standardization of weights and some ceramics, and the obvious civic works, there is little evidence for a Pan-Indus control structure (no places of central authority, monumental architecture, or temples). A second factor is that both Proto-Elamite and the Indus script use the compounding of common signs (especially logograph + number) to create new signs that, while unique, are composed of high frequency signs.

As has been shown in this chapter some variations in sign design can be signaling variations sign value with resulting variations in sign use,

while some variation are only graphic variations. In cases where variations cannot be demonstrated to be either graphic or graphemic the signs are kept separate awaiting further analysis. These uncertain signs appear in the sign list as low frequency signs (often as singletons), and have the effect of artificially inflating the count of singletons (Figure 3.11).

High frequency signs can be the result of the abundance of certain artifact types at a site. For example, a comparison of the sign frequencies from Mohenjo-daro and Harappa show variations in rank order and inventory of the most frequent signs. The 10 most common signs from Mohenjo-daro and Harappa are given in Table 3.1. The rank of each sign at

Table 3.1 Ranked order of the 10 most common Indus signs

Sign No.	Harappa	Mohenjo-daro	Total
740	1	1	1,696
002	6	2	763
700	2	63	565
032	5	4	507
033	4	8	445
220	7	3	443
400	3	23	432
240	8	6	331
520	10	5	282
235	19	9	243

Mohenjo-daro and Harappa is given along with the sign graph, sign number, and total frequency for each entry. The question of why these sequences are different can be answered by a careful examination of the artifact inventories from each site. The presence of large numbers of TAB:B and TAB:I artifacts at Harappa, and the high frequency of signs 700, 033, 032, and 400 are not a result of coincidence, but rather a recognizable pattern.

In fact, TAB:B and especially TAB:I texts very frequently contain the sign 033 + sign 700 (033-700) or the sign 032 + sign 700 (032-700) sequences. This is the same effect that causes such high frequencies of both sign 740 and sign 002 linked to the large numbers of seals at Mohenjo-daro. It is useful to examine the sign inventories from these sites with signs 002, 740, 700, 400, 031, and 032 removed. This results in the lessening of two effects: 1) the high frequency signs tend to dominate the lower frequency signs in analysis; and, 2) artifact specific signs tend to exaggerate difference between sites and artifact types. As 82% of the sign occurrences come from SEAL and TAB artifact types, their sign inventories have a pronounced effect on the overall frequencies. If we are to get at the heart of the Indus script it is necessary to look beyond the obvious and examine the details of sign distributions.

Indus writing: Myths

The myth of the uniformity of the Indus system of writing can be debunked in several ways. The following discussion of sign distributions examines the differences in the distributions of Indus signs, by artifact type and by site.

The distributions of signs in Figure 3.12 demonstrates that the Indus script is not uniform geographically. Certain signs (176, 240, 220, 003,

002

031

032

033

400

700

740

033+700

032+700

002+740

176   240   220   003   590

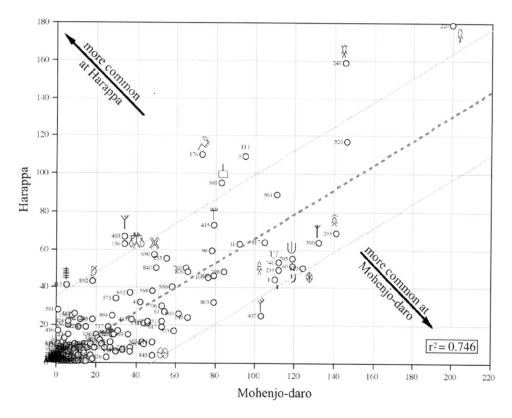

Figure 3.12 Comparison of sign inventories from Mohenjo-daro and Harappa.

590, 405, 156, 413, and 892) occur far more frequently at Harappa, while others (407, 820, and 845) are more frequently found in the inscriptions from Mohenjo-daro. These signs are not the rare signs but rather the more common ones. These differences are minor for the majority of signs, with signs 176, 220 and 240 being notable exceptions. The Indus script is not uniform but with a correlation coefficient of 0.746 (Figure 3.12) these differences cannot be characterized as systemic, but rather there are a handful of signs that occur more commonly at one site or the other. Figure 3.13 compares sign inventories from SEAL:R and SEAL:S artifact types from Harappa and Mohenjo-daro.

It can be seen from Figure 3.13 that SEAL:S artifacts from these sites have very similar sign inventories, while SEAL:R artifacts have many differences (r2 = 0.853 and 0.61 respectively). For SEAL:R artifacts there are eight signs that are more common at Mohenjo-daro than at Harappa (001, 820, 220, 407, 798, 920, , and 617), with only signs 692, 817, and 154 being more common at Harappa. The similarity of sign inventories from

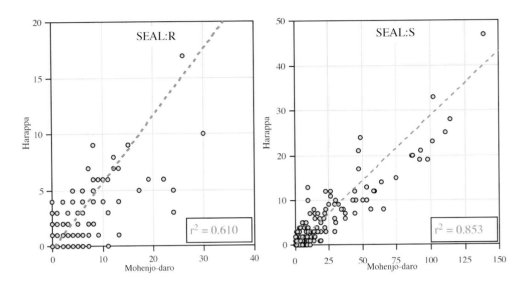

Figure 3.13 Frequency of signs by seal type from Mohenjo-daro and Harappa compared.

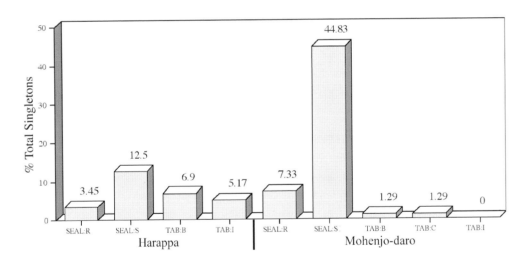

Figure 3.14 Singletons by artifacts type.

SEAL:S artifacts points to a uniform subject matter and possibly language between these two sites. The differences in the SEAL:R inventories seem to indicate a difference in subject matter. There are at least two possible explanations for this difference. First, SEAL:R artifacts could have different functions at Mohenjo-daro and Harappa. Second, as was discussed in Chapter 1 seals were used in the control of trade (as TAG artifacts would seem to indicate) then SEAL:R artifacts might be labeling local trade items (thus the site specific inventories), and SEAL:S artifacts might be labeling Pan-Indus items (a unified sign inventory). It is also possible that SEAL:R artifacts had a limited set of uses relating to cycle of production and system of exchange, while SEAL:S artifacts had a larger inventory of uses with only a minor overlap in function.

The occurrences of low frequency signs are not uniformly distributed across artifact types. As shown in Figure 3.14, regardless of site of origin, seals in general have the highest proportion of singletons. SEAL:S artifacts from Mohenjo-daro have the highest proportion of singletons by an order of magnitude – with ≈45% of all singletons coming from Mohenjo-daro SEAL:S artifacts. The relatively conservative sign inventories of TAB artifacts may be attributed in part to the repetitiveness of the TAB texts and their limited subject matter, but this does not explain the low percentage of singletons in SEAL:S texts from Harappa. Again, this relates to the function of the artifacts, and the fundamental differences in sign inventories.

TAB artifacts may have been used as ration chits or a form of money (Wells 1999:35), with the repetitive use of sign 700 paired with sign 032, sign 033, sign 034, and sign 035 (32-35) relating to various values in a possible system of Indus volumetric measures. This association is supported by the many examples of sign 0700 paired with sign 032, sign 033, sign 034, and sign 035 on POT:T:g artifacts, although this relationship is not absolute. It is possible that wages were paid with grains dispersed from a centralized storage facility. There is little archaeological evidence bearing on this issue other than standardized ceramics and the ubiquitous pointed base goblets in later levels.

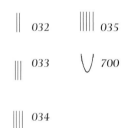

I would suggest that SEAL:S artifacts might have greater proportions of singletons for two reasons: First, their more complex messages and limited space require more compounding, and second, as the Indus trade relations expanded the Indus script would have to describe a greater number of things and so new signs needed to be invented. New things can be described either by spelling (some of these would be compounded spellings) or with new logographs.

Chronological relationships

Just as the occurrence of singletons is not uniform for all artifact types, they are likewise unevenly distributed chronologically. An example of this is the sign distributions from Mohenjo-daro's DK.G area. In Figure 3.15 the relationship between the total number of signs and the number of singletons by archaeological phase can be seen.

The distribution of singletons is not uniform, and in a general way mimics the overall distribution of signs. There are three exceptions to this: the

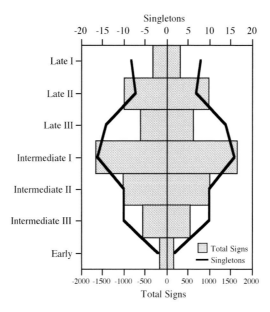

Figure 3.15 Chronological distribution of singletons from Moehenjo-daro, DK.G Area.

Intermediate III, the Late III, and the Late I phases where the number of singletons is higher than expected. The chronology of the Indus civilization is poorly defined, and so it is difficult link these variations to specific cultural or historical influences. In any case the distributions of singletons is complex with many variations spatially, temporally, and among artifact types.

Allographic variations over time

The chronological data published in the early 20th century for Mohenjo-daro and Harappa (Marshall 1931; Mackay 1938; Vats 1940) have been criticized for their crude field methodology and incomplete publication (see Chapter 1). Nevertheless, this corpus remains the largest and best documented set of data describing the chronology of the Indus texts. Altogether these publications list chronological and spatial data for 1,270 texts. The recent excavations at Harappa (Meadow et al. 1990–2001) list

chronological information for 308 artifacts, but only 139 of these can be ascribed to a specific phase (≈200 year period). More than half of the 308 artifacts (157) are fragmentary ceramic texts and of little use in epigraphic studies. Only 15 of the 308 artifacts are SEAL artifacts (SEAL:R = 6; SEAL:S = 9) and 136 are TAB artifacts. With the Vats (Mound F) and Mackay (DK.G) data, texts can be seriated into seven chronologically separate groups, but the relationship between these divisions is not certain.

Sign 740 is the most common Indus sign (n = 1,696) and it has six recognizable variations. These variations can be plotted over time and their distributions compared - as in Figure 3.16. Each graph has the same scale for its x axis. The most obvious feature of this figure is that 740b is the most common variety. Also noticeable is the shift

740 (for sign 740 a-f see Figure 3.16.

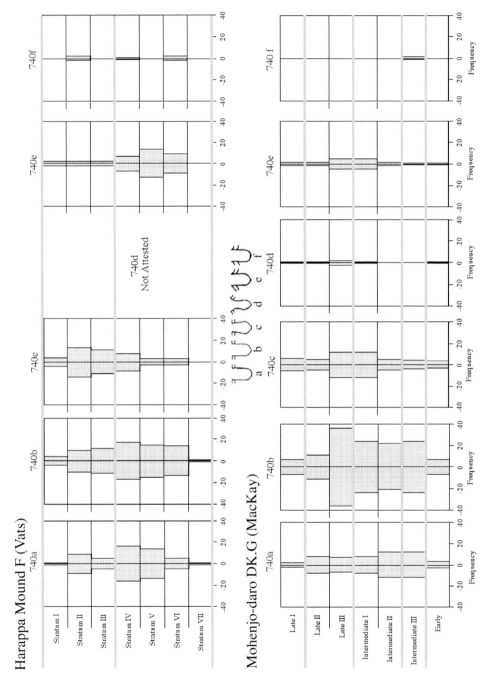

Figure 3.16 Sign 740 graphic variants over time from Mohenjo-daro and Harappa.

740   in popularity of 740a and 740c, with 740a being more common in the earlier periods, and 740c in the later periods (Figure 3.16). This is generally
true at both sites, but Mohenjo-daro is stylistically more conservative in
that 740b monopolizes the sign inventory with other varieties playing only
minor roles. At Harappa the sign inventory is less concentrated, and even
minor varieties (740a, b and especially e) can make up significant proportion of the inventory during the period of their maximum use. These are
the sorts of distributions that are expected from graphic variations.

The variations in the distributions of the graphemes in Figure 3.17 are
very different than those of the graphic variations in Figure 3.6. The
graphemes have distributions that are more mutually exclusive than
graphic variants. In other words, the distributions of signs are proportion-
ally constant when compared to the total number of signs), while many
variants have distributions that are mutually exclusive (see Figure 3.9:
signs 740c and 740e).

The distributions of sign 740 reinforce the results of the contextual
analysis that led to the categorization of all varieties into a single
grapheme represented by a standard graph: sign 740. This sort of analysis
can be performed for many of the Indus signs, and is another source of
data relating to the relationship between sign variants, but again it is
restricted by low sign frequencies.

Initial, medial, and terminal signs

The frequency of sign positions within texts (initial, medial, or terminal)
can be easily calculated. There are 1,999 texts (11,509 characters) that
have three or more signs and for which the texts are complete. These data
are useful in several ways. First, they can identify signs that occur entirely
or primarily (or never) at the start or end of inscriptions. As shown in
Chapter 4, the organization of Indus texts is far too complicated to be fully
described by such a simple technique, but sign preferences for certain
positions within text can identify important differences between signs
526   with near identical graphs. For example, the case of signs 526 and 527
was discussed previously in this chapter. These signs were identified as
two separate graphemes based on the analysis of their contexts, but the
527   separation of 526, and 527 was tentative, and they were maintained as
separate signs awaiting further evidence. Sign 526 occurs in 10 texts for
which its position can be determined as follows: initial = 0, medial = 0,
and terminal = 10. Sign 527 occurs in 38 texts for which its position can
be determined as follows: initial = 1, medial = 5, and terminal = 32. These
data support the separation of signs 526, and 527 into two distinct, but
related, graphemes.

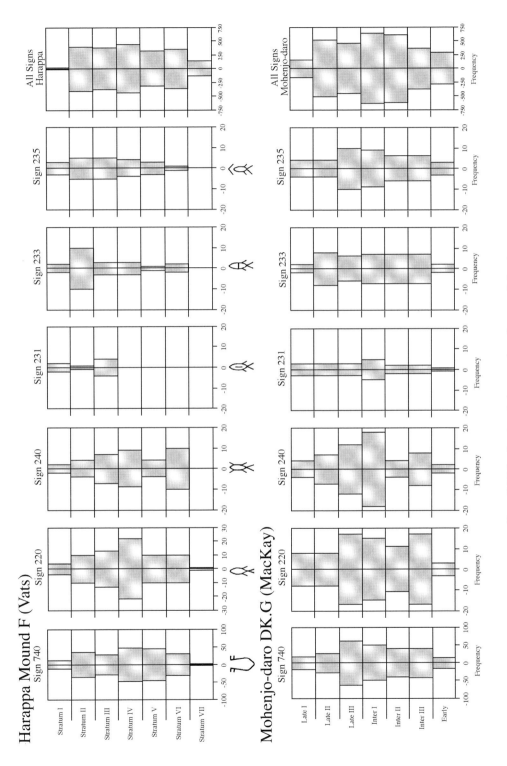

Figure 3.17 Graphemic variations over time of common Indus signs.

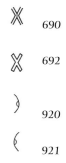

690

692

920

921

A similar problem arose with the analysis of signs 690 and 692. For these sign the counts are: sign 690 initial = 8, medial = 55, and terminal = 13; sign 692 initial = 42, medial = 6, and terminal = 3. Sign 690 is primarily medial (72.4%) while sign 692 is primarily initial (82.4%). They are not only different graphemes, but have very different uses in Indus writing.

These sorts of differences can also be seen in signs 920 and 921. Sign 920 has the following distribution: initial = 57, medial = 42, and terminal = 4; and 921 has: initial = 4, medial = 8, and terminal = 2. Again the division of these signs into two distinct graphemes seems to have been the right decision.

Conclusion

In this chapter we have examined in detail a methodology for creating a sign list for the Indus script. This method began with the grouping of signs on the basis of graphic design. Graphic variations were identified through the analysis of their contexts, and the resulting graphemes were analyzed for their chronological and spatial distributions. Additional considerations included artifact type, positioning in texts and pairings with other signs (including numerals). This methodology led to the creation of a sign list with 676 signs, but as has been pointed out in this chapter, not all of these signs are certain to be separate graphemes. Instead, part of the sign list consists of sets of related signs that cannot be defined either as graphic variations or graphemes with certainty. Following a policy of maintaining detail, signs that fall into this category are maintained as separate signs awaiting further analysis. Figure 3.7 lists the ways in which Indus signs are constructed. These categories are also integrated into the Indus sign list. The number of elements used to construct signs (components) and the frequency of signs are to a high degree inversely proportional (Figure 3.10). Complex signs with many components normally have low frequencies. This pattern is also evident in both the proto-Elamite and proto-Cuneiform scripts, and resulting in a high proportion of singletons in the sign list (Figure 3.15, see Chapter 4). In addition to having large proportions of singletons, these three scripts (Indus, proto-Elamite, and proto-Cuneiform) share other features: a small number of very high frequency signs, many allographic variants, and logographic conflations including numbers.

This chapter examined the distributions of signs in detail. Far from being uniform, these distributions showed that the Indus script is very complex in its regional usage, and that only the inventories from SEAL:S artifacts are significantly correlated between at all major sites. Differences between sites in terms of sign inventories can be attributed to difference in artifact type, and this is also true for different artifact types from the same site. For example, the sign inventories of TAB:B and TAB:I artifacts from Harappa are markedly different. The nature of these differences is also important, as they use similar signs to write their texts, but in different proportions, with some signs being very common on specific artifact types. There are also differences in the signs used at the various sites. About half of all Indus signs are found at only one site as follows: Mohenjo-daro = 196 (134), Harappa = 103 (71), Lothal = 6 (6), Chanhujo-daro = 8 (7), Kalibangan = 11 (10), and Other = 10 (8) signs. The number of singletons is given in brackets.

Just as important is that Mohenjo-daro and Harappa share 281 signs, and Mohenjo-daro, Harappa, and Lothal share 118 signs. These signs form the majority of the Indus texts. While singletons comprise a large number of signs in the sign list (235 signs or about 35%), they represent a small part (0.13%) of the 17,423 sign occurrences recorded in the ICIT database. This sign list cannot be considered the final or definitive Indus sign list. Rather it marks just another stage in the ongoing process of analysis of this complex and interesting system of ancient writing.

4

THE PROCESS OF DECIPHERMENT AND STRUCTURAL ANALYSIS

Every written document not only embodies the message 'I am meant to be read'
but also instructions, however indirect, as to how this can be done. In other words,
the systematic makeup of writing contains a key to its own decipherment.

-Florian Coulmas (2003)

In this chapter we explore the nature of ancient writing systems especially the similarity and differences between what is known of these other systems, and what can be observed for the Indus script. Since its discovery the Indus script has presented a challenge to epigraphers. The sign distributions are highly patterned, and that there is structure in the texts is obvious to all those that have worked with them. For example, those familiar with the Indus texts can recognize signs that are out of their normal order. This was evident in the construction of the ICIT database. Many typing errors were discovered simply through the visual inspection of the texts. These patterns are detectable on two levels - the order of signs in the texts, and how specific sets of signs cluster. The first of these (sign and sign cluster order) is suggestive of syntax, while the second (sign cluster combinations) is suggestive of morphology. The definition and discussion of these two features is the focus of the second part of this chapter. The first part focuses on other ancient writing systems - how they developed and how they work - and what was known about them when they were deciphered.

Ancient scripts and decipherment

Arguments have been made on the internet and in self-published e-journals that the Indus script is not writing but rather merely a symbolic system not linked to a specific language (Farmer et al. 2004). The argument is that the texts are too short, there are too many singly occurring signs (singletons) and too few high frequency signs, no commonly repeating signs, and no perishable or monumental texts.

Many scholars currently working on the Indus script have dismissed this theory as highly unlikely and poorly conceived (personal communications from M. Coe, G. Possehl, A. Parpola, D. H. Kelly, S. Bonta, and others 2006). More importantly, many of arguments and several of the issues raised by this theory are dealt with in this book, with the data presented here refuting this theory with regards to the nature of the Indus system of writing.

At least 2,500 Indus texts have been available for study since 1940 (Marshall 1931; MacKay 1938; Vats 1940). These circumstances have lead to a series of attempted decipherments using a variety of different methodologies. The results have been as varied as the number of would-be decipherers (see Possehl 1996:76-161 for a partial list). Several facts emerged from these decipherments. The first is that no two decipherments agree on more than a few sign values even when they are assuming the same root language. The second fact is that there is no agreement on the details of the Indus sign list. Sign lists vary in length from 62 (Rao 1973, 1984) to 683 (Wells 1999). Third, beyond a general agreement that the texts are mostly read from right to left, there is little agreement as to the mechanics of the script. In fact, with some notable exceptions (Knorosov 1968; Lal 1975; Parpola 1994; Bonta 1995; Wells 1999) little attention has been paid to sign distributions and macro structures (syntax) in the texts. Decipherments have suffered from a lack of typological, temporal and geographic control (see Kelley and Wells 1995; Wells 1999 for details). That is, they generally lump all texts into a single analytical group without regard for the type of artifact the text was inscribed on, its site of origin, or the age of the artifact. This has resulted in some contradictory and confusing results. This is especially true of decipherments that rely on very general sign lists, which have the effect of systematically removing detail of sign relationships from the texts (Knorosov 1968; Parpola 1994; Mahadevan 1970) and in some cases creating relationships that do not exist between signs (Parpola 1994). As major differences in sign inventory (subject matter) do exist between sites, and artifact types, a methodology that ignores these variations is bound to have many inconsistencies. To further complicate their respective decipherments most researchers base sign reading on the visual identification of the sign as some animal, person, or object. This identification can vary greatly between researchers. It is often assumed that the signs are being used by the ancients for their rebus value, which is then guessed at. The resulting sign values often have little to do with the original sign graph. Parpola's 'fish' = 'to glitter' = 'star' formula is only one example of this process (Parpola 1994). Finally, no decipherment offers proofs of readings, and most decipherments are so idiosyncratic that only their

originators can use them. It is little wonder that of the 60 or more attempts at decipherment of the Indus script (Possehl 1996:76-161) none have received a favorable reception from the academic community.

In a recent discussion of decipherment Houston and Coe (2003:151-152) give five criteria that must be met before a successful decipherment can take place. In paraphrase they are: 1) a large well-published database; 2) correct identification of a known language; 3) one or more bilingual texts; 4) a well understood cultural context; 5) pictorial references if the script is logographic. The problems faced in the decipherment of the Indus script at first seem insurmountable in this light. Fortunately, Houston and Coe (2003) overstate their case, and there are several examples where one or more of these criteria were not met and a successful decipherment still occurred. The most obvious example is the decipherment of Linear B that met none but the first of their criteria. Further, the identity of the language (Houston and Coe's primary criteria) of Linear B was only discovered at the point of decipherment (Table 4.1). Although they overstate the importance of having all of these factors in place, their five factors form the core of what epigraphers hope for when approaching the decipherment of a script. I would add to the list two additional factors: 6) an comprehensive sign list; and, 7) a clear understanding of the basic mechanics of the script derived from structural analysis. The availability of these seven factors define which techniques might be productive in the analysis of the undeciphered writing system under consideration. Additionally, these criteria can be used to assess the prospects of deciphering Indus writing, which is the goal of the following discussion.

One feature of Table 4.1 is that none of the writing systems listed met all five of the Houston

Table 4.1 Some details about selected ancient scripts

Script	Type	Period	Signs	Context	Corpus	Language	Bilingual	Pictures Deciphered
Egyptian	Sp. L-S	3500-300 BC	800	x	x	/	x	x
Proto-Cuneiform	L	3600-3000 BC	600	/	x		x	
Akkadian	L-S	2334-2154 BC	600	x	x	x	x	/
Cypriot	S	650-150 BC	56	/	x	x	x	x
Luvian	L-S	1500-700 BC	497	x	x			x
Linear B	L-S	1900-1400	87	/	x			
Isthmian	L-S	250-500 AD	210		x	/		
Mayan	L-S	250-1400 AD	1000+	x	x	x	/	x
Undeciphered								
Meroitic	A	712-656 BC	25	x	x		x	/
Etruscan	A	700-500 BC	24	x	x		x	
Linear A	L-S?	1750-1450 BC	418	/	/			x
Proto Elamite	L-S	3050-2900 BC	≈1000	x	x	x		
Linear Elamite	S	≈ 2150 BC	80	/	/	x		
Rongorongo	?	Before 1600 AD	120	x	x	x		
Zapotec	L?	600-400 BC	90	x	x	x		/
Indus	L-S	2600-1700 BC	700	x	x			/
Phaistos	?	1850-1600 BC	56					/

Key: Sp. = special; L = logographic; S = syllabic; A = alphabetic; x = criterion fully met; / = criterion partially met; blank = criterion not met.

and Coe (2003) criteria. The only criterion met by all successfully deciphered scripts is that of a large and adequately published corpus of texts. Equally obvious, Linear B, Luvian, and Isthmian (sometime called Epi-Olmec) met few of these criteria yet were still successfully deciphered. The inverse is also true: several scripts that meet many of these criteria remain only partially deciphered (Meroitic, Etruscan, Rongorongo, and Proto-Elamite). The unevenness of these results highlight an important fact concerning the process of decipherment. It is not the number of criteria met that controls our ability to decipher, but rather the specific details and combinations of criteria for a given script. The presence or absence of a bilingual, for example, is often given as a critical factor for a successful decipherment to occur, but three ancient scripts have been deciphered without the aid of bilinguals. No single factor determines whether a writing system can be deciphered.

The criteria and the Indus script
Adequate corpus of inscriptions (criterion 1)
The presence of an extensive and accurate corpus for the script under consideration is a feature shared by all deciphered ancient scripts. Adequate is a subjective measure and depends on the nature of the artifacts and the writing system. For the sake of this discussion an adequate corpus is one that contains all or most of the known inscriptions, in a format that is accurate and legible, and contains sufficient number of pieces to represent all elements of the writing system. In some cases a corpus consists of drawings and in other cases photographs, but in either case the reproduction must be legible and accurate, or the resulting analysis will not yield a reliable decipherment.

In the case of the Indus script, decipherment has been stalled because most decipherments have relied on replacement fonts (Koskenniemi et al. 1970; Mahadevan 1977) that were not representative of the texts. These publications present the texts in a manner that divorces them from their archaeological provenience (cultural contexts). Several hundred texts might be enough for a decipherment if these texts are long and associated with related imagery (Maya). Conversely, many thousands of texts may not be adequate if they are short and no related imagery exists (Proto-Elamite and Indus). Further, drawings with errors can create an insurmountable obstacle to decipherment.

The ICIT database contains 3,835 texts from 48 sites with at least one recognizable Indus sign, and about 2,341 artifacts have complete texts. Whether the ICIT constitutes an adequate corpus remains to be determined.

Known language (criterion 2)

One factor most epigraphers would agree is critical to a decipherment is the knowledge of the language of the script at least to the language family level. For the decipherment of Classic Mayan writing it was known that the texts were written in a Maya language. Which language exactly remained unknown until the 1990s when there was a slow realization that most texts were written in an early form of Ch'olti' or Ch'orti' (Coe and Van Stone 2001:15). This was ascertained from the affixing patterns of verbs. Many of the Classic Maya texts were already deciphered and read in a general way for more than 20 years. Knowledge of the exact Maya language of the texts was not a prerequisite for decipherment, and for many years it was believed that the southern texts were in Ch'olan, and the northern texts were in Yukatek. This misunderstanding had no effect whatsoever on the decipherment. The Maya example also demonstrates that a script can express a single language, while the people who use it speak a variety of different, albeit related (Mayan), languages.

The decipherment of Linear B is an example of the language of a script being discovered at the point of decipherment. We now know that these texts were written in Greek with some special (abbreviated) spelling rules. But, this fact was unknown to Ventris until after he began to work with already known syllabic values. It became evident to him that the assembled syllables were spelling Greek words that approximated place names known from later historic texts (ko-no-so ≈ Knososs, and a-mi-ni-so ≈Amnisos). One helpful feature of Linear B texts is that logographs are often paired with syllabic spellings of the same word. Many logographs could be guessed at from their form, and important features such as gender markers could be identified. Further, known syllabic values and logographic interpretations led to many proposed sign readings.

The initial conclusion that Linear B script was written in some form of Greek was tested by Ventris, but he did not expect it to lead anywhere. Interestingly, Ventris had never before considered Greek because he, and everyone else in the field, thought it to be an impossibility. When Ventris deciphered Linear B he did it with a combination of insight, hard work, revolutionary methodology, and some luck. He also relied heavily on the work of others, especially Alice Kober and later John Chadwick.

The problem of the Indus language is at about the same state as the Linear B language before Kober began her research - many suggestions, some interesting theories, but nothing conclusive. The most serious proposals have been a language of the Dravidian family, including Proto-Dravidian, (Knorosov 1968; Fairservis 1992; Lal 1975; Parpola 1994), Sanskrit (Rao 1973), para-Munda, an unknown language (X), and several languages (Witzel 1999). This situation is analogous to Linear B in that the language will have to be discovered by a decipherment. How productive the decipherment is will depend on the accuracy of the identification of the proposed root language. One important fact is that the language(s) people spoke at a given time and given place need not have been the language of the writing system, as with Maya, Latin, and Sumerian. It may also be a lingua franca, or a code not based on a specific language. All of these possibilities require serious consideration.

It is interesting that none of the Dravidian based decipherments agree on the readings of a single sign with the exception of the fish sign (220). This is in part because of the methodology (poor quality sign fonts, lack of geographic and artifact differentiation, and preconceptions of the structure and spelling rules), but also because values were in every case assigned to signs as if they were pictographs. These values rely on the subjective interpretation of the sign graph as a real world object, and therefore vary a great deal from researcher to researcher. This methodology was used on Indus texts because it had been applied with some success in a limited way to the decipherment of Proto-Cuneiform texts. The difference here being that the Indus texts are all from the period when the writing system was already developed, the metonymic processes had likely already occurred, and the basic sign inventory had become somewhat fossilized in mainstream use, because the majority of the Indus texts are from ca. 2300–1900 BC. In other words, the Indus script had already made the transition from a predominantly logographic script (where the sign for fish looked like a fish) to a system where a sign which looks like a fish may have multiple values only some of which will be homophonic and related through rebus as is show in detail in Chapter 6. This process is examined in detail later in this chapter. One final

problem results when additional signs are interpreted based on their contexts in order to help make sense of signs already read using the process described above. This results in nonsensical reading of texts (see Kelley and Wells 1995:22-23 for examples).

In short, the language of the Indus script has yet to be convincingly demonstrated. It is highly probable, given the vast expanse of the Indus Civilization and the fact that it was composed of many regional cultures, that more than one language was spoken during the Bronze Age in the Greater Indus Valley. But this does not mean that the script was written is several languages. The results of structural analysis may clarify this issue. It is not necessary to know the language of the script to analyze its structure, and so no assumption as to the language of the Indus script is made here. This topic is returned to in Chapter 6.

Bilinguals (criterion 3)

Bilingual texts are texts with parallel (related) passages in two scripts on one object or in the same place. In an ideal situation (the Rossetta Stone - actually a trilingual) one or more scripts are known and one or more others are not. This allows the unknown script to be deciphered. The advantage of a lengthy bilingual is obvious. In several cases bilinguals have lead to a successful decipherment, most notably Cuneiform and Egyptian Hieroglyphic. In other cases the bilingual is less useful and more difficult to recognize. A good example of this is the Landa alphabet (Coe and Van Stone 2001:20), which was key in Knorosov's work on the Maya script. This is not a true bilingual, but rather a partial syllabary with syllables equated with certain letters in the Spanish alphabet. No bilingual was used in the decipherment of Linear B, and none is known for the Indus Script.

A well-understood cultural context (criterion 4)
It is difficult to define what a well understood cultural context is. More precisely, we are interested in how writing is used and how inscribed artifacts are used in a particular place and time. For example, the presence or absence of monumental inscriptions tells us a great deal about that culture. First, we know that writing was practiced by those with enough resources to create monumental inscriptions, and therefore the existence of a literate elite can be postulated – as can scribes and other specialized craftsmen. Yet, given the nature of the archaeological record, the absence of texts does not mean there was no writing. This can be demonstrated by the existence texts on perishable material from many ancient cultures (Mayan, Chinese, Egyptian, Mycenaean, Rapanui and Indus to name a few). The best example is Linear B, for there would be few Linear B texts if the tablets had not been inadvertently fired when the buildings they were found in were destroyed. From the Indus Valley evidence for perishable texts comes from a tag found at Mohenjo-daro (DK12145, M-0426) that has the impression of a wooden doweling on the reverse (Figure 4.1). Along with the grain of the wood, a text with eight or more signs can be discerned. The text continues in both directions beyond the limits of the tag. Mackay (1938:Plate XC 17c) gives the photo of the text on the reverse of the tag. What Mackay (1938:353-4) tells us is: "On the inside of the sealing there are also some markings which look remarkably like pictographic signs (c), though, unfortunately but little remains of them owing to the breaking of the sealing...if, however, the inscription had been incised upon the wooden rod, the characters upon the sealing should have been in relief, whereas they are the opposite. There is, however, the possibility that the original writing, if writing it be, was in some thick ink

which stood out enough to impress it self upon the reverse side of the sealing." In addition to writing with ink or paint on wood, other types of perishable material may also have been used in the Indus Valley (for example, unfired clay and leafs). Many Classic period Maya temples had lengthy texts in plaster integrated into their façades or carved in wooden lintels. Only the remaining fragments testify to their existence.

At best, all we can hope for is that we have a good cultural context for whatever writing survives. The cultural context of Indus writing is not perfectly understood. For example, the function of 'miniature tablets' is not known with certainty, if indeed they have a single function. Parpola (1994:107) suggests they may be votive offerings. Wells (1999:33 and Figure 2.3) suggests some of them may be tokens in a system of rationing – a kind of proto-currency. Although there is overwhelming evidence (Chapter 1) that seals have several economic uses, there is a great deal of resistance to this idea among those that consider them as objects d'art (too beautiful to have an economic function). In my opinion, Indus writing had a primarily economic function, the exact nature of which is poorly understood. What is clear from the archaeological record is that seals were not used as personal identification or symbols of status (Fairservis 1992:5). First, there are no seals, or any other writing, found in any Indus burial. This is unexpected for highly treasured symbols of prestige, or for a magical talisman. Seals are, however, often found in trash, room fill, workshop areas, and in virtually every part of Indus sites – as if discarded when no longer needed. They had no value beyond the uses of their owners. Their use was relatively short lived and probably tied to bureaucratic functions of production and trade.

The distribution of Indus artifacts is not entirely without patterning. In several contexts

Figure 4.1 Inked or painted text from Mohenjo-daro drawn from Mackay 1938:Plate XC 17c.

at Mohenjo-daro (Mackay 1938) the distribution of seals are highly correlated to the distribution of Indus weights (Figure 4.2). These are also instances where seals and other inscribed artifacts cluster in specific houses and specific rooms in houses (Figure 4.3). The evidence of TAG artifacts also points to a use in both regional and international trade. While there are many lacuna in our understanding of the function of writing in Indus culture, it seems to have had a primarily economic function.

Pictographic or pictorial references (criterion 5)

Texts with associated scenes are very useful to a would-be decipherer. An interesting example is the Classic Maya monuments of Mesoamerica. For several generations archaeologists and epigraphers spoke of the peaceful Mayan priest kings, living tranquilly in their isolated ceremonial centers, gazing at the stars and carving texts marking the long passage of cosmic time. This is a romantic image, which today we know to be utterly untrue. In spite of many representations in Maya art of war, capture, and sacrifice, the "peaceful Maya" paradigm was widely accepted for 50 years or more. The point of this example is that it is not enough to have pictorial representations, researchers also have to make appropriate use of them.

In the ECIT database 5,040 artifacts are inscribed with various textual and iconographic

elements. These include scenes of the Indus people involved in various activities (n = 52), and various types of animals, plants and geometric symbols (Figures 1.1–1.3). A few of these give us insights into the ritual and ceremonial lives of the Indus people. Whether these elements are linked to the texts is not easily determined. It is important to realize that there is no obvious connection between the Indus texts and imagery. It is possible that the combination of the text and image on the Indus artifacts represent two independent messages. It is highly unlikely that the iconographic components are simply decorative, as they are highly patterned suggesting some purpose, but the lack of a definable relationship between texts and image seems to indicate they carry independent messages.

A comprehensive sign list (criterion 6)

As demonstrated in Chapter 3 the creation of an Indus sign list is not a trivial matter. Further, the final definition of Indus graphemes effects all levels of analysis, and especially structural analysis. As can be seen in Figures 4.4 sign graphs need not be the best definition of graphemes. The sign list is an intermediate step, and can only be fully defined after decipherment, but a comprehensive sign list is a critical first step in decipherment as it defines the units of construction in the writing system.

A simple count of the number of signs in a writing system can tell us what type of system it

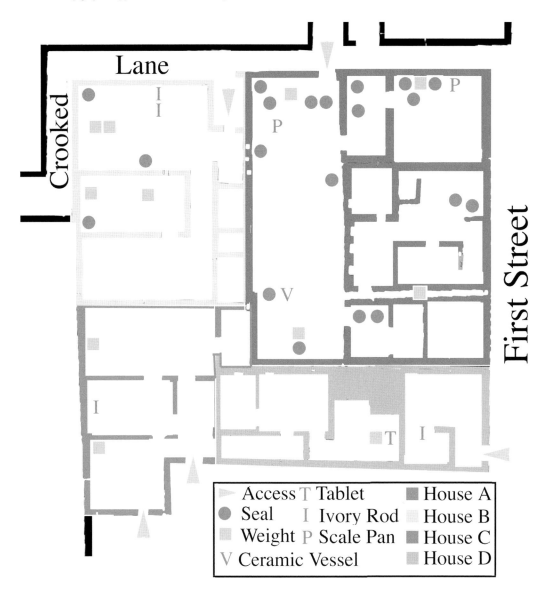

Figure 4.2 Mohenjo-daro, DK.G, Block 3, Intermediate Period showing building access,
and the distribution of weights and inscribed artifacts.

*Figure 4.3 Mohenjo-daro, DK.G, Blocks 7, 9, and 10, Late Ia and Ib phases
showing the distribution of kilns, wells, weights and inscribed artifacts.*

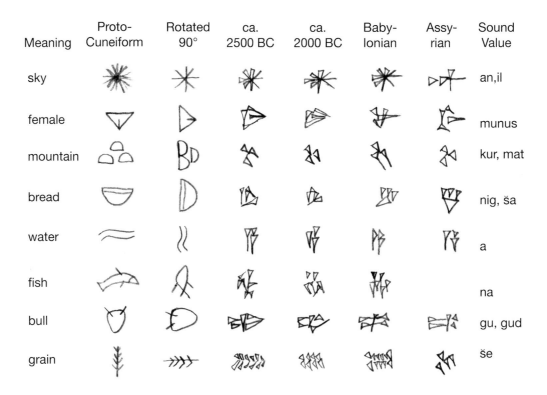

Meaning	Proto-Cuneiform	Rotated 90°	ca. 2500 BC	ca. 2000 BC	Baby-lonian	Assy-rian	Sound Value
sky							an,il
female							munus
mountain							kur, mat
bread							nig, ša
water							a
fish							na
bull							gu, gud
grain							še

Figure 4.4 Metamorphosis of Cuneiform over time.

is (Table 4.2). For example, about 35 or fewer signs would indicate an alphabetic system (Meroitic and Ugritic), about 40-90 signs would indicate a syllabic system (Cypriot, Linear B, and Persian), about 200-1000+ signs would indicate a logo-syllabic system (Cuneiform, Mayan, and Egyptian Hieroglyphic), and thousands of signs would indicate a logographic system (Chinese). There are also intermediate forms (Daniels and Bright 1996). The count of signs can be complicated by the mechanics of the system. For example, cuneiform is said to have between 900 to over 1,000 signs (Coulmas 2003:45). In some systems (Indus and Maya) conflations and infixing can inflate sign counts. This is an important issue with the Indus Script, where both of these mechanisms can be easily

identified. As shown in Chapter 3 many of the singletons found in the Indus Script can be identified as being composed of common signs conflated into a single unit, perhaps to save space, but more likely for linguistic reasons.

The mechanics of the script (criterion 7)

Many ancient scripts are logo-syllabic, that is, they combine word signs (logographs) and syllable signs to form phrases and sentences. Yet, if we examine these writing systems in detail we can immediately see major differences in the mechanics that individual systems employ. Further, some systems change over time, usually becoming less pictographic and increasingly abstract (Figure 4.4). This is exactly the case with Cuneiform and Hieroglyphic Egyptian writing.

In the case of early Sumerian writing signs were pictures of objects - normally economically important plants and animals, manufactured items such as bread, human anatomical features (head and mouth), and other important items (mountain and female).

In the case of early Sumerian writing, signs were pictures and in their earliest forms the signs resemble the objects that they represent. The first abstract signs are numbers (cones for 1 and spheres for 10). Overtime, two main factors influence the development of cuneiform (Coulmas 2003:43): 1) the signs become less pictorial because of the restrictions of the medium (wet clay); 2) the number of existing signs grows and signs are employed in new ways. For example, the sign for star (Figure 4.u) was semantically expanded by metonymy to mean 'sky' and eventually also 'god' (Coulmas 2003:46). The first factor resulted in signs becoming divorced from their pictorial values and associated with abstract values not linked to their semantic values. This allowed the system to be expanded, using homophones and the rebus principle to semantically encompass unrelated words. However, this also resulted in signs with multiple semantic values, and created some confusion, as meaning was a matter of context. To further complicate reading, near homonyms were also included in the process of transfer. The sign for 'arrow', ti, was also used for writing ti(l) 'life' (Coulmas 2003:47).

As the system expanded signs began to have non-homophonic values, as in the example above for the 'star' sign. Coulmas (ibid) gives the example of the sign for 'mouth', (Figure 4.a), ka, having

Table 4.2 Number of signs in various types of writing systems

Writing System	No. Signs
Idiographic	
Chinese	5,000+
Logo-Syllabic	
Maya	1,200
Egyptian	800
Sumerian	600+
Hittite	497
Syllabic	
Linear B	87
Cherokee	85
Cypriot	56
Persian	40
Alphabetic/Consonantal	
Sanskrit	50+
Russian	36
Anglo-Saxon	31
Arabic	28
English	26
Meroitic	25
Hebrew	22
Etruscan	20

the additional values of inim 'word', and dug, 'to speak'. Further, signs are combined to form conceptually related words: mouth (Figure 4.a) plus bread (Figure 4.b) = food (Figure 4.c). In the fully developed system the sound gu can be expressed using 14 different signs - all with different meanings. This is further complicated by the fact that (Figure 4.d) gu3 not only means 'voice' but also 'tooth' and 'mouth'.

It can be seen how this system could rapidly become unusable. In order to clarify the intended meaning it was necessary to find a way to differentiate the different semantic values from the

 4.a   4.b   4.c   4.d

unitary sign graph. In the case of several scripts this is done using phonetic compliments (hints to the semantic values), and determinatives (semantic classifiers). These additions clarified the meanings of the signs and allowed the system to express more of the language without the invention of new signs.

In Egyptian hieroglyphic the same sign stands for the words 'open', 'hurry', 'mistake', 'become bald', 'light', and the city of Hermopolis (Zauzich 1992:28-29). How can the scribe choose among these various readings? Confusion is eliminated within this writing system by the use of semantic determinatives. These are signs that signify the class of the object but are not themselves pronounced during reading. In Egyptian hieroglyphic writing semantic determinatives are common.

In Classic Maya inscriptions semantic determinatives are rare, but because polyvalence is common it is necessary to find some means of differentiating graphically similar signs. The solution employed by Maya scribes to clarify the intended meaning was the use of phonetic compliments. Using these signs in various ways the Maya scribes could clarify the meaning of polyvalent signs. Nowhere is the problem created by dissimilar allographic variants more clear than in Classic Maya writing where completely different signs that have exactly the same value.

As for the Indus script we know nothing of the variations, either spatial or temporal, in the mechanics of sign use. The vast majority of the writing comes from the part of the Integration Era (Mature Harappan) that dates from 2300 BC to 1900 BC. During this 400 year period we have very few sets of texts that can be chronologically arranged, and those that can seem to be generally homogenous. There is some geographic variation, but there is also a good deal of interregional homogeneity (Chapter 3). The main goal of this chapter is to define some of the mechanics of Indus writing. In general, it can be said with some certainty that Indus writing is most often read from right to left (80.84%). There are several examples of boustrophedon (0.16%), left to right (2.62%), and top to bottom (0.01%) readings, but these are rare. In the ICIT database direction of reading could not be established for 16.27% of texts most often because they were fragmentary.

We can expect that the Indus script will utilize a similar inventory of sign classes as those used in other ancient scripts – logographs, syllables, semantic determinatives, phonetic complements, and special markers – although they may be employed in unique ways. We must also be aware that new classes of signs could also be employed, or signs may be combined in unusual ways. The forgoing discussion has stressed the similarities in the general structure of the mechanics of ancient scripts, but it must also be pointed out that they differ in the details of how these various classes of signs are used. In detail, ancient writing systems share very little in the implementation of the basic inventory of sign classes, and we can expect this to also be true of the Indus script. It is not possible, for example, to simply overlay the pattern of Sumerian or Linear B on the Indus texts in order to decipher the Indus script. What is necessary is to analyze the patterns of sign distributions in order to discover sign classes and their method of employment. The structure of these relationships may allow us to identify the root language of the Indus script, as the patterns in the texts reflect the logic of the language it expresses.

Structural analysis

Structural analysis as defined by Kelley (1976, 1982) is a method that strives to define related segments in texts through the analysis of parallel inscriptions. That is, by comparing inscriptions with some shared sign sequences, but which are not identical in other respects, interchanging elements (replacement sets) and variations in sign usages (spellings?) can be defined and isolated for further analysis. Replacement sets can either be words or phrases with the same syntactic value of the sign cluster it replaces for (verb or noun etc.), or can be alternate spellings of the sign cluster in question.

Several forms of structural analysis have been used in attempted decipherments of the Indus script (Knorozov 1968; Mahadevan 1970, 1982, 1986; Koskenniemi and Parpola 1979, 1980, 1982, Koskenniemi 1981; Koskenniemi et al. 1970; Parpola 1994). All of these analyses assumed a Dravidian language and used computer programs for their structural analysis. These attempts achieved interesting but significantly different results. This was partly due to their radically different sign lists (the Russians used 250 signs, the Finns 386, and Mahadevan 417) and also partially due to difference in their computer code. More significantly when they bridged the gap between the results of structural analysis and derived readings for signs many interpretive differences arose. In all cases the results of the computer-based analysis were cast aside in favor of subjective identifications of signs as real world objects, irrespective of variations in sign placement within the structure of the texts. These subjective identifications combined with the assumption of a root language, and assumed rebus values, gave rise to readings of signs as words. These identifications rely heavily on subjective and individualistic criteria and often cannot be replicated by other researchers. It is interesting to note that many decipherments offer reading of signs as words (implying at least a heavily logographic system) but offer sign lists

with 250 to 400 signs (on the low end of logo-syllabic). The question arises: Where are the syllabic signs? By the end of this chapter this question is at least partially answered.

Bridging the gap between the analysis of patterns and the reading of signs is not a simple task, and is not necessarily the next logical step in the analysis of the texts. Structural analysis should allow the identification of Indus words and phrases, and associated clusters of signs with like syntactic values. These identifications are independent of root language and serve to confirm the type of script (logographic, or syllabic, logo-syllabic, alphabetic, etc). This helps in the analysis of sign function (syllable, logograph, or determinative), and the range of use (affix, word building or word). Additionally, considerations of polyvalence (more than one value for a single sign) and the common practice in some scripts of having several signs with distinct graphs, but with the same phonetic value (allographs) must be integrated into the analysis of signs. The derived meanings of signs must explain the details of structural analysis. For example, a sign identified as a logograph representing a human and given a corresponding value (as with sign 090 = "man" from Parpola 1994:277) should be consistently in an appropriate syntactic position in texts in terms of the proposed root language.

Analyzing Indus texts

The following analysis draws upon the 3,835 artifacts (17,358 signs) of the ICIT database as its source dataset. What these artifacts share in common is that they all have at least one recognizable Indus sign visible somewhere on them. Of these texts, 2,341 are complete inscriptions. Table 4.3 summarizes the distribution of texts by site and artifact type. Figure 4.5 gives the frequency of texts by number of signs.

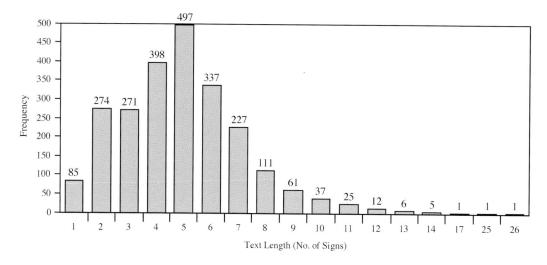

Figure 4.5 Number of signs per artifact for complete texts in the ICIT database.

Further, the analysis of sign inventories presented at the end of Chapter 3 demonstrated that various types of seal and tablet texts have different sign inventories. Therefore, artifact types must be a consideration when analyzing texts.

What this table makes clear is that the majority of the complete Indus texts come from Mohenjo-daro and Harappa, and from SEAL:S artifacts. TAB artifacts comprise a major sub-component (n = 763 for all TABs) of the data available for analysis. It is important to note that a greater percentage of Lothal and Kalibangan texts are from TAG artifacts, and as these artifacts are normally fragmentary, the representation of these sites in Table 4.3 is somewhat less than expected based on the overall count of artifacts from these sites. Because the vast majority of texts come from Mohenjo-daro and Harappa, much of the following analysis focuses on these two sites.

The classification of texts

It is possible to classify Indus texts in a variety of ways. The most obvious is by site by artifact type.

There are signs and texts whose distributions are restricted in this manner, and at some point in the analysis of the texts these attributes must be considered. If we compare the sign inventories from Mohenjo-daro to those of Harappa we find they are most similar for SEAL:S artifacts. Conversely, the correlation between any other artifact type at a specific sites is not high. This is likely because they contain different subject matter and therefore signs are present in different proportions. These aspects of sign distributions are important for two reasons: 1) we expect that like artifacts will have similar subject matter because they have the same function, and consequently similar sign inventories will occur if the underlying languages is the same. In the case of SEAL:S artifacts this seems to be the case, supporting the use one language at both sites, but this is untrue for any other type of artifact; 2) if different types of artifacts have different sign inventories this can be attributed to differences in subject matter, but what is the reason that the same types of artifacts at Mohenjo-daro and

Table 4.3 Tabulation of complete texts in the ICIT database

Site	Frequency	Type	Frequency
Mohenjo-Daro	1,238	SEAL:S	1,125
Harappa	870	TAB:B	388
Lothal	72	TAB:I	229
Kalibangan	58	SEAL:R	212
Chanhujo-daro	46	TAB:C	146
Banawali	12	POT:T:g	59
All Other	53	All Other	183

Harappa have different sign inventories? They must either have different subject matter or be using different dialects or languages. The second possibility is ruled out by the high correlation between SEAL:S artifacts, and so similar artifacts from these sites must have different subject matter. What this analysis teaches us is that artifact type and site are useful characteristics for classifying Indus texts, but we need to look further if we are to discover the nature of the difference in subject matter.

The results of structural analysis demonstrate the existence of groups of texts that share basic characteristics in their content and organization. This allows the construction of a typology that categorizes texts into one of five groups. Subsets are structurally related. The following typology of Indus texts focuses on the content of the inscriptions, setting aside for the present all other characteristics. Table 4.4 summarizes this typology.

The distribution of the categories is not uniform among sites or artifact types. The pattern is one in which TAB:I and TAB:B artifacts from Harappa are dominated by short patterned texts (≈55% in both cases), with few other types in significant proportions, and by VN texts. The exception being single segment texts on TAB:I artifacts from Harappa. TAB:B and TAB:C artifacts from Mohenjo-daro have significantly higher proportions of single segment texts, and the short and long patterned texts are more evenly distributed.

Seal texts from both sites are more consistent in their proportions of text types.

Setting aside the artifact types the following can be said about the distributions of the various types of texts: The comparison of segment texts (both single and multiple) shows that they have about the same proportions at both Mohenjo-daro and Harappa. This is not true for patterned texts. Short patterned texts are far more common at Harappa (47% vs. 32% at Mohenjo-daro). Conversely, long patterned texts are far more common at Mohenjo-daro (28% vs. Harappa at 13%). Another anomaly is the distribution of long complex texts, with 5.5% at Mohenjo-daro and 1.78% Harappa. The rest of the text types have similar distributions between sites. Each group of text types is discussed in detail in the following sections of this chapter.

Segment texts

There are several recognizable patterns of sign use in the Indus texts. Patterned texts, for example, consist of a well-defined sequence of sign clusters repeated in a more of less fixed order. Single Segment texts consist of only one of these clusters. Multiple Segment texts consist of two or more sign clusters. They are normally found in the same position in Patterned texts.

Figure 4.6 (bottom) lists nine Single Segment (SS) seal texts, the top of this table lists a mixture of Multiple Segment (MS) texts (i.e. M-0371 and

Table 4.4 System of classifying Indus texts

N=2,335 Segments	Code	Length	n =	% of N	Most Common Mohenjo-daro	Harappa	Proportionally Important Mohenjo-daro	Harappa
Single Segments	SS	2 to 5	486	20.81	TAB:B and C	TAB:I and SEAL:S	ALL	SEAL:R and S
Multiple Segments	MS	5 or more	19	0.81	SEAL:R	SEAL:R	NONE	NONE
Patterned								
Short Patterned	SP	3 to 5	829	35.5	SEAL:S	TAB:I and B	ALL	ALL
Long Patterned	LP	6 or more	463	19.83	SEAL:R	SEAL:R	ALL	SEAL:S and R
Complex								
Short Complex	SC	2 to 5	251	10.75	SEAL:S	SEAL:R and TAB:B	NONE	NONE
Long Complex	LC	6 or more	111	4.75	TAB:C	SEAL:R	NONE	NONE
Unclassified								
Too Short	TS	1 to 2	176	7.54	TAB:B	SEAL:R	NONE	NONE
Incomplete	omitted	n/a	1496	n/a	n/a	n/a	n/a	n/a
Sign 700								
Sign 700+Numeral	VN	2	333	91.73	NONE	TAB:1andB	NONE	TAB:IandB

4.v

4.w

679

002

817

4.x

4.y

H-158) and Long Patterned (LP) texts (i.e. M-869 and H-008). The vertical arrangement of Figure 4.6 (Top) is meant demonstrate the normal order of text segments. Likewise, the bottom of this figure has the single segment texts arranged in their apparent intended order. Single Segment seal texts can be used to recreate long and short patterned texts, as in the following example demonstrates: M-0792, SEAL:S (Figure 4.v) can be recreated using other seals: CH1293 sign 679, Ksr-2 (Figure 4.w) and M-0825 sign 002, sign 817.

One possible explanation for this phenomenon is that short texts encode only part of a complete message, and that in use short texts of this type would be combined to create longer messages. This would allow a certain amount of flexibility in cases where a defined set of segments could be used in various combinations to construct the appropriate message for the sealing task at hand. There are, however, no surviving examples of this technique being used to create TAGs. But as there are few surviving TAGs this cannot be construed as an absolute refutation of the possibility.

Multiple Segment (MS) texts containing two or more segments that occupy the same position in Patterned texts, are often separated by sign 001 presumably in its word divider role (H-158 in Figure 4.6). In the same way that M-0792 could be formed from three Single segment texts, H-158 can be approximated using DK6140, SEAL:S (Figure 4.x) and DK10567, SEAL:R (Figure 4.y).

At the bottom of Figure 4.6 there are listed nine examples of Single Segment texts, but there are in total 486 of this type of text, or a little over

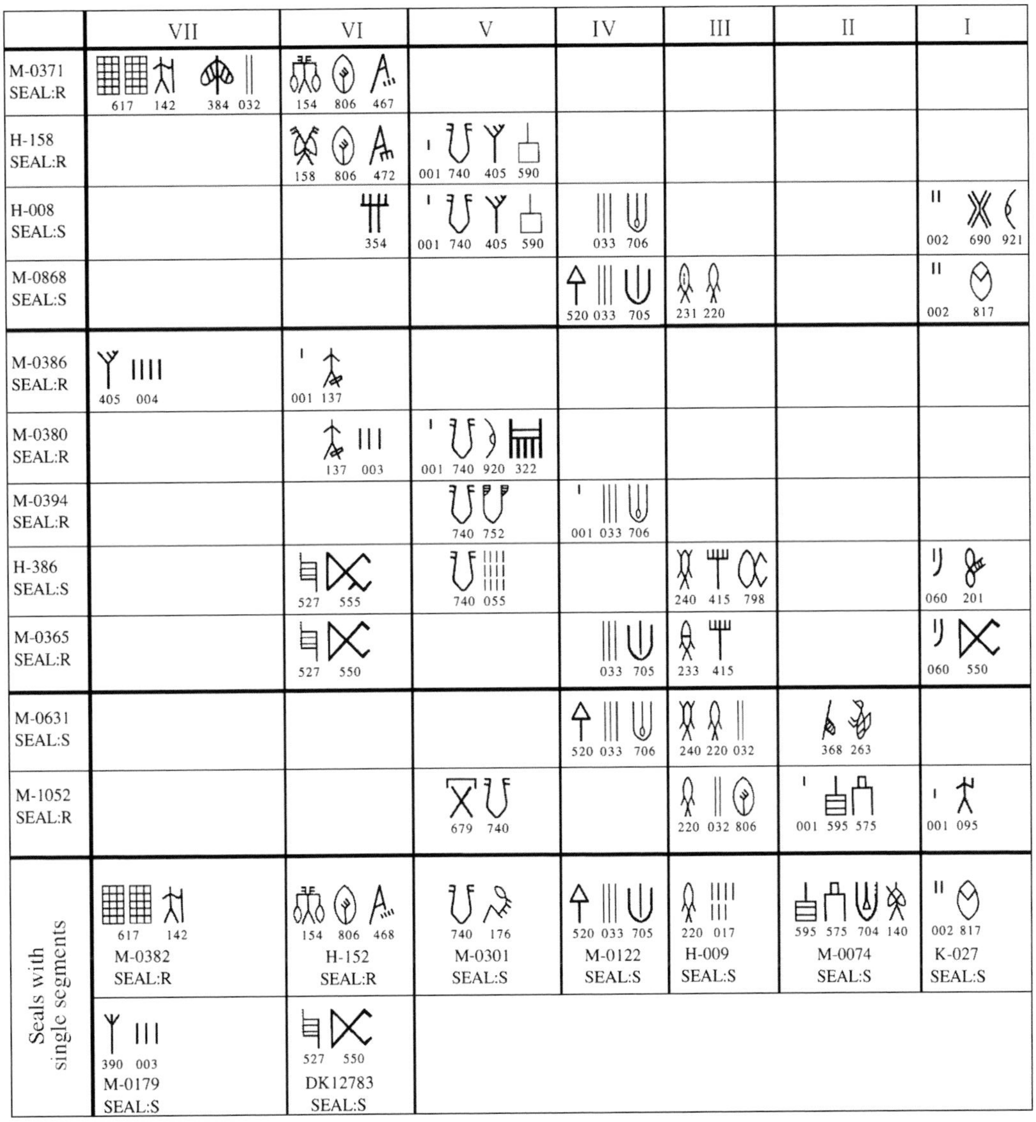

	VII	VI	V	IV	III	II	I
M-0371 SEAL:R	617 142 384 032	154 806 467					
H-158 SEAL:R		158 806 472	001 740 405 590				
H-008 SEAL:S		354	001 740 405 590	033 706			002 690 921
M-0868 SEAL:S				520 033 705	231 220		002 817
M-0386 SEAL:R	405 004	001 137					
M-0380 SEAL:R		137 003	001 740 920 322				
M-0394 SEAL:R			740 752	001 033 706			
H-386 SEAL:S		527 555	740 055		240 415 798		060 201
M-0365 SEAL:R		527 550		033 705	233 415		060 550
M-0631 SEAL:S				520 033 706	240 220 032	368 263	
M-1052 SEAL:R			679 740		220 032 806	001 595 575	001 095
Seals with single segments	617 142 M-0382 SEAL:R	154 806 468 H-152 SEAL:R	740 176 M-0301 SEAL:S	520 033 705 M-0122 SEAL:S	220 017 H-009 SEAL:S	595 575 704 140 M-0074 SEAL:S	002 817 K-027 SEAL:S
	390 003 M-0179 SEAL:S	527 550 DK12783 SEAL:S					

Figure 4.6 Single segment seal texts and their sequence of combination in longer seal texts.

20% of the complete Indus texts. Multiple Segment texts are much rarer, with only 19 examples. Not all of these use the telltale sign 001 divider and so they can be difficult to identify.

It is possible that Single Segment seal texts were intended to be used together to create longer complete messages. If so each of these seals contain a different element (syntactic unit) of the message, and separately would individually make no sense. This could present a considerable obstacle to decipherment. Attempts to make sense of the Indus texts needs to include

One Sign Initial Clusters

	Sign No.	817 ◊	861 ◊	820 ⊛	692 ⋈	920)	550 ⋈	Total
Initial Cluster Terminal Markers	2 ‖	143	113	77	1			334
	1 ǀ			14	4	1	1	20
	60 ǀǀ			26	40	55	24	145
	Total	143	113	117	45	56	25	499

Figure 4.7 Frequency of pairings of signs in two sign initial clusters.

this possibility in the consideration of text form. What Figure 4.6 (bottom) establishes is the order that these nine elements are found in, and that this order is mostly constant.

Patterned texts

Short (2-5 signs) and long (6+ signs) patterned texts are common (Short Patterned = 829 and Long Patterned = 463) and together comprise more than half of the complete texts in the ICIT database. Before beginning the discussion of patterned texts it is necessary to clarify the identification of Initial Sign Clusters. Following this long patterned texts, followed by short patterned texts, are discussed.

Initial sign clusters

Many of the longer Indus texts begin with recognizable clusters of signs. There are pairs of signs that occur frequently at the beginning of Indus texts. These pairings are not random, in that there is a strong preference for certain signs to locate exclusively with others (Figure 4.7). There are many examples in Indus texts of other signs collocating with sign 001, sign 002, and sign 060 two of these signs (sign 001 and sign 002) can be demonstrated to have other functions in certain contexts. The functions and values of these three signs are not known, but they clearly mark a syntactic boundary in texts where they are functioning as Initial Cluster Terminal Markers. The linguistic identity of these signs is speculated upon in Chapter 6. Before further exploring their function as Initial Cluster Terminal Markers, it is necessary to define what other functions sign 001 and sign 002 might have.

001 ǀ

002 ‖

060 ǀǀ

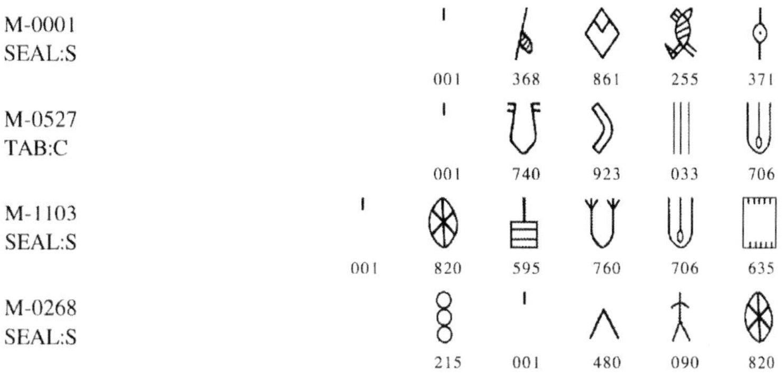

M-0001 SEAL:S	I				
	001	368	861	255	371
M-0527 TAB:C	I				
	001	740	923	033	706
M-1103 SEAL:S	I				
	001	820	595	760	706	635
M-0268 SEAL:S			I		
	215	001	480	090	820

Figure 4.8 Possible syllabic contexts for sign 001.

Additional functions of sign 001 and sign 002

i) As a word divider

For sign 001: (Figure 4.e) In this example sign 001 separates two well known short segment texts that occur separately as independent texts. Here sign 001 seems to be functioning as a word divider, and is certainly not functioning as an ICTM.

H-027 SEAL:S   4.e

For sign 002: (Figure 4.f) as with the example above, here sign 002 separates two well know segments and is functioning as a word divider and not a ICTM.

M-1155 SEAL:S   4.f

ii) As a numeral

For sign 001: (Figure 4.g) Here sign 002 is functioning as an ICTM, while sign 001 is right adjacent to a fish sign cluster in a known contexts for numerals.

M-0266 SEAL:S   4.g

For sign 002: (Figure 4.h) In this texts sign 002 occurs right adjacent to a fish sign, a position normally occupied by stroke signs when they are functioning as numerals (see Chapter 5). Further, it is also part of a cluster of numerals. In Chapter 5 the case is made for) as the number 5. This is a case of positional notation, with a numeral cluster forming a high magnitude number.

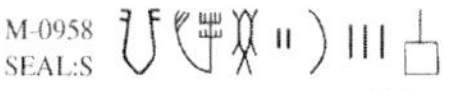

M-0958 SEAL:S   4.h

iii) As a syllable

For sign 001: The inscriptions that seem most likely examples of the syllabic contexts of sign 001 are listed below. There few explanations other than this for the position of sign 001 in the terminal (n = 3), or near terminal (n = 1) position. It is not functioning as a numeral, word divider, or Initial Cluster Terminal Marker (Figure 4.8).

Table 4.5 Locations of Initial Cluster Terminal Markers in texts

Frequency	1st	2nd	3rd	4th	5th	6th	7th	8th	9th	10th	Total
Sign 001	10	48	45	35	24	7	7		3	1	180
Sign 002	11	423	188	69	23	11	10		1		736
Sign 060	1	170	19	7							197

Percentage	1st	2nd	3rd	4th	5th	6th	7th	8th	9th	10th
Sign 001	1.5	57	26	9.4	3.1	1.5	1.4		0.1	
Sign 002	5.6	27	25	19	13	3.9	3.9		1.7	0.6
Sign 060	0.5	86	9.6	3.6						

4.k

4.l

For sign 002: (Figure 4.k) The definition of syllabic signs in an undeciphered script is problematic at best, but the case can be made for this example. First, the two left adjacent signs are part of a common sign cluster (Figure 4.l). All three signs occur separately in other contexts. Sign 002 is not functioning as an Initial Cluster Terminal Marker, and is not in the normal position for a numeral. The remaining possibility is that it is being used as a syllabic sign, or logograph. In either case it is a third function for sign 002. I favor the syllabic interpretation for two reasons: 1) sign 002 is graphically simple and seems a good candidate for a monosyllabic sign; and, 2) it is part of a long string of signs that do not fit the usual pattern of Indus texts (as is shown below. It seems likely that these are strings of syllables (spelling words) and not strings of logographs.

Sign 60

060

One interesting aspect of the various functions of signs 001 and 002 is that they do not seem to be shared by sign 060. If the positions at which Initial Cluster Terminal Markers located in texts are tallied, the results are very uneven (Table 4.5). Sign 060 never locates further left than the 4th position in any text, while signs 001 and 002 locate up to the 10th and 9th positions respectively. While sign 060's focus is the 2nd position (86%), sign 001 is less focused (57%), and sign 002 is the most dispersed. This distribution suggests that initial sign clusters can only be four signs long (three signs plus an Initial Cluster Terminal Marker). Examples of signs 001 and 002 in positions 5-10 are likely contexts where they are functioning as something other than an Initial Cluster Terminal Marker (syllables, numbers, or word dividers). An alternative explanation is the initial clusters can be very long when terminated by signs 001 or 002. In either case Initial Sign Clusters greater than four signs long (including the Initial Cluster Terminal Marker) should be viewed as possible cases of an Initial Cluster Terminal Marker being used for one of its other values.

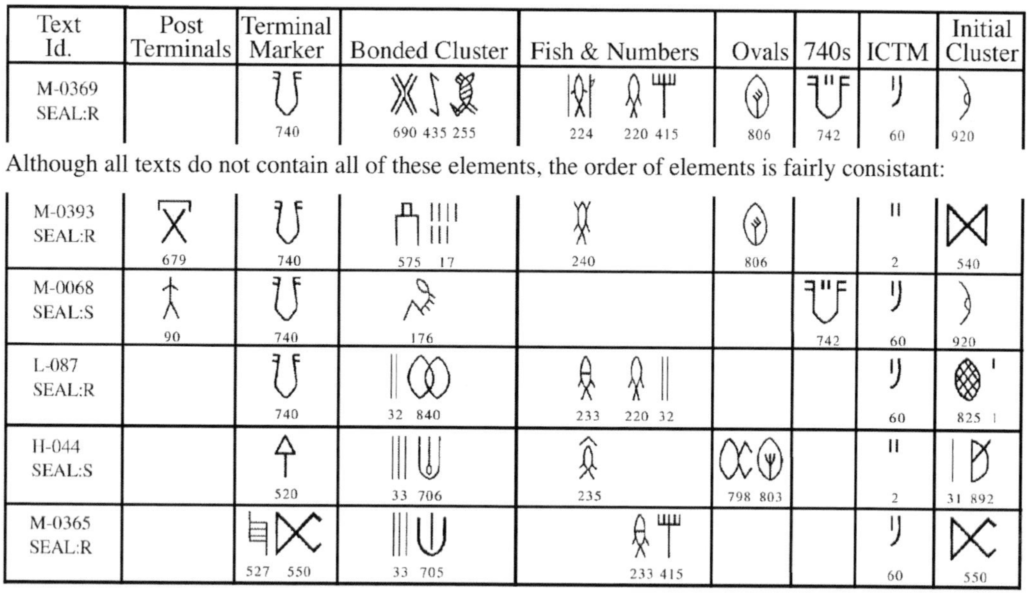

Text Id.	Post Terminals	Terminal Marker	Bonded Cluster	Fish & Numbers	Ovals	740s	ICTM	Initial Cluster
M-0369 SEAL:R		740	690 435 255	224 220 415	806	742	60	920

Although all texts do not contain all of these elements, the order of elements is fairly consistant:

Text Id.	Post Terminals	Terminal Marker	Bonded Cluster	Fish & Numbers	Ovals	740s	ICTM	Initial Cluster
M-0393 SEAL:R	679	740	575 17	240	806		2	540
M-0068 SEAL:S	90	740	176			742	60	920
L-087 SEAL:R		740	32 840	233 220 32			60	825 1
H-044 SEAL:S		520	33 706	235	798 803		2	31 892
M-0365 SEAL:R		527 550	33 705	233 415			60	550

Figure 4.9 Components of long patterned texts.

Having recognized that not all occurrences of signs 001 and 002 are Initial Cluster Terminal Markers, the analysis of the internal structure of the patterned texts can proceed.

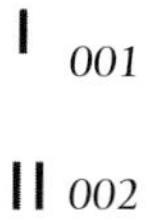

I 001

II 002

Fixed sign orders and repeated sign clusters

Defining sign clusters and their order

i) Long Indus texts (six or more signs) are often composed of sets of sign clusters that occur in a fixed order as follows: Initial Cluster; Initial Cluster Terminal Marker; signs 741, 742 and 745; Ovals; Fish and Numbers; Bonded Clusters; Terminal Markers; and Post Terminals. For example, M-0369 (Figure 4.9).

741

742

745

ii) Variations in sign order. Not all texts follow exactly the sign order given above. In some cases single signs or sign clusters are shifted, especially Fish and Numbers in reverse order with Ovals (Figure 4.10).

iii) Duplicate elements. In some cases elements are duplicated within a single inscription. In these cases the sign sequences are known from many other examples were they do not occur in conjunction with other bonded clusters.

1) Bonded clusters. Multiple bonded clusters in the same texts are relatively common, but they still often occur between the Fish and Numbers

Text Id.	Terminal Marker	Bonded Cluster	Ovals & Numbers		Fish & Numbers	ICTM	Initial Cluster
H-012 SEAL:S	740	690 435 255		803	220 240 235	2	817
H99-4064 SEAL:S	740	405 590	32 900 3	806	235 220 32	2	690 921

Figure 4.10 Variations in component ordering in long patterned texts.

Text Id.	Terminal Marker	Bonded Clusters		Fish & Numbers	Ovals	ICTM	Initial Cluster
H-268 SEAL:S	740	585 17	33 706		803	2	220 455 920
E2475 SEAL:R	740	407 590	31 752	33 705	220 415	798	

Figure 4.11 Multiple bonded clusters in long patterned texts.

and the Terminal Markers. They may be list of (enumerated) items (Figure 4.11).

2) Terminal markers. As with multiple Bonded Clusters, Terminal Marker can also occur more than once in a text. When this occurs it is normally in the same order as single Terminal Markers (Figure 4.12).

3) Duplicated sequences. In very rare case sequences of sign clusters occur that consist of elements of the overall sequence. These are arranged in the same sequence in longer texts (Figure 4.13).

Short patterned texts (2-5 signs) contain two or more of the sign cluster defined in (i) above (Figure 4.14). They are the most numerous type (n = 829), and are found equally distributed at

Mohenjo-daro and Harappa. They are proportionately most common on TAB artifacts from Harappa, but form an important component of all texts from all artifact types. Other than their terseness they are identical to long patterned texts. There is a great deal of variation in how sign clusters are used to form short patterned texts.

Complex texts

There are some texts attested in which the organizational scheme in less easy to define. They consist of sign sequences of various lengths, but although they use the same sign inventories as other inscriptions, the signs are arranged in a completely unique sequences when compared to segmented and patterned texts.

Short complex texts (3-5 signs) occur on 251 artifacts. Although these types of texts can be

Text Id.	Terminal Markers			Bonded Cluster	Fish & Numbers		Ovals	ICTM	Initial Cluster
H-386 SEAL:S	527	555	740	IIII IIII IIII 55	220	415	798	II 2	201

Figure 4.12 Multiple terminal markers in long patterned texts.

Text Id.	Sequence 2 Fish+BC+TM			Sequence 1 Oval+TM		ICTM	Initial Cluster	
DK8242 SEAL:S	520	72	233	740	798	II 2	861	832

Figure 4.13 Duplicate sequences in long patterned texts.

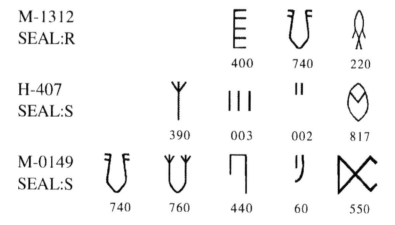

Figure 4.14 Short patterned texts.

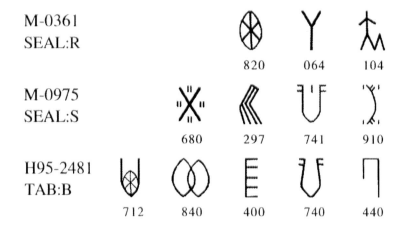

Figure 4.15 Short complex texts.

found on all artifact types they do not form a substantial group on a single artifact type. They are slightly more common at Mohenjo-daro than Harappa. The texts in Figure 4.15 are typical of this type of text.

Long complex texts (6+ signs) occur 111 times in the ICIT database. They are most common on TAB:C artifacts which are found exclusively at Mohenjo-daro. They are relatively rare at Harappa and not found at all on TAB:I artifacts from that site. The texts in Figure 4.16 are typical of this type.

Complex texts are important to the study of Indus inscriptions because of the possibility that they are syllabic spellings. Their analysis is undertaken in detail in Chapter 6.

Too short or incomplete to classify

To begin with, incomplete texts (n = 1,496) are not included in this study. The primary reason being that it is impossible to analyze them completely. Some of the incomplete texts are used (especially the long ones) for comparison to complete text when individual sign cluster are

analyzed, but they are not part of the typology of texts described here. Some texts are too short (1-4 signs) to classify (n = 176), but they nevertheless form a significant component of the complete texts and are an important part of this study. Because these texts are complete they must be either complete messages on their own, or be segments used to construct longer messages. This is especially true of text consisting of only one sign. It seems logical that single sign texts should be logographs or multiple component signs. A closer look at the artifacts types of single sign texts reveals an interesting distribution (Figure 4.17).

The focus of these texts is noticeably different than that of the corpus in general, with bangles (BNGL) and ceramics (POT:T:g and POT:T:s) comprising far greater proportions of one sign texts. The POT:T:s texts (n = 16) are entirely from Harappa and repeat only three

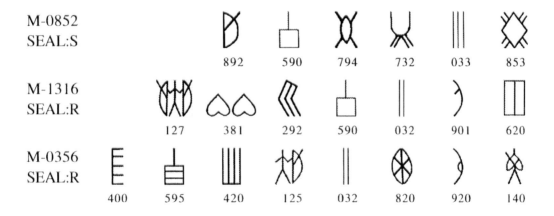

Figure 4.16 Long complex texts.

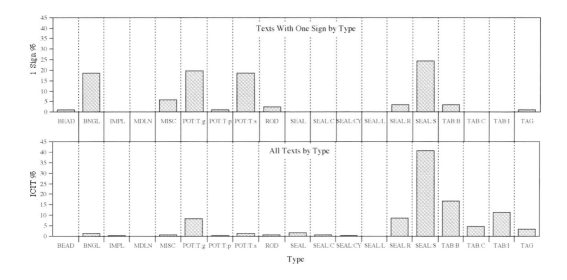

Figure 4.17 Comparison of frequency of texts by artifact type.

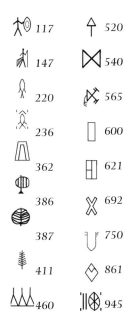

signs: sign 416 x4, sign 013 x4, sign 440 x8. We can see from the seal impressions that these 16 texts were created with only three seals (all SEAL:R). The POT:T:g and MISC texts with one sign are reminiscent of potters' marks, consisting largely of stroke signs (signs 1–35). One sign texts from SEAL artifacts tend to use more complex signs (sign 945, sign 565, sign 117, sign 147, and sign 236 etc.). Simple signs used in SEAL texts are restricted to 'picture signs': sign 387, sign 411, and sign 386 (logographs). All but one example of the bangle (BNGL) texts come from Mohenjo-daro, as do the majority of SEAL texts.

Two sign texts present a special problem for analysis in that they may contain fragments of pattern texts that cannot be identified as such with certainty: sign 520, sign 460, sign 520, sign 220, sign 621, sign 226, and sign 400, sign 226, for example. Here the assumption is made that these are short patterned texts. This accounts for the vast majority of two sign texts. The remainder are either doubled signs (sign 750, sign 705 and sign 540, sign 540 both POT:T:g) or signs that do not fit into the Patterned text category: sign 362, sign 861 SEAL:R, sign 600, sign 143 and sign 692, sign 451 SEAL:S for example.

One and two sign texts can be analyzed for the number of components each text contains. The concept of components was introduced in Chapter 3. The greater the number of components the more complex the sign is. For example the one component sign sign 220 becomes the three component sign sign 236 with the addition of (Figure 4.m) and (Figure 4.n). Figure 4.18 compares the number of components per text for texts with one or two signs.

The mean number of components per sign for one sign texts is 1.78, but nearly double that for two sign texts (3.39). One factor influencing this difference is the large number of one sign texts that consist of numerals (all numeral signs have one component), but even with the numerals removed the mean number of components per sign increase only slightly to 1.87. There are variations in this value between artifact types with one sign texts. Many one sign texts are on BNGL, BEAD, MISC, POT:T, IMPL and other (non-intaglio) inscribed artifacts. Single sign seal texts draw upon the more complex signs (SEAL:S = 2.42 and SEAL:R = 2.0). The most complex artifact type is TAB:C with a value of 4.2, and the least complex is MISC (1.2), POT:T:g (1.3) and BNGL (1.5). The values are most likely related to the fact the main functions of the low scoring artifacts is not the communication of their message, while this is the purpose of SEAL and TAB artifact types. Consequently, the texts of SEAL and TAB artifacts must convey whole ideas. The low scoring texts, however, may only been functioning as mnemonics, or marking items at stages within the cycles of production and distribution.

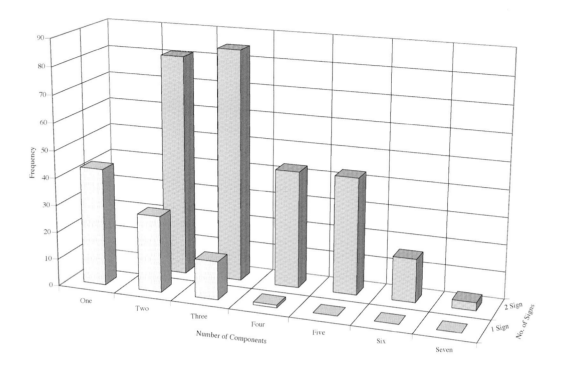

Figure 4.18 Comparison of the complexity of one and two sign texts.

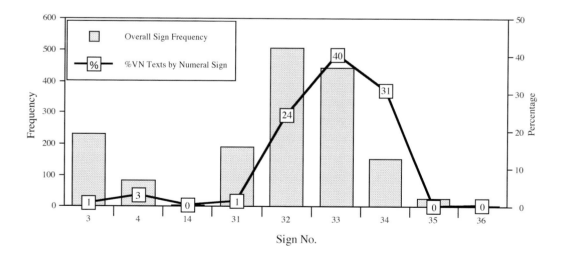

Figure 4.19 Comparison of numeral sign frequencies, and the percentage of sign 700 + Number texts using numeral signs.

Table 4.6 Frequency of text type pairings for artifacts with two texts (see Table 4.4 for abbreviations)

Code	SP	LP	SC	LC	SS	MS	TS	VN	Sub
SP	11	9	43	-	6	-	26	155	250
LP	-	4	10	7	-	-	20	8	49
SC	-	-	5	5	10	-	15	34	69
LC	-	-	-	2	-	-	4	3	9
SS	-	-	-	-	5	-	12	47	64
MS	-	-	-	-	-	-	-	-	-
TS	-	-	-	-	-	-	13	14	27
VN	-	-	-	-	-	-	-	-	-
Sub	11	13	58	14	21	-	90	261	468

Set 5: Sign 700 + numeral

$\bigvee$ 700

Of the 565 examples of sign 700 sign, 363 are from complete texts, and 333 of these (92%) consist of sign 700 and an associated numeral. In some cases these sign pairs are imbedded in longer texts (n = 34). In most cases these sign pairs are the only signs in the texts with associated texts on the reverse (obverse?). While most of the sign 700 + number texts occur on TAB:B and TAB:I artifacts from Harappa, is a small number (n = 5) of the sign 700 + number texts are on POT:T:g artifacts. The significance of this connection is discussed in detail elsewhere (Chapter 5 and Wells 1999:34-35). There are not enough examples for a detailed study, but it is possible that the Indus volumetric system is involved. It is clear from Figure 4.19 that sign 700 collocates preferentially with specific numerals (signs 033 and 034). Signs 031 and 032 are not used in sign 700 + number texts as much as would be expected from their overall frequencies. These variations point to fact that signs 031-034 do not have the same values in VN text as they so in other types of texts. sign 700 + number texts are often found on artifacts with two or more inscriptions on their various sides. These occurrences are part of a special set of artifacts with multiple texts and are discussed in the following section.

VN signs can occur in longer texts too (i.e. H-811, H-774 and H94-2273). One sign sequence that is repeated on TAB:B artifacts from Harappa is (Figure 4.z). This sequence occurs 20 times in the ICIT database with minor variations and here the TAB effect must be considered. In all cases sign 700 + number sequences are in the terminal position of these texts.

Multiple texts artifacts

There are 506 complete Indus artifacts with inscriptions on more than one side. The vast majority of these artifacts come from Harappa (391 = 77%)

and only 98 (19%) from Mohenjo-daro. There is also a strong preference for TAB:B (218) and TAB:I (181) artifacts. They are relatively uncommon on seals (SEAL:S 55, SEAL:R 5). As to what text types co-occur, Table 4.6 (see Table 4.4 for abbreviations) summarizes these pairings for the 468 two-text artifacts. In this table Short Patterned and + Number texts dominate. One feature of this table is the complete lack of Multiple Segments texts co-occurring with any other texts. It is the only category completely absent from this table.

Only 38 artifacts have more than two sides inscribed. Of these only SS/TS/VN form a significant cluster (19), with SP/SC/VN (5) and SC/TS/VN (3) texts forming minor clusters. All other examples (11) have a frequency of 1. The two most common text types to occur on multiple text artifacts are VN (261) texts and SP (250). They pair in 155 case and form the largest set of paired text types. These pairs are entirely restricted to TAB:B and TAB:I artifacts.

Syllabic vs. logographic signs

Signs that occur in one sign texts and cannot be further deconstructed (i.e. into known signs) are good candidates for logographs based on the assumption that this represents spoken language (see Chapter 6). These signs are not compound signs, and should be interpretable as complete concepts or words (i.e. fish, leaf, tree, etc.). Although the Initial Medial terminal (Figure 4.20) is not absolutely regular, most of the signs occur in restricted contexts. The best understood example being sign 740. This sign is discussed in the definition of Patterned texts, where it was defined as a Terminal Marker (TM). Other signs also share this context (see Chapter 6 for a complete list): 390 sign, 407, sign 405, and sign 520. These signs are most probably logographs, as are the signs in Figure 4.20, although the exact identification of what they represent cannot be know without resorting to speculation.

Of all the TMs only one uses more than one sign: one of 525/526/527 sign, paired with one of 550/554/555. These signs pair in 58 texts, the most common being 527 with both 550 (n = 28) and 555 sign (n = 20). The fact that it takes two signs to perform a function normally fulfilled by a single sign raises the possibility that these signs are syllables, in some cases with additional markings (sign 554, sign 555). Of signs 550/554/555, only 550 is found in the initial position in texts paired with sign 060. Interestingly, the text of the SEAL:S M-0063 consists of: sign 525, 555, 060, 550. I would posit that sign 550 is a syllabic sign, with 554 and 555 being minor variation in the quality of 550, and are likewise related syllabic signs.

390
405
407
520
740

525   526   527

550   554   555   060

Sign No.	Graph		Total	Init	Med	Term	Set
220		n=	443	40	239	8	11
		%	64.79	9.03	53.95	1.81	
384		n=	26	4	16	1	24
		%	80.7692	15.38	61.54	3.85	
405		n=	112	1	54	25	28
		%	71.43	0.89	48.21	22.32	
411		n=	5	0	2	1	28
		%	60	0	40	20	
440	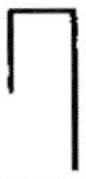	n=	48	8	20	3	32
		%	64.58	16.67	41.67	6.25	
455		n=	37	5	15	3	34
		%	62.16	13.51	40.54	8.11	
700		n=	565	63	37	276	57
		%	66.55	11.15	6.55	48.85	
740		n=	1696	9	351	758	59
		%	65.92	0.53	20.7	44.69	
790		n=	52	13	17	7	63
		%	71.15	25	32.69	13.46	
850		n=	47	7	24	4	65
		%	74.47	14.89	51.06	8.51	

Figure 4.20 Signs that occur in one sign texts and are not deconstructable.

Signs 525/526/527 sign are also paired with other signs (in addition to 550/554/555) most commonly following 388 sign (n = 4), but also following sign 195 (1), sign 456, (1) and sign 140 (1). In Figure 4.20 (potential logographs) signs 384 and sign 455 are listed and their elaborated forms sign 388 and sign 456 collocate with 525/526/527. Since signs 525/526/527 are signs that collocate with logographs, and as they are not found in other contexts, they must be either syllabic signs or determinatives.

While syllabic signs are difficult to define, there are two signs that are common and are found in contexts that allow their tentative identification as syllabic signs: 400 (n = 432) and 090 (n = 168). The most common context for both signs is following terminal markers. It has been suggested that in these contexts they are case markers (Lal 1979; Mahadevan 1982) or determinatives (Parpola 1994). One problem with these suggestions is that both signs occur together in terminal contexts. Secondly, because determinatives classify nouns they would occur only in restricted positions in texts, and as these signs occur in initial, medial, and terminal positions they cannot be determinatives. Another explanation is needed, and the possibility that they are syllabic signs seems likely.

Another possible way of identifying logographs is by the use of numerical infixes. All signs in Figure 4.20 that are capable of infixing are found affixed with signs 001-004 (for example, sign 790 + 001-004 = 832, 829, 831 and 833). The same pattern is followed for signs 740 (741, 742, 745 and 748) and 700 (701 and 703). This does not mean that all signs with numeral infixed are logographs, only that there are several characteristics shared by these signs that seems to support the identification of them as functional equivalents.

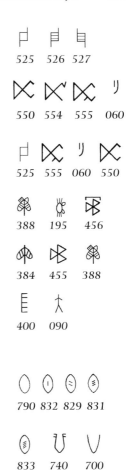

Special function additions

The elements described in Chapter 3 as enclosures (Figure 3.7) have various effects on the positioning of the sign they enclose. That is, they can affect the syntactic values of the signs they modify. There are 63 enclosed signs in total. Table 4.7 lists the frequency occurrence of enclosure signs. The effects of enclosure signs vary with both the sign enclosed and the type of enclosure. These variations can be tracked to some degree by comparing the Initial Medial terminal data of the enclosed sign with the unenclosed sign.

Two approaches are taken here: first, the Initial Medial terminal data for fish signs (both enclosed and unenclosed) are compared; second, caged sign are compared for variations in their Initial Medial terminal data.

Fish signs

There are seven fish signs examined here, six are enclosed and one is not. Although every type of enclosure is found, low frequencies make analysis for

Table 4.7 Enclosure signs frequency of occurrence

Type	Table 3.4 No.	No. Signs	No. Occurrences
Brackets	7a	21	93
Strokes	7b	24	138
Cages	7c	19	44

Sign	Type	Total				Mohenjo-daro				Harappa			
		Freq	I	M	T	Freq	I	M	T	Freq	I	M	T
220	basic	443	40	239	8	200	12	130	2	179	26	84	5
221	enclsd	6	1	4		1		1		2	1	1	
222	enclsd	13		11		12		10					
223	enclsd	3				2				1			
224	enclsd	1			1	1			1				
225	enclsd	1								1			
226	enclsd	36	2	3	18	25	1	1	14	3	1		

Figure 4.21 Sign 220 and its enclosed varieties.

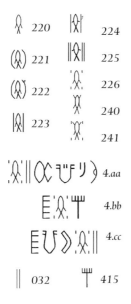

some signs difficult. Figure 4.21 list the frequencies and Initial Medial terminal data for sign 220 and all enclosed varieties of it. In this table sign 220 can be seen to be most often a medial sign with low frequency initial and terminal placement. Site-specific data shows that sign 220 located initially far more often at Harappa than at Mohenjo-daro. Terminal locations are equally rare at both sites. Sign 221 has a similar distribution to 220, but with only six examples attested this could be coincidence. Sign 222 is slightly more common with 13 examples, all from Mohenjo-daro, and all medial. Signs 223, 224 and 225 cannot be analyzed because of their low frequencies. Sign 226 is the best opportunity for comparison to 220. Here the pattern is overwhelmingly terminal with majority of examples coming from Mohenjo-daro. Sign 226 behaves as a terminal marker in some cases: M-0387, SEAL:R (Figure 4.aa) and Rpr 1, SEAL:R (Figure 4.bb), but can still locate medially in contexts similar to sign 220: M-1438, SEAL:R (Figure 4.cc). It still locates left adjacent to signs 032 and 415.

Of the 275 enclosed signs 44 are fish signs. Fish signs are, however, the only group for which examples of all enclosures are applied to the same root sign. Although these data are sparse in places, the general pattern points a greater use of enclosures at Mohenjo-daro (n = 41) than at Harappa (n = 7). Further, major changes in positioning within the texts seem to occur with the addition of cage enclosures. This pattern also holds true for signs 240/241 with nine of 10 examples of 241 terminal and all but one example coming from Mohenjo-daro. The reason for the geographic variations in enclosure use are unknown, but it might relate to the need to adapt existing signs to new uses. It is also possible that idiomatic uses could cause localized variations in sign construction.

Variations in enclosures over time

Figure 4.22 shows the distribution of enclosures by archaeological phase at Mohenjo-daro (DK.G). Also given is the mean text length by phase. The low frequency of enclosed signs in the Early period is attributable to sample size, as the Early period was only reached during deep diggings and represents only a tiny proportion of the total excavated volume. The distribution of enclosures by phase is uneven, with the highest frequency in the Intermediate III phase, and a dramatic decreases in the Late I and II phases. This distribution does not mirror the total frequency of signs (Figure 3.15). That is, the proportion of enclosures to total signs are very different by phase, especially in the Intermediate III and Late III.

Another interesting aspect of this distribution is that it is correlated to the mean length of texts by phase (r = 0.734). Increase in the number of enclosures used in a phase is inversely proportional to mean text length in a given phase.

A possible toponym

The closest thing to a monumental inscription in the Indus corpus is the Dholavira sign board (Parpola 1994). The text consisted of nine signs formed by arranging pieces of crystalline stone inlayed into a wooden plank, with signs about 30 cm high. Discovered in a side chamber near one of the main entrances to Dholavira and bears the following texts: (Figure 4.o). It has been suggested that it hung over the entranceway of the gate. I would postulate that some of these signs could be spelling the ancient name of

4.o

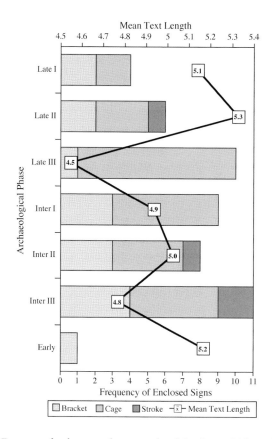

Figure 4.22 Frequency of enclosures and mean text length by phase at Mohenjo-daro (DK.G).

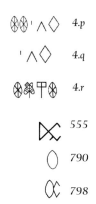

Dholavira. Further, the signs spelling the name of an important site should be repeated elsewhere in the Indus corpus. This is in fact exactly what happens. The sign sequence (Figure 4.p) is repeated on five artifacts (Figure 4.23). The sequence has two elements: (Figure 4.q) and sign 821. This is known because (Figure 4.q) occurs without sign 821 and visa versa. The identities of the other signs: (Figure 4.r) and the terminal sign 798 are not as clear, but there placement suggests that sign 798 is a word sign, either syllabic cluster (sign 790 + sign 555) or logograph (i.e. isolated at the end of the text), and (Figure 4.r) is a separate introductory phrase (four signs and nine components). The sign sequence (Figure 4.q) may be three syllabic signs spelling Dholavira's ancient name.

Conclusion

The purpose of this chapter has been to examine in details of the structure of Indus texts, and to look for patterns of sign use within the structure of the texts. Several important structures were defined leading to the identification of the

Id.	Type	Inscription
DK7535	IMPL	
DK7856	IMPL	
DK7854	IMPL	
Dlv-2	MISC	
Hd-3	POT:T:g	
L-274	POT:T:g	
Krs-1	SEAL:R	
C-24	SEAL:S	
DK10551	SEAL:S	
DK6390	SEAL:S	
H-718	TAB:B	
H96-3175	TAB:I	
M-1384	TAG:L	

Figure 4.23 Other contexts of repeated signs found on the Dholavira signboard.

Text Id.	Post Terminals	Terminal Marker	Bonded Cluster	Fish & Numbers	Ovals	740s	ICTM	Initial Cluster
M-0369 SEAL:R		740	690 435 255	224 220 415	806	742	60	920
Signs: 11		1	3	3	1	1	1	1
Components: 18		1	1+1+2 = 4	3 + 1 +2 = 6	2	2	1	2

Figure 4.24 Components by segment for a long patterned text.

macrostructure of some Indus texts, and giving rise to a typology of texts based on their content. The linguistic nature of these macrostructures are examined in Chapter 6. It was also demonstrated that specific types of texts locate preferentially on certain artifacts. Given that different artifacts had demonstrably different functions, these patterns suggest that differences in subject matter may be and important factor in the composition of Indus texts. That certain sign clusters (i.e. sign 700 + number) have a restricted use is undeniable, and yet the vast majority of common Indus signs occur on several artifact types (including sign 700).

In this chapter I have outlined the basic epigraphic principles relating to structural analysis. Further, I have given examples of how these principles can be use in the analysis of Indus texts. This has resulted in: 1) the definition of a typology of Indus texts; 2) the identification of some polyvalent signs; 3) the identification of both syllabic and logographic signs. This information serves to demonstrate the underlying mechanics of the Indus script.

The concept of components makes it clear that the number of sign in a text is not an accurate measure of the amount of information contained in the texts. Although the number of components normally increases with the number of signs in a texts, the existence of up to six components in one sign points to the inadvisability of making a direct link between number of signs and message complexity. The question of why signs have multiple components, i.e. to save space, aesthetics, or linguistic considerations, is not always clear. There is no reason that all of these factors cannot be affecting sign form at the same time. The data given in this chapter (and in Chapter 3) suggest that linguistic considerations are the main factor, and that space and aesthetics are secondary considerations. For example: sign 104 but never (Figure 4.s), and sign 132 but never (Figure 4.t). So while the components of compound signs are likely selected for their values, their arrangement may be controlled by aesthetics, available space or order of reading. It is also possible that the attached elements (i.e. comb or shoe) have a logical association with their placement.

Given these circumstances the analysis of texts can be very complicated: first, dealing with text type and macro structures; second, identifying associated sign clusters; and finally, considering the number of components for each sign (Figure 4.24). This is a long patterned text (Long Patterned), with seven of eight of the elements that comprise Long Patterned texts (lacking only post terminal signs), and contains 11 signs and 18 components (1.64).

The meta-structures of Indus texts are in my opinion likely to be either elements or sub-elements of syntax. The individual signs are likely syllables or logographs spelling words and phrases. These structures and their elements are discussed in terms of their relationship to language in Chapter 6.

5

Indus Numeral Signs

This chapter examines the evidence for the system of numerals used in the Indus script. As was shown in Chapter 2 there are several systems of numerals in use in south and southwest Asia in the third and fourth millennium BC that were part of a system of potters' marks. These systems are in some cases geographically distinct and in other cases overlapping, but none are universal beyond the most basic components (graphic universals). They consist of straight stroke signs, curved signs, dot signs, and signs that are combinations of these elements. The Indus system, at least on ceramics, was shown in Chapter 2 to consist of stroke signs and curved signs, and to be much simpler system than its counterparts in Baluchistan and the Iranian Plateau. However, the system of numerals used in the Indus script is considerably more complex. As can be seen in Figure 5.1 there are several signs whose identity as numerals is not transparent from the shape of their sign graphs. In short, the Indus Script system is more complex than the potters' marks system, but utilizes some of the same signs. Some symbols have a wide distribution and a long history of use (sign 900), other symbols are graphic universals (sign 031), and still others are unique to the number system of the Indus script (sign 415). The complete system of Indus numerals consists of four sets of distinctive numerals: short linear strokes, long linear strokes, short-stacked strokes, and special numerals. The numbers that these special numerals represent are not certain, but that they represent numbers within the overall system of Indus numbers is obvious from their contexts in the inscriptions.

031

415

900

For comparisons this chapter looks at a selection of deciphered scripts (Linear B, Proto-Sumerian, and Proto-Elamite) for which systems of numerals are common and well defined. These texts are compared to parallel examples from the Indus inscriptions in order to identify shared structures. Secondly, Indus texts with numeric components are examined in order to assess the function of these numerals. While the use of the Indus system of numerals can hardly be considered accountancy, there is an unmistakable pattern of numeral usage similar to that known for economic texts from other ancient scripts. The detailed understanding of the number systems of Proto-Elamite, Ancient Maya writing, and other ancient scripts were not considered decipherments. This is also true of the Indus script. Yet, the use of numerals in the Indus script can help us achieve a deeper understanding the structures of these scripts, and their root languages.

Sign Number	Sign Graph	Total	Mohenjo-daro	Harappa	Lothal	Chanhujo-daro	Kalibangan	Banawali	Other	Initial	Medial	Terminal	Number Type
1	I	191	110	44	22	2	3		10	7	119	13	
2	II	763	422	205	58	29	21	6	22	10	523	12	
3	III	231	95	109	7	9	4	1	6	80	72	1	Short
4	IIII	85	42	32	3	2		1	5	16	37	1	Linear
5	IIIII	41	27	8	2	3	1			11	13		Numerals
6	IIIIII	3	3							1	1	1	
7	IIIIIII	5	3	1				1			3		
13	II/I	25	6	15	2	1			1	12	6		
14	II/II	5	1	3				1		2	1		
15	III/II	6	2		2	1	1			2	1	1	Short
16	III/III	40	22	12	2	1	2		1	4	14	2	Stacked
17	IIII/III	76	46	21		3			6	9	44		Numerals
18	IIII/IIII	5	2	3						2	2		
19	IIIII/IIII	5	1	3					1	1	1		
31	|	190	92	63	8	5	19	1	2	38	66	12	
32	||	507	174	280	18	7	20		8	110	182	29	
33	|||	445	139	284	3	8	4		7	118	151	24	Long
34	||||	153	6	146					1	87	3	16	Linear
35	|||||	27	17	9	1					2	9	2	Numerals
36	||||||	5	1	3		1				1	2	1	
415	⊥	165	79	73	5	1	1		6	41	76	5	
900	)	95	61	26	2	2	2	1	1	14	55	1	Special
65	⌐	15	11	2	1		1				9	1	Numerals
55	IIII/IIII/III	56	27	11	12	2	1		3	8	29		
Total Numbers		3139	1389	1353	148	77	80	12	80	576	1419	122	
Total Signs		15150	7616	6479	660	319	348	50	395				
% Numbers		20.72	18.24	20.88	22.42	24.14	22.99	24.00	20.25				

Figure 5.1 Numeral signs attested in the ICIT database.

It is helpful in the process of decipherment to be able to differentiate between texts based on their subject matter. In the case of economic texts this is especially important because the placement of numbers within the syntactic framework of languages is often restricted.

The case for numeracy

There are at least two lines of evidence relating to the issue of numeracy in the Indus texts. The first is the comparison of Indus texts to other ancient texts for the purposes of assessing correspondences in form and content. The second line of evidence is the presence and contexts of the proposed Indus numerals. Both of these lines of evidence are pursued in the following discussion.

For the purposes of this discussion a numeral is defined as: a symbol that stands for one or more numbers. For example, in Proto-Cuneiform texts the numeral Figure 5.a that normally has a value of 10 when counting discrete objects, takes a value of 18 when used to measure fields, and a value of 6 with dry measures of cereal. Therefore, Figure 5a is the numeral and 6, 10 and 18 are the numbers it stands for depending on the context (Nissen et al. 1993:131-132). In Proto-Cuneiform the system of numerals is complex and the values of numerals can be linked to the context of their use.

●   *5.a*

Other ancient scripts

In 1900 and again in 1904 Sir Arthur Evans excavated more than 3,000 clay tablets in an unknown script from Knossos, Crete. The Linear B script, as it came to be known, remained mostly unpublished until 1952. Alice Kober (1946, 1948) made some early advances using structural analysis, but her death in 1950 prevented her further progress with the decipherment. Michael Ventris took up this task in 1951-1952 (Ventris and Chadwick 1953). Parpola (1994-1945) describes Ventris's approach as follows:

Ventris's methodology consisted above all in completing, as fully as possible, the syllabic grid started by Alice Kober. In addition, he prepared statistical analysis of the frequency of each sign in different positions within the words. Thus he could spot the characters that were almost exclusively limited to the initial position and therefore probably stood for pure vowels.

Ventris was also able to identify the post-fixed connective particle and some prefixes based on his statistical and distributional analysis. Additionally, he used clay tablets of the same type and age from Ugarit to guess that certain words were personal names, locatives, and occupations. At this point Ventris could use his partially complete syllabic grid to reconstruct place names, which in turn were used to expand his grid. As it turned

(a) Linear B   (b) Proto-Cuneiform

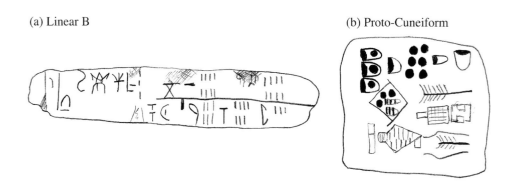

Figure 5.2 Economic texts from the Linear B and Proto-Cuneiform systems.

out about 75% of Ventris's syllabic grid was correct. At this point he turned for help to John Chadwick and together they continued to expand their grid and word list until virtually all of the texts could be read, at least in part.

Ventris had three advantages over Indus epigraphers: 1) all of his texts came from a limited time period (1900 to 1625 B.C.); 2) the Linear B texts are longer than Indus texts; and, 3) the texts from Pylos were all inscribed in a single year and related in content. Ventris correctly guessed that the script was logo-syllabic, and eventually realized that it expressed an archaic form of Greek.

What then does a typical economic Linear B text look like? Figure 5.2a gives a Linear B tablet and a reading for its text. The signs (Figure 5.b) are read "barley 9". Notice that the standard measure is omitted (or rather implied). This text was meant to be read: "9 standard rations of barley". These texts list people, animals, weapons, and other commodities owned by the palace. Linear B texts employ several different systems of measurement. Discrete items were counted, but other items were weighed. Additionally, separate volumetric systems were employed for liquids and grains. In Linear B texts seemingly equivalent values such as (Figure 5.c; wheat) and (Figure 5.d; wine) have quite different values, while (Figure 5.b; wheat) and (Figure 5.e; barley) have equivalent volumetric values. The implication of this pattern for our interpretation of the Indus script is a cautionary tale.

Proto-Sumerian and Proto-Elamite both employed more complex systems of numerals involving not only different systems of measurement, but also different values for the same numeric signs (Nissen et al. 1993:28–29). In Proto-Cuneiform texts for example, when measuring cereals the numeral (Figure 5.f) has a value of 60, but a value of 300 when used in texts measuring surfaces (fields). This phenomenon is called polyvalence. Proto-Cuneiform employs 60 numerals in at least 13 discrete groups, and Proto-Elamite uses 14 numerals in at least five groups (Damerow et al. 1989:74–75). In both cases the system being employed is understood from the context of the texts that is by which noun they are associated.

Are there analogous texts in the Indus inscriptions? Figures 5.2 and 5.3 show very similar sign sequences from Proto-Cuneiform and Indus. For example (Figure 5.g) might read eight units of an unknown commodity. In the case of Indus texts there are often introductory sign sequences of 1–3 signs, again mimicking the structure of other ancient economic texts.

It seems unlikely that structural patterns in Indus texts that mirror the patterns found in other ancient numeral texts are coincidental, indicating that these Indus texts also have a numerical (perhaps economic) subject matter. Figure 5.2 and 5.3 demonstrate that this correspondence is systematic on two levels. First, all of these scripts have a Number + Noun construction in their accounting texts (they share a structure), and second the forms of the signs being enumerated are similar in that they are often phytomorphic. For example, barley is depicted as (Figure 5.h) in Linear B and (Figure 5.i) in Proto-Sumerian. That does not mean that the (Figure 5.j) sign stands for barley in the Indus texts, only that the pattern suggests it is representing some economically important item, perhaps a plant (and it is a logograph). Other generic similarities exist in the use of phytomorphic, zoomorphic, and anthropomorphic signs in all scripts.

Another point is that the inventory of numerals is about the same for the Linear B and Indus texts. In Linear B texts the numerals given range from 1–9, and 1–10 in Indus texts. In the Proto-Sumerian and Proto-Elamite texts increasing values are represented by separate but morphologically related signs such as (Figure 5.k). In the texts (Figure 5.l) and (Figure 5.m) there are both short linear and long linear numeral signs are associated with the same (noun) anthropomorphic sign. These may be related in the same way that the small and large circle are in the Sumerian texts. Proto-Sumerian uses a number system in which numerals can be combined with other signs to create ligatures with both numeric and semantic components. As far as numeric ligatures are concerned there are plentiful examples of equivalent signs in the Indus script: sign 832, sign 830, sign 831, sign 741, sign 742, and sign 745. These ligatures use a subset the entire inventory of Indus numbers. This points to the close association of specific numerals with specific signs, especially sign 740 and sign 790 with signs 1 to 4.

Indus numbers and the signs most commonly found in association with them can be defined using the ICIT program (see Figure 5.1). Those numerals omitted from this figure use numbers with additional markings

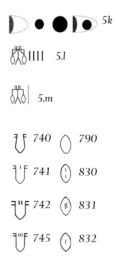

Figure 5.3 Indus and Uruk texts compared.

such as capped numerals, enclosed numerals, attached numerals, infixed numerals or numerals conflated with other signs. The analysis of these signs must follow the analysis of the numerals, but the large number of these signs in Indus texts suggests that they play an important role. Unfortunately, their small frequency of occurrence means their analysis must rely on comparisons to the overall system of numerals. This subject is taken up again later in this chapter.

The basic Indus number system consists of 24 signs occurring 3,139 times, or about 21% of all sign occurrences (Figure 5.1). Numbers are found primarily on POT:T:g (213), SEAL:R (301), SEAL:S (1305), TAB:B (496), TAB:I (412), TAB:C (142), and TAG (126) artifacts. These totals contain the counts for signs 001, 002, 031, 032, and 033 they are consequently inflated by non-numeric (polyvalent) uses of these signs and by the repetitive nature of TAB texts (the TAB effect).

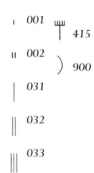

There is reason to believe (based on contexts) that other signs may have numeric values especially sign 415 (Bonta 1995) and sign 900 (Wells 1999), which occur in 165 and 95 inscriptions respectively. There is also reason to believe that stroke signs do not have numeric functions in every case: sign 001, sign 002, sign 031, sign 032, and sign 033. For example, sign 001 seems to have four identifiable functions (see Chapter 4). Other numeral signs (especially sign 031, sign 032, and sign 033) seem to have both numerical and syllabic functions. Polyvalence creates some problems when trying to identify economic texts, especially where the contexts are ambiguous.

Further evidence supporting the case for numeracy in the Indus script can be found in the frequency of signs on various types of artifacts. Leaving aside POT:T:g artifacts (because of their high frequencies of texts consisting only of numerals), the mean text length for specific artifact types is fairly highly correlated to the mean number of numerals found on the same artifact types (r2 = 0.72). That is, the proportion of numeric to non-numeric signs is fairly constant across artifact types. It was argued in Chapter 1 that seals were used to control the transportation of goods and in the cycle of production (amongst other uses).

It would be reasonable to expect TAG artifacts to have a high frequency of numerical signs. Many, but not all, tag texts use numeral signs. There are 169 Tags listed in the ECIT database. Of these 119 have at least one readable Indus sign. In all 90 TAGs have inscriptions with one or more numerals. There are 125 numeral signs of the 515 legible signs (≈24%). The 34 TAGs without numerals may be linked to the control mechanisms of the Indus bureaucracy, representing situations where items need to be sealed, but where the contents were either obvious or known by some other means.

POT:T:g artifacts have the largest proportion of numeral signs of any artifact type in the ICIT database (33% of all signs found on this type of artifact are numerals). TAB:I and SEAL:R artifacts likewise have relatively large proportions of numerals (≈20%). The lowest proportions of numerals are found on TAB:B and TAB:C artifacts (both with 15%), SEAL:S (18%), and the remainder of minor artifact types (19%).

Positional notation

The question of the scale of Indus economic activity is of obvious importance to a discussion of numeracy in the Indus texts. The expectation is that large-scale exchanges require systems of notation capable of annotating such transactions. One strategy employed in ancient and modern systems is to express larger numerical values in positional notation. For example, in Linear B the number 1,357 would be written (Figure 5.n) using four numerals (Chadwick 1987:13). In Proto-Sumerian the number 135,000 would be written (Figure 5.o) using five numerals (Nissen et al 1993:37).

There are few obvious cases of positional notation in the Indus inscriptions (Figure 5.4). This is in part due to the fact that some Indus numerals (discussed earlier) have non-numeric functions, but also in part because it is uncertain if Special Numerals (discussed below) are functioning solely as numerals. Additionally, it is difficult to determine whether or not some signs have multiple functions and what all of their functions might be. The problem of polyvalence is a vexing one that cannot easily be resolved. Polyvalence is only now becoming well understood in Proto-Sumerian texts (Friberg 1999). To add to the confusion some texts, mostly from Harappa (13 of 15), use unique staggered numerals (Figure 5.4), but they are very rare.

A necessary first step to resolving the functions of numerals is to identify which contexts are numerical and which are not. In order to better understand Indus numerals it is necessary to devise some method for determining the different systems of measurement and analyze which numerals are used in which systems (or if the Indus texts use only one system). The full resolution of the problem of polyvalence in the Indus script is beyond the scope of this book, but it is possible to make some progress.

Special numerals

The following discussion of special numerals is important to our consideration of positional notation because if these signs are numerals in some or all of their occurrences, then the number of examples of positional notation increases significantly. Of the special numerals sign 900 is the most important to our investigation of positional notation. Care should be

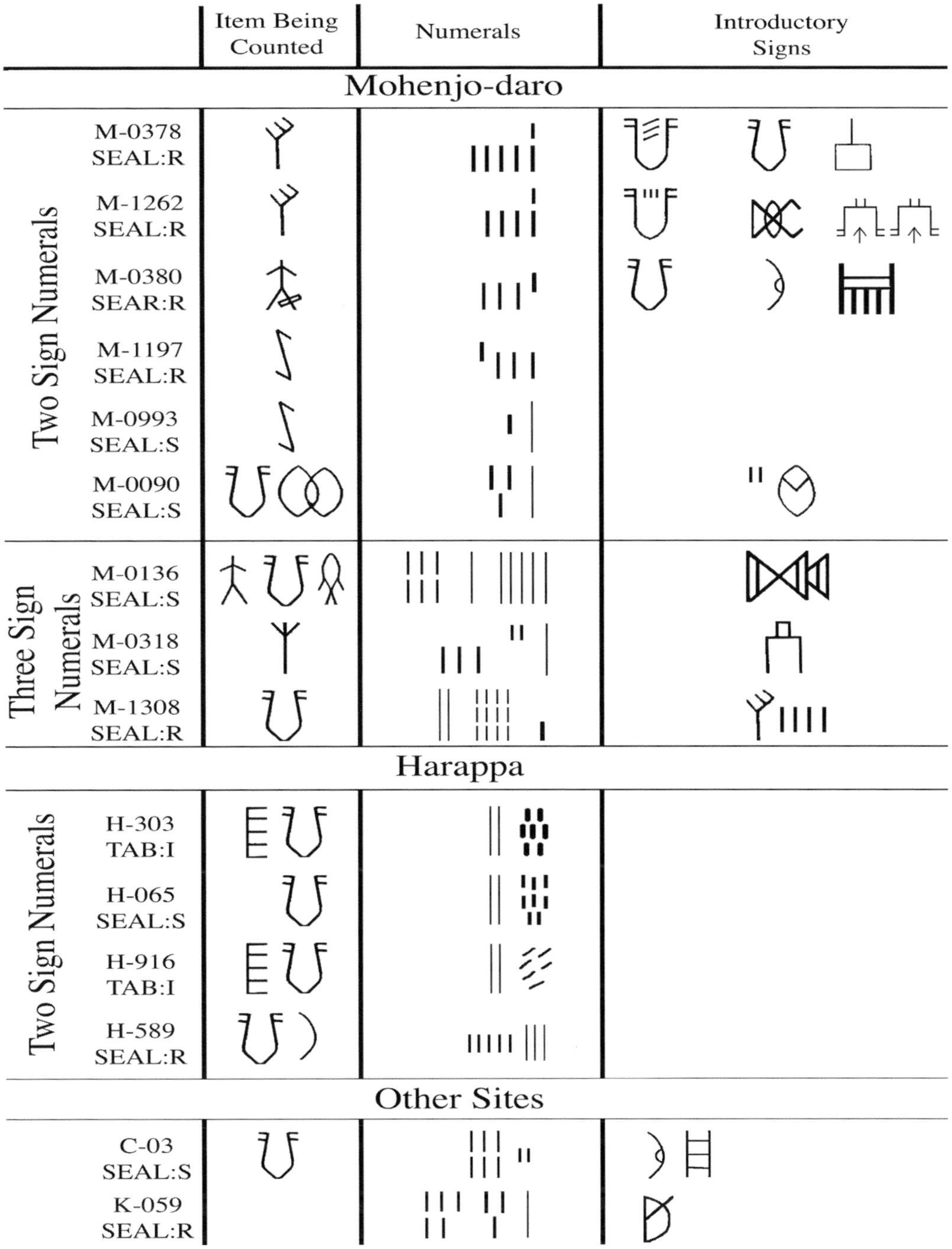

		Item Being Counted	Numerals	Introductory Signs
Mohenjo-daro				
Two Sign Numerals	M-0378 SEAL:R			
	M-1262 SEAL:R			
	M-0380 SEAR:R			
	M-1197 SEAL:R			
	M-0993 SEAL:S			
	M-0090 SEAL:S			
Three Sign Numerals	M-0136 SEAL:S			
	M-0318 SEAL:S			
	M-1308 SEAL:R			
Harappa				
Two Sign Numerals	H-303 TAB:I			
	H-065 SEAL:S			
	H-916 TAB:I			
	H-589 SEAL:R			
Other Sites				
	C-03 SEAL:S			
	K-059 SEAL:R			

Figure 5.4 Examples of positional notation from Indus texts.

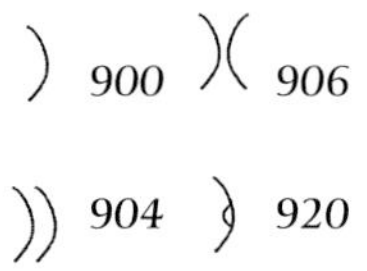

) 900   )(906

)) 904   ) 920

𝔘 𝔄 *5.p*

𝔘 𝔄 ||||) *5.q*

||
002   ) 900

|||
|| 015

||||
||| 017

) 900

||) ||| *5.r*

) |||||||| *5.s*

taken not to confuse sign 900 with sign 920, sign 904, or sign 906. These signs require separate consideration.

If sign 900 is a numeral, then the number of examples of positional notation increases dramatically (Figure 5.1). The evidence that sign 900 is a numeral, in at least some of its occurrences, comes from two sources - the specifics of a single context; and the general behavior of the sign:

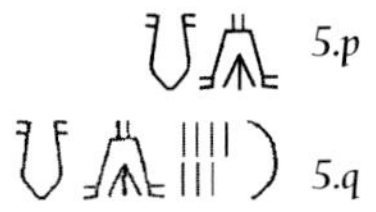

1) one sign sequence that is very informative (because of its replacement sets) is (Figure 5.p; signs 740/585) which is often preceded by the numeral sign 017. The full texts are given in Figure 5.65. In at least one case sign 017 is replaced by sign 900 + sign 002 (Figure 5.65, H-472). This would suggest that sign 900 has a value equal to sign 015. Unfortunately, the contexts of sign 585 + sign 017 are not that simple. In one example (Figure 5.q) occurs. But note the sign order: In the sign 900 + sign 002 example sign 900 is adjacent to (Figure 5.p), but in the other example it is separated by 017 from the terminal signs (Figure 5.p). These contexts raise the possibility that (Figure 5.p) comes in quantities of sign 017 + sign 900, and sign 900 + sign 002, suggesting that sign 900 stands for the number 5 (perhaps when space is a concern). Alternately, sign 017 + sign S900 and sign 900 + sign 002 could be examples of positional notation.

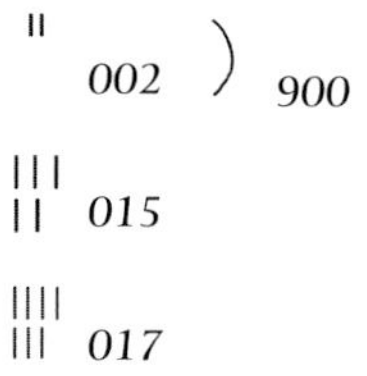

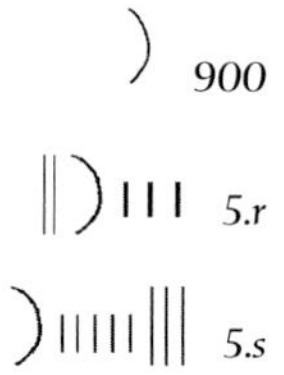

2) sign 900 is often found associated with clusters of numerals. Two such examples are H-141 in the cluster (Figure 5.r); and H-589 in the cluster (Figure 5.s). These are not the only examples of sign 900 in close association with clusters of numerals, there are many such examples (n = 38). In these contexts sign 900 does seem to be functioning as a numeral.

If the arguments that sign 900 is a numeral (at least in some of its contexts) are accepted then the inventory of positional notation in Figure 5.5 can be added to those given in Figure 5.4.

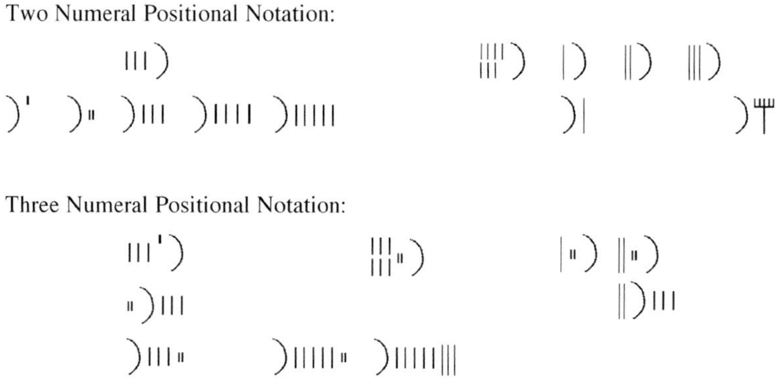

Figure 5.5 Examples of positional notation using sign 900.

Two Numeral Positional Notation:

Three Numeral Positional Notation:

These patterns are similar to the ones for numerals found in Figure 5.4, and this suggests that in these contexts sign 900 is functioning as part of a set of numerals. The evidence for sign 900 as a numeral is persuasive, based on many contexts and replacement sets.

Another sign with possible numeric function is sign 415 (Bonta 1995). This identification is possible because sign 415 frequently replaces for numerals (n = 91), as the replacement set in Figure 5.7 demonstrate.

There are many more examples of this sort of replacement. With the exception of three possible examples, in numerical contexts sign 415 collocates exclusively with sign 220 (Figure 5.86). In terms of numerical contexts, they are most often from Mohenjo-daro (n = 40) and Harappa (n = 44), with only seven examples coming from other sites. The second most common context of sign 415 is in the sign cluster (Figure 5.t). Sign 100 seldom (n = 3) collocates with any of the numeral signs other than sign 415. This is clearly a non-numerical context of sign 415. There are two possible examples of positional notation in sign 415 texts (one from Harappa (Figure 5.u); and one from Lothal (Figure 5.v)), but neither is convincing.

There are two other sets of signs that are informative about the numeric functions of sign 415 and sign 900. The first of these is an anthropomorphic sign often found conflated with other signs - sometimes numerals: (Figure 5.w)

5.w

These signs are, in some cases, constructed by attaching numerals to the basic sign 090. This supports the argument that both sign 900 and sign 415 have a numeric function in some cases, although sign 090 also collocates (but does not conflate) with non-numerical signs, especially sign 740 and sign 400. The second set of signs with this type of construction pattern are:

(Figure 5.x). In this example only the short linear stroke signs and possibly sign 415 and/or sign 400 are added to the basic sign. This example supports the identification of sign 415 as a numeral and sign 472, sign 473, and sign 474 as varieties of (Figure 5.ee) + sign 415. This case is not strong enough to collapse 472, 473, and 474 into a single sign in the sign list, but they must be considered as possible allographs in all further analysis.

Figure 5.6 Evidence for sign 900 as the number five.

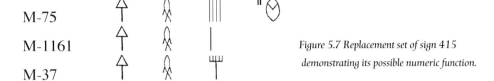

M-75

M-1161

M-37

Figure 5.7 Replacement set of sign 415 demonstrating its possible numeric function.

The evidence for sign 065 as a numeral is much weaker than that for any other Special Numeral signs (Figure 5.1). This is partly because there are only 15 examples of this sign. In eight of these 15 texts it is part of the sign pair sign 220 + sign S065. Despite the fact that signs that precede sign 220 are often numerals, there is nothing obviously numerical about these contexts. In seven of 15 occurrences of sign 065 it is found in the initial sign cluster in the texts. In most texts containing sign 220, this sign (220) occurs in the second or in the final position in those texts. So while the collocation of sign 065 raises the possibility that it is a numeral, the unusual positioning of this sign within the texts raises some doubt about this identification.

The final Special Numeral is sign 055. It is included under this heading because it occurs in a wide variety of contexts, and because the numeral for 11 is not attested, which has the effect of isolating this sign from the rest of the system of Indus numerals. A brief review of the texts containing sign 055 demonstrates the wide variety of contexts it can be found in (some numerical and some not). For example, compare the two texts: M-399 (Figure 5.y) and H-131 (Figure 5.z).

One interesting result that comes out of the analysis of sign 055 is that Indus sign clusters occur in different orders and locations within a given text, both in relation to each other and to sign 055. This implies a certain amount of flexibility in sign order. This pattern is similar to the placement of sign clusters in economic texts from other ancient scripts where lists of items are often enumerated. Because of its distribution sign 055 is also a good candidate for a number sign with a polyvalent syllabic value.

It can be seen from the proceeding discussion that the use of Indus numbers is complicated, as it is in most ancient scripts. What the forgoing discussion makes clear is that there are significant similarities between the patterns of usage of numerals in ancient economic texts and the patterns of usage in some Indus texts. These similarities strongly suggest that at least some Indus texts contain numerical information. Some Indus texts (H-25 (Figure 5.aa)) have several counts of items recorded in a single text, and some of these counts employ positional notation.

065

220

055

5.y

5.z

5.aa

Sign No.	Freq.	Graph	151 / 80	156 / 103	154 / 38	158 / 34	220 / 443	231 / 82	233 / 182	235 / 231	240 / 331	390 / 243	405 / 112	407/9 / 134	520 / 282	740 / 1696	700 / 565	705/6 / 286	575 / 72	585 / 58	Other	Total	
1	191	'					2	1	3	5	3				1	1		6	1		81	99	
2	763	"		2	1		22	12	17	31	71			1	1	1		5			233	397	
3	231	|||		35		1	17	1	1			20	2			1	3				77	158	Short
4	85	||||		1			3					16	6	14			8	1			9	58	Linear
5	41	|||||		2								7	3	4				3			4	23	Numerals
6	3																										2	2	
7	5																						3						3	
12	3	¦																			3	3	
13	25	¦¦																			15	15	
14	5	¦¦					1										1				3	5	
15	6	¦¦¦										1									1	2	Short
16	40	¦¦¦					12					10	1	3		2					2	30	Stacked
17	76	¦¦¦¦					1					4	2	1		9			13	27	8	65	Numerals
18	5	¦¦¦¦										1	1								3	5	
19	5	¦¦¦¦¦											1			1					1	3	
20	1	¦¦¦¦¦																			1	1	
31	190			3	9			3		1		9				3	4	3	5			61	101	Long
32	507								57					2	2	8	1	52	87	2			140	351	
33	445	|||	3			1	2				3				15	2	137			4	104	271	Linear
34	153	||||					1					2					105				6	114	Linear
35	27	|||||										1	1			7					8	17	Numerals
36	5																					2					2	4	
37	2																													
39	1																														
415	165	⊥					140		2										1		96	239	
900	95	)				1										37				1	28	67	Special
65	15	⊦							7												3	10	Numerals
55	56	¦¦¦¦	2				1									9					5	17	
Totals	3146		8	49	1	3	262	14	31	31	86	64	19	31	21	129	346	22	15	32	896	2060	65.48

Figure 5.8 Right adjacent Indus numbers and associated signs from Mohenjo-daro and Harappa.

What is being counted?

If the model outlined above for ancient numerical scripts (number + noun) is applied to the Indus script then a limited number of signs associated with numerals can be postulated to be nouns. In the case of Indus texts the reading order is from right to left in the majority of cases, and numerals normally precede the nouns they modify. Figure 5.6 gives the frequency of combinations of numerals and nouns for the most common pairings. It is obvious from this table that the distribution of Indus numerals is uneven, and that certain numerals have a preference for certain signs. This is not surprising given the existence of a standardized system of weights and standardized sizes for many ceramic vessels. Texts with numeral signs found on ceramic vessels (POT:T:g artifacts) are mostly short and long linear strokes (especially sign 1-4 and 31-34; Figure 5.9). The preference of specific numbers for use on specific artifacts suggests a purpose linked to the functions of these artifacts. Additionally, the most frequent numerals are polyvalent signs (001, 002, 032, 033, and 415).

The signs listed as paring with numerals in Figure 5.8 are likely candidates for nouns. If so this tells us something interesting about the syntax of the Indus texts. First, these signs are all normally terminal signs with the exception of the fish signs. Inscriptions exist with two sets of numeral + sign pairings (C-40, H-131, and M-38 etc.), but these are rare. The significance of numeral placement is discussed later in this chapter.

The fact that numeral signs of the same type cluster on similar artifact types points to a fundamental unity of function. In other words, like signs are used in similar proportions on specific artifacts. Figure 5.9 compares the distribution of numeral signs for SEAL:R, SEAL:S, and POT:T:g artifact types. Sign numbers of numerals are placed on the circle representing those sign frequencies. The size of the circle is proportional to the frequency of numerals found on POT:T:g artifacts.

Figure 5.9 shows that the use of number signs on SEAL:R and POT:T are related (cluster 2) in their use of long stroke signs, while SEAL:S artifacts are not. Further, SEAL:R and S artifacts are related (cluster 1) in their use of short stroke signs, while POT:T artifacts are not.

Bracket signs

There are several signs related to sign 900 (n = 95): 901 (2), 902 (1), 903 (1), 904 (61), 905 (11), and 906 (13). Of these, three (901–903) have frequencies too small to be analyzed as to their function (i.e. numeric vs. nonnumeric). The rest (904–906) can be examined for their relationship to other signs, especially signs that pair with numerals. For example, in 10 of the 11 occurrences of 905 it pairs with sign 032, but because sign 032 has

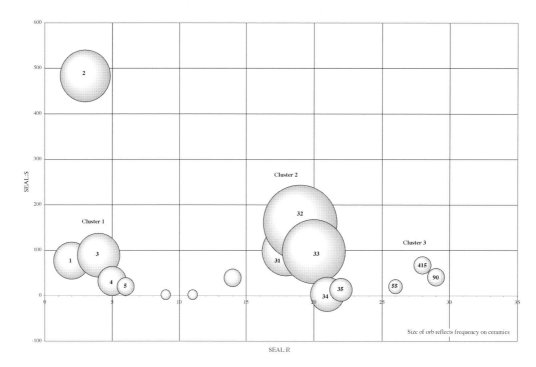

Figure 5.9 Comparison of numeral signs by artifact type (size of orb reflects frequency on ceramics).

				003
			032
				055
))	904
))	905
)(	906

a numeric and non-numeric use this association does not necessarily iden-tify sign 905 as a numeral. The contexts of the sign 032/905 pairings is ambiguous and the question of whether or not 905 is a numeral in any or all of its uses remains unresolved. Sign 906 occurs 13 times in the ICIT database but pairs with numerals in only two texts (sign 055 once and sign 003 once). There is nothing numeric about the other contexts. This strong-ly suggests that 906 is either not a numeral or polyvalent.

Sign 904 occurs 61 times in the ICIT database. In 22 of these examples it is either adjacent to a single numeral sign (n = 12) or part of a sequence of numeral signs (n = 10). The most suggestive context is M-495 (TAB:B): (Figure 5.bb). This is only one of three texts on this artifact, but the other two do not contain sign 904. All of this data taken together points to sign 904 as being a numeral in at least in some contexts.

Compound signs with numerals

There are 31 Indus signs that compound with numerals in 861 examples (Figure 5.10). These are only the examples for which there is no doubt about the identity of the numerals being compounded. It is clear from this

Sign No.	Freq.	Graph	790 / 52	465 / 1	90 / 168	700 / 565	740 / 1696	645 / 24	Total	Other Compound Signs With Numerals	Total Other	Grand Total	
1	191	'	33		4		200		237	(compound signs)	35	272	**Short**
2	763	‖	2			10	41		53	(compound signs)	11	64	
3	231	‖‖	17	8		11	40		76			76	**Linear**
4	85	‖‖‖	2	8	2		3		15	(compound signs)	3	18	
5	41	‖‖‖‖		2					2			2	**Numerals**
6	3	‖‖‖‖‖											
7	5	‖‖‖‖‖‖											
12	3	(stacked)	1					2	3			3	
13	25	(stacked)											
14	5	(stacked)	1						1			1	
15	6	(stacked)								(compound sign)	1	1	**Short**
16	40	(stacked)					5		5	(compound sign)	1	6	**Stacked**
17	76	(stacked)											**Numerals**
18	5	(stacked)											
19	5	(stacked)											
20	1	(stacked)											
31	190	│	16		72	200		2	290	(compound signs)	109	399	**Long**
32	507	‖						3	3			3	
33	445	‖‖											**Linear**
34	153	‖‖‖											
35	27	‖‖‖‖											**Numerals**
36	5	‖‖‖‖‖											
37	2	‖‖‖‖‖‖											
39	1	‖‖‖‖‖‖‖											
415	165	(graph)		7	13				20			20	
900	95	)			2				2			2	**Special**
65	15	(graph)											
55	56	(graph)											**Numerals**
Totals	3146		72	25	93	221	289	7	707		160	867	**Totals**

Figure 5.10 The use of numerals in compound signs.

figure that the numerals being compounded are far more restricted than those used as individual numeral signs (Figure 5.6). Short stacked stroke signs are seldom compounded, only 1.3% of the 867 signs tabulated in Figure 5.10, this is a curious circumstance given that short stacked numerals take less space than the short linear numeral signs, thus reinforcing that these are two distinct set of numerals.

Signs that compound with numerals, like signs that collocate right adjacent to numerals, are good candidates for nouns - items that can be counted. In many cases these signs are found in medial contexts. It is unlikely that numerals used in compound signs are used only for their numeric values; we can expect the same range of use for these signs as those exhibited by equivalent uncompounded numeral signs. Some of the same signs found in Figure 5.5 are also found in Figure 5.10, although the range of associated numerals is more restricted.

Sign 740 plus numeral clusters

The most common numeral signs collocating right adjacent to sign 740 are signs 032 (n = 52) and 900 (37) (Figure 5.8). Less frequently we find the following signs: 017 (9), 055 (9), 035 (7), 031 (4), 007 (3), 016 (2), 033 (2), 001 (1), 002 (1), 003 (1), and 019 (1). Only 92 of the 1,722 occurrences of stroke signs collocate with sign 740. If sign 900 is included the total increases to 129, but these uses are not systematic.

These contexts suggest at least four possible explanations: 1) sign 740 represents an item that can be counted (noun); 2) in these contexts numerals are being used for their phonetic values - raising the possibility that these numerals are monosyllabic or have monosyllabic polyvalent values; 3) the numbers represented by these numerals are homophones (or near homophones) and are being used in these contexts for their alternate semantic (rebus) values; 4) these signs may have unrelated (polyvalent) values - for example, sign 055 may in one context have a meaning of "12", in other contexts might mean "many" or "rain", in a third context it might stand for a CV syllable derived from any of its other meanings. It is not necessary to choose one solution from these options, as any of these possibilities could be operating for a given numeral. The first goal is to identify as many different contexts for numerals as possible, and to eventually derive meanings that are compatible with these uses. It seems likely from these and other contexts that the numeral signs 001, 002, 031, 032, 033, 055, and 900 (and probably others) have both numeric and nonnumeric, perhaps syllabic, values in the Indus script. The fact that sign 740 collocates with numeral signs in 129 examples suggests that it is being counted (it is a noun). This has implications for defining the syntax of the Indus

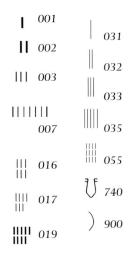

texts - other signs that replace for numerals and habitually collocate with nouns may be adjectives.

Numerals and the Indus language

The preceding discussion has established the uses and extent of Indus numerals. Several features of this system of numerals have characteristics that may be useful in limiting the number of possible languages of the Indus script. For example, numeral signs in Indus texts normally precede the signs (nouns) associated with them. This fact is known for certain from the many short inscriptions that contain only a single numeral and one associated sign. Numbers precede nouns, and perhaps other adjectives do as well. This idea bears directly o the identification of sign 900 and sign 415 as numerals.

There are cases where this order is reversed. The most common example is in texts containing the 033/705 and 033/706 sign clusters. These clusters often collocate with the terminal marker 520. One explanation for this order is that the numeral sign is being used for its syllabic (3 = 'mun' in Tamil) or logographic value (i.e. 3rd or 30th), rather than their numeric value. Another example of optional sign order is found with sign 032 (sign 033 n = 445; sign 032 n = 507). While sign 032 is found in all of the same numeric contexts as 033 (032/700, 032/220, and in numeric clusters), it is also found as the initial sign in 63 texts, and as the terminal sign in 12 texts. Conversely, sign 033 (excluding 033/700 examples) is initial in 26 and terminal in seven texts. These signs share similar contexts, but in very different proportions - sign 032 has a marked preference for initial positioning compared to sign 033. Initial and terminal counts are inflated in Figure 5.1 by the many examples of both 032/700 and 033/700 texts (the TAB effect). These contexts are not included in the above discussion. Nevertheless, initial, medial and terminal nonnumeric contexts are plentiful for both signs 032 and 033. For example: H-5, SEAL:S (Figure 5.cc) and M-852, SEAL:S (Figure 5.dd).

Obviously, given this complex situation, statements about the location of numerals in Indus texts must be restricted to contexts for which the identification of numeral signs as functionally numerals is more or less certain. The most secure contexts are those that find many of the numerals right adjacent to the same sign or sign cluster (Figure 5.8). The statement that numerals precede the signs that they modify is accurate in this context. It can also be said with confidence that the Indus number system counts to 10 and all numerals from 1 to 10 are attested, although the numeral ten is attested only once. Since signs 032 and 033 are initial and terminal in nonnumeric contexts, linguistic elements in the candidate language must

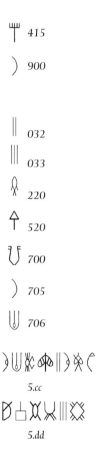

415

900

032

033

220

520

700

705

706

5.cc

5.dd

make sense of these relationships. Further, the normal syntax may be VSO or VOS, and therefore verb initial languages are preferred. This is an important point because verb initial languages are exceedingly uncommon.

A major advancement in the decipherment of the Linear B script was the recognition by Kober that signs that were almost exclusively initial were pure vowel signs (Parpola 1994:45). The Indus script has 121 signs that are exclusively initial. Most of these signs are singletons (80), and the rest have similarly low frequencies (none have a frequency greater that 10). Further, the most common of these are compound signs, and so unlikely to be pure vowel signs. Some of the most common predominantly initial signs are numerals, but this is misleading because of the large number of texts that consist of an initial number and one other sign (more than 90 texts not counting sign 700 contexts). The question of the significance of these results to the identification of Indus language is taken up again in Chapter 6.

6

THE INDUS LANGUAGE

The purpose of this chapter is to identify as close-ly as possible the language(s) of the Indus script. Data relating to this issue comes from several sources: historical linguistics, the distribution of modern languages, archaeological data, and the structure of the Indus texts. As discussed later there are sub-state words in the Vedic texts (post date the Indus civilization) and a few loan words in Mesopotamia texts that are contemporary with the Indus Civilization. These data supply infor-mation relating to different aspects of the Indus language. For, example, from the archaeological data we know that the Indus script was in use from at least 2600 BC to 1700 BC, and therefore any candidate language must have sufficient time depth to have been in use during this peri-od. Because of the time depth involved it is unre-alistic to look to modern languages for compari-son with the structural analysis. Instead we must turn to the work of historical linguistics for reconstructions of 'proto' forms of languages and to other ancient records. However the quality of the reconstruction of the various Proto languages is uneven for Proto-Indo-European, Proto-Dravidian and Proto-Munda.

As to the significance of the modern distri-bution of languages, this has been dealt with in detail elsewhere (Parpola 1994; Wells 1999) and need not be repeated here in detail. In sum-mary, Parpola (1994) points out that the majori-ty of Indians today speak Indo-European (IE) or Dravidian (Dr) languages, and there is a distinct north–south division in the distribution of these two language families (Figure 6.1). He points to

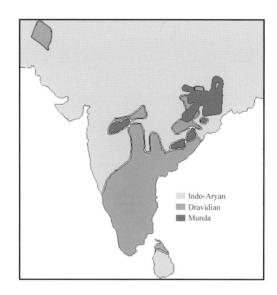

*Figure 6.1 Simplified language map of
the Indian subcontinent.*

the distribution of specific linguistic features (i.e. inclusive/exclusive 'we') as evidence that PDr was the indigenous language in the areas domi-nated by IE speakers today (Parpola 1994).

His theory being that when Dr languages were replaced by IE languages (with the coming of the Aryans), certain features of the former lan-guage were adopted and retained by the later. One could then map these features as a proxy for the former distribution of Dravidian languages. This leads Parpola (1994) to postulate that the entire area of Indus civilization spoke (and wrote) some form of Proto-Dravidian (PDr). Parpola goes on to analyze the Indus texts as PDr.

I find Parpola's (1994) argument initial convincing as he has several sets of data that support his main argument. However, these data have been criticized. A problem with this argument is that there are ca. 1,700 years between the end of the Indus civilization and earliest language data for Dravidia, and it is difficult to know the exact point in time when an innovation like retroflex consonant was introduced. Further, the *in situ* borrowing of this feature is not certain; it could have been acquired anytime and spread geographically over time through diffusion.

A more recent reconstruction (Witzel 1999) has suggested that the Indus people spoke several languages. Witzel, is a Sanskrit scholar and used the sequence of borrowings into the Vedas (the earliest post Indus material) as his main source of data. He begins by dating the books of the Rg Veda based on style and content. He then identifies the various loan words in each chronological set. He discovers that the earliest loan words into the Rg Veda are not Dravidian, but most of the words come from an unknown language related to Munda (Para-Munda in his nomenclature; Witzel 1999). He makes the assumption that the Vedic people entered the Indian sub-continent from the northwest based on his analysis of place names and (after the middle of the second millennium BC), spread south and east to about the limit of their modern distributions. His argument is that the earliest borrowings were made in the north of the Indus valley (from local languages such as Para-Munda) and later borrowings from the southern Indus areas (Dravidian). Another language that has influenced the substrate of Vedas is Language X (X) that centers on Uttar Pradesh. There are also the remanents of other languages in the Vedic texts (such as proto-Burushaski). The distributions of modern languages (Figure 6.1) reflects this relative positioning (except for X and Para-Munda).

The arguments presented here, and those published elsewhere, are from necessity conjectural. No one language has been definitively demonstrated to be The Indus language. The language map of the Indus valley was likely complex and variable over time. That there is one language written by the Indus people throughout the period from 2600 to 1700 BC cannot be conclusively demonstrated. There is simply not enough chronological control to track the fine scale developments and variations in the Indus texts. What can be said form the inscriptions is that there is a good deal of intersite regularity in text form and content, and that most of the variation can be explained by differences in subject matter between artifact types.

As was pointed out in Chapter 3 the sign inventories of various artifact types are complicated. SEAL:S artifacts have very similar inventories between sites (r2 = 0.853 for Mohenjo-daro and Harappa), but other types show more intersite variation (SEAL:R, r2 = 0.61 for Mohenjo-daro and Harappa). I suggest that the best explanation for this pattern was that the Indus texts were written in one language (SEAL:S sign inventories), but that variations in subject matter between artifact types at the same and among different artifact types of different sites were attributable to differences in subject matter. Regardless of the several languages that were spoken within the Indus area in the 2nd and 3rd millennium BC, the Indus texts are sufficiently similar in sign order and usage, to allow the assumption that the vast majority of Indus texts (especially from Mohenjo-daro and Harappa for the Mature Harappan period) are written in one language. The language(s) of the Indus texts (or their descendants) are no longer spoken in this area.

Nevertheless, the most likely candidates for the Indus language, based on geographic proximity are: Proto-Dravidian (PDr), Proto-Elamo-Dravidian (PED), Proto-Elamite (PE), Proto/Para-Munda (PM), Proto-Indo-European (PIE) and Language X (X). This list can be narrowed somewhat based on arguments presented by Parpola (1994). First, the arrival of the Aryans (PIE speakers) can be set on the basis of archaeological data and linguistic data (Parpola 1994) to 1000 BC give or take a few hundred years. They are, therefore, too late chronologically to be considered. Further, the dominant morphological pattern in Indus texts uses suffixes and prefixing and possible infixing. This pattern can be seen in several places in the texts, but the most obvious is the addition of Post-Terminal (PTs) clusters to Terminal Markers (TMs). These additions are not inflectional as they do not conform to the patterns of inflectional paradigms (Kober 1946).

Kober (1946:268–289) in her seminal work on inflection in Linear B, gives five assumptions regarding systems with inflection (inflection is the change in word forms that mark distinctions such as case, gender, voice, mood, number person or tense): 1) that the language in question had inflection (root+stem suffix+ending); 2) that the inflected language must have paradigms of some kind; 3) that when inscriptions contain lists of words, in this case each followed by a ideogram and a number, such words are nouns, or what passes for nouns in the language; 4) nouns appearing in the same list in any given inscription are all in the same case; and, 5) that if nouns in the language were declined, a specific form in any given list is the form of the given case for whatever declension is represented by the noun in question. (declension is a class of nouns or adjectives having the same inflectional form)

In terms of the Indus script, this type of analysis leads to the identification of sign 740, sign 520 and sign 526, sign 550 as possible suffix endings. Assumption (4) above fits well with texts such as: Figure 6.a. But problems arise in short texts when sign 740 is the only sign following the Initial Cluster (IC) (see Chapter 4) or when it is the only sign in the text. The occurrence of a case without a root (indicating the meaning of the word) is not possible. This leads to the conclusion that sign 740 is a logograph and represents a word that requires no further elaboration to convey its meaning. The possibility that Post Terminals are inflectional endings is returned to later in this chapter.

520

526

550

740

Case I item₅ item₄ item₃ item₂ item₁ IC

6.a

M-0356, DM255, SD-Stupa-NW, -8 ft.
Long Complex

Graph	Sign No.	Freq	Init	Med	Term	Comp
	140	103	**32**	**33**	2	2
	920	139	**57**	**42**	4	2
	820	202	**113**	23	10	2
	32	507	**110**	**182**	29	1
	125	50	13	**23**	2	3
	420	5	0	**3**	0	1
	595	46	2	**21**	7	2
	400	432	2	27	**263**	1

H-020, 3170, Mound F-N9/5,Stratum II, -5 ft.
Long Patterned

Graph	Sign No.	Freq	Init	Med	Term	Comp
	550	111	**26**	**39**	2	1
	60	204	0	**157**	1	1
	806	117	**45**	**44**	0	2
	32	507	**110**	**182**	29	1
	220	443	40	**239**	8	1
	255	120	22	**55**	2	2
	435	63	0	**39**	3	1
	690	109	8	**55**	13	1
	176	193	49	**90**	1	2
	740	1696	9	**351**	**758**	1

Figure 6.2 Comparison of long complex and long patterned texts with sign location and component data.
Signs listed in order of reading from right to left.

Even with these important reductions in candidate languages there are at least five languages to consider (including Language X; Masica 1971). This list can be narrowed further. If we accept McAlpin's (1981) reconstruction of Proto-Elamo-Dravidian, the split of PED into PDr and PE at about 3000 to 5000 BC based on the presence or absence of terms for agricultural items and writing. This early split rules out PED as a candidate language. Further, it seems likely that this split occurred as a result of the geographic separation of two populations of PED speakers. It seems logical that the geographic split would result in PE speakers on the Iranian plateau and PDr speakers further west in Baluchistan and the western Indus valley. This would mean that PDr was one of the languages spoken in the Indus valley around 3000

BC, and eliminates PE as a candidate language.

This leaves PDr, PM and X for further consideration. The likely source area for Munda is to the east of the Indus area. Its geographic proximity means that it cannot be removed from the list of possible Indus languages based on geographic separation. The argument has been made that the spread of Munda speakers is linked to the arrival of rice cultivation in the Indus valley. The dating of this event is disputed, and the evidence sufficiently inconclusive that PM cannot be eliminated on this basis.

The forgoing discussion is general and the details of the various arguments are not given here. Interested readers should access the original material for the details of the various arguments (Zvelebil 1974; McAlpin 1981; Parpola 1994; Wells 1999; Witzel 1999).

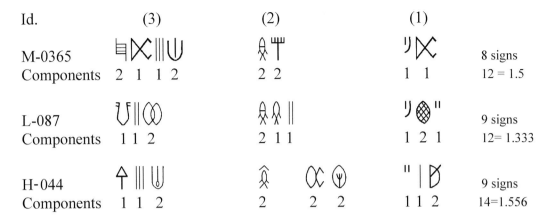

Figure 6.3 Syntax of patterned texts.

Characteristics of the Indus Script

Syntax

It has been demonstrated (Chapter 4) that the Indus script is logo-syllabic and that the main mechanism of sign construction are the compounding of signs and the addition of non-sign (design) elements to existing signs (Figure 6.3). Further, compounding is not haphazard, and the placement of the compounded elements has a logical basis and a linguistic motivation.

Sign distributions within texts are likewise patterned. Some signs have preferences for specific locations within texts (initial, medial, terminal), and these preferences are maintained even in Complex texts (Figure 6.2; cf. Table 4.4).

The fact that signs maintain their order and habitually cluster in specific 'zones' within texts, attests to the presence of both logographs and syntax. Very short texts aside (Table 4.4), Indus texts consist of two or more definable elements of syntax. This structure is most evident in Patterned and Segmented texts, but can also be demonstrated for Complex texts (Figure 6.2). There are subsets of texts that consist of only one syntactic element (single segment texts) and these consist of two to five signs that have equivalent values in longer texts (Figure 4.6). These structures suggest that Indus texts can consist of one to three elements of syntax depending on the context of use (and available space). Texts can consist of abbreviated forms: sign 740, sign 900, sign 156, sign 031, or sign 220, sign 015 for example, or long lists: Figure 6.a. The various types of texts (Table 4.4, except Set 5) are not restricted to specific artifact types. Figure 6.3 lists three examples of patterned texts analyzed for syntax.

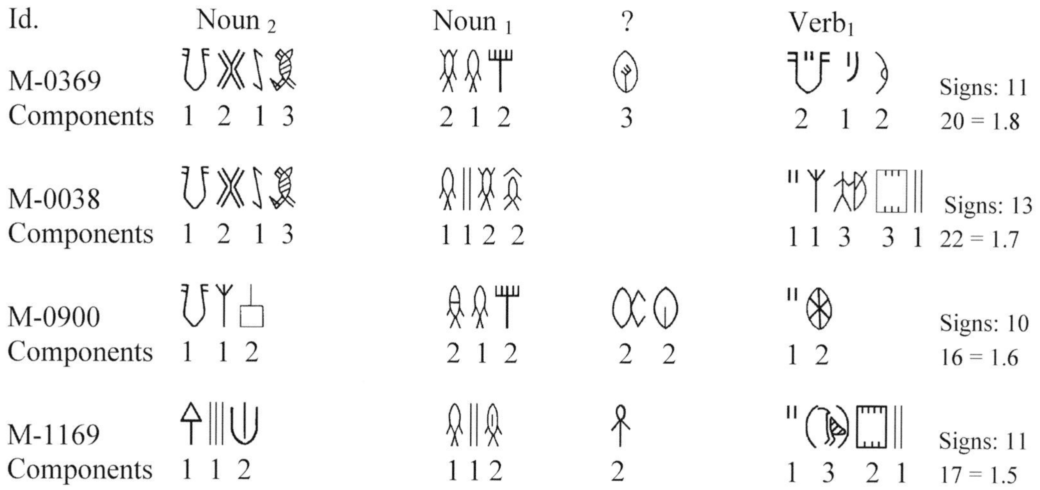

Id.	Noun 2			Noun 1			?		Verb₁				
M-0369													Signs: 11
Components	1	2	1	3	2	1	2	3	2	1	2		20 = 1.8
M-0038													Signs: 13
Components	1	2	1	3	1	1	2	2	1	1	3	3 1	22 = 1.7
M-0900													Signs: 10
Components	1	1	2		2	1	2	2	2	1	2		16 = 1.6
M-1169													Signs: 11
Components	1	1	2		1	1	2	2		1	3	2 1	17 = 1.5

Figure 6.4 Proposed syntactic identities of text sub-elements.

These examples are representative of patterned texts. Note that numerals follow their associated signs (or are infixed?) in (3) and precede them in (2). While the analysis in Chapter 4 demonstrated that there is considerable variation in this pattern, the basic sequence of initial, medial and terminal elements is fairly constant in long texts. Variation in the sequence of numerals may be attributable to polyvalent values of some numerals.

Although the identity of specific units of syntax has not been absolutely established, the occurrence of numerals primarily in association with medial and terminal sign clusters suggests a verb initial structure and this is be used in the following discussion as a working hypothesis. This is based on the well-established pattern of numerals and nouns clustering in texts (i.e. things are counted). The number of elements present in texts varies, as does the order of the medial sub-elements (Fish, numerals, ovals). The complexity of text construction and polyvalence (especially numerals) combine with other

factors (such as lists, introductory statements, abbreviated texts, etc.) makes the full analysis of the syntax of every Indus text difficult. However, the more common and repetitive structural types (Table 4.4) can be analyzed for their syntactic structure (Figure 6.4). At least some of the inscriptions will be whole sentences.

The length of the elements in these texts can vary in the number of signs and components. The exact syntactic placement of the oval signs is not certain, and they may be prefixes to the fish sign clusters or agglutinative elements of the initial clusters. The oval sign clusters vary somewhat in length, and their order is also variable, i.e. oval signs can follow fish sign clusters (Chapter 4). This secondary positioning suggests that oval signs are associated with the fish sign clusters, and that the order is flexible or effected by an unknown set of rules (Figure 6.5). In the text given in Figure 6.6 sign 806 occurs twice,

 806

Figure 6.5 Flexible order of oval and fish signs.

Figure 6.6 A text where sign 806 occurs twice.

once as expected between the initial cluster and the fish signs, and once in the terminal cluster. This is a third context of 806 and is related to its best-known context, as discussed in Chapter 3. While 806 is likely a logograph, it can locate in three contexts within two (Noun1 and Noun2) syntactic elements in Indus texts. The initial contexts of sign 806 and sign 803 are all restricted to texts that lack initial clusters (segmented). This further supports the identification of the verb initial syntax of the Indus Script.

Numerals

Indus numerals occur in great variety and can be enclosed, marked and conflated as other Indus signs. Leaving aside these special (low frequency) occurrences, numerals are restricted to four main groups: short linear, short stacked, long linear and special numerals (Chapter 5). Each of the three stroke based systems counts slightly differently: short linear 1-7; short stacked 2-10; and long linear 1-7 and 9. It is unlike (but possible) that there are two systems of counting (1-7, i.e. base 8 and 1-10) perhaps for different purposes. More likely there is a shift to the stacked numerals to save space for values above 7. For a discussion of the twelve stroke sign see Chapter 5.

Numeral signs have a non-uniform distribution (Figure 6.7). The sign counts for signs 1 and 2 are inflated by their polyvalent values, especially their use as Initial Cluster Terminators. Sign counts are inflated at Harappa by the many tablet texts with sign 700 plus numerals 31-34.

803

806

 700

There is a high probability that the Indus number system is base 10, but the frequencies of the high value signs is low (for sign 19, n = 5, and for sign 20, n = 1), and so the possibility of a base 8 system cannot be ruled out completely. This situation does not help determine the identity of the language of the Indus script other than to prefer languages with either a base 8 or a base 10 system.

Morphology

The morphology of Indus words is another subject that bears directly on the identity of the language of Indus texts. Those supporting the Dravidian hypothesis predict a mostly agglutinative system. Parpola (1994) has demonstrated that the pattern of post-terminal additions is not consistent enough to be gender, person or tense. They function more like clitics and post-positions do in Dravidian languages.

As can be seen in the examples in Chapter 4 the Indus texts often consist of recognizable sign clusters with signs arranged in a predictable order. This is especially true for Patterned and Segmented texts. The analysis of these formulaic texts results in the identification of sign clusters that must either be words or short phrases. The resultant sign clusters can likewise be analyzed for variations in sign usage, including possible affixes. There are two environments that affixing can be easily identified: following initial cluster terminal markers (ICTMs) and terminal markers (TMs) (Chapter 4). Given our limited sample of Indus texts, it seems probable that we likewise have a limited sample of the vocabulary and of the various systems of affixing (i.e. limited by subject matter and the shortness of the texts). This results in the over representation of some element (affixes) in the script as well as the under-representation of others. Unfortunately, we have no idea of the correct proportions of these elements.

Terminal marker signs and affixing in the Indus script

The most common sign in the Indus script is sign 740. It occurs 1,696 times, but only 348 (20.5% of these are affixed. Most of these examples of the affixing of sign 740 are limited to sign 400 (n = 210) and sign 090 (n = 93). All other affixes total 45 examples (Figure 6.81).

090

400

740

The distribution of Terminal Markers collocating with affixes is likewise skewed, with only sign 400 having a broad distribution, but at low frequencies. Other TMs besides 740 are common enough to have examples of several types of Post Terminals (520 and 390) if this was a system of linguistic affixing. Affixes in other ancient writing systems marks tense, person, gender etc., but also mark polyvalent signs to clarify their meaning (phonetic complements and determinatives). One way of distinguishing between these various

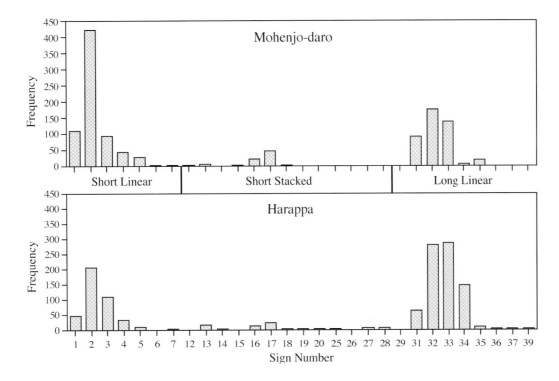

Figure 6.7 Distribution of numerals at Mohenjo-daro and Harappa.

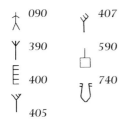

6.b

6.c

6.d

elements is through the analysis of the contexts. For example, are specific contexts always affixed in a consistently.

This type of analysis is most productive where bonded clusters collocate with a variety of Terminal Markerss and Post Terminals. For example, the Bonded Clusters sign 390, sign 590, sign 405, sign 590 and sign 407, sign 590 associates with the Terminal Markers sign 740 and the possible Terminal Marker sign 820. Further, these combinations also include the Post Terminals sign 400 and sign 090 associated with the sign 740 texts. The vast majority of the constructions of sign 390, sign 590 are simple sign 740, sign 390, sign 590 preceded by Verb1 and/or Noun1. For example: M-0900 Figure 6.b. All examples of Figure 6.c come from Harappa (TAB:B = 11; SEAL:S = 1) with nine TAB:B examples using the Bonded Cluster sign 405, sign 590 and the rest using sign 390, sign 590. The only example of another affix being used comes from Mohenjo-daro: M-0851 Figure 6.d. This distribution is typical of Indus affixing. Because 11 of 12 of the examples from Harappa come from just two molds (the TAB effect), we

Terminal Markers

Post-Terminals	Site	740	520	526/550	390	151	156	154	158	159	595	# of Affixes	PT Sign Total	% of Sign Used as PT
90	Mohenjo-daro	55	1									56	78	71.79
90	Harappa	38										38	59	64.41
400	Mohenjo-daro	20	4	7	2				5	2	2	42	80	52.50
400	Harappa	190	11	2		4	14	4	12			237	341	69.50
400/90	Mohenjo-daro	2										2	2	100.00
400/90	Harappa	10										10	10	100.00
621	Mohenjo-daro	4										4	18	22.22
621	Harappa											0	2	0.00
679	Mohenjo-daro	10										10	14	71.43
679	Harappa											0	3	0.00
790	Mohenjo-daro	6										6	28	21.43
790	Harappa											0	15	0.00
564	Mohenjo-daro	6										6	10	60.00
564	Harappa	2										2	5	40.00
405/61	Mohenjo-daro	2										2	24	8.33
405/61	Harappa	3										3	4	75.00
Total Affixes		348	16	9	2	4	14	4	17	2	2		418	
Sign Total		1696	282	61	243	80	103	38	34	6	46		2589	
% Affixed		20.52	5.67	14.75	0.82	5.00	13.59	10.53	50.00	33.33	4.35		16.1	

Figure 6.8 Indus 'affixes' from Mohenjo-daro and Harappa. (PT: Post-Terminal).

cannot say with certainty that the use of sign 400 at Harappa is pointing to geographic (dialect) as opposed to subject matter differences (TAB vs. SEAL). There is no recognizable motivation for the addition of affixes. This conclusion is very important in the identification of the underlying language.

What is clear from Figure 6.8 is that only about 16% of the possible combinations of Terminal Marker and Post Terminal signs are used and many of these combinations are present only in low frequencies. Further, the frequency of the most common affix sign 400 is inflated by the many examples from TAB:B artifacts from Harappa, and (except for one example of sign 090) only sign 400 collocates with more than one Terminal Markers.

The restricted distribution of affixes suggests that either because of the restricted sample of texts the system is under-represented, or the system is not marking a complete set of word modifying elements. Rather they seem to be a restricted set of markings that modify the value of the Terminal Markers. That is, determinatives and phonetic complements are used optionally. We know this because there are many examples of near identical texts form the

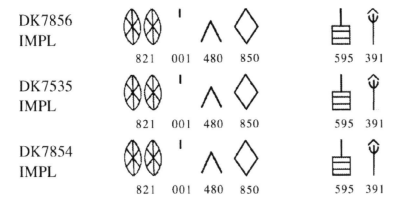

Figure 6.9 Possible locative for Dholavira.

same artifact type where one uses an affix and one does not: H-075, SEAL:S Figure 6.c and H-533, SEAL:S Figure 6.e. The implication is that Post Terminals are optional. This might occur in a situation where the context of artifact use makes the Post Terminals (normally required by linguistic convention) unnecessary. For example, if sign 740 was the generic term for a ceramic vessel, and sign 400 denoted a specific type of vessel, the sign becomes redundant when used to seal that specific type of vessel. Another example would be in cases where space is restricted and the value of the Post Terminals to the understanding of the message is negligible (i.e. called for by linguistic conventions by unnecessary in this context of use).

Indus, PDr and PM morphology

The following descriptions of the construction of Indus, PDr and PM words relies heavily on McAlpin (1981) and Anderson (2001). These works give a relatively comprehensive and understandable summary of (P)Dr and PM including the derivation of nouns and verbs, the number system, adjectives and syntax. The following overview of the material contains only the details that seem relevant to the discussion of the Indus script. For more details regarding PDr, Elamite and PED see McAlpin (1981) and reference therein.

The (P)Dr noun

The basic structure of the Dr noun is: ROOT (+derivational augment(s)) (+morphological augment(s)) +Case (+postpositions). Elements in brackets are optional and depend on the details of use (McAlpin 1981:32-33). Noun roots normally take the form (C)V(C) (C: consonant; V: vowel) and the true monosyllabic root takes the form VC.

Case endings can take the following forms: Ø, -V, -VC, -VCV or -(C)CV. Derivational augments normally take to form VC, while postpositions can take a variety of forms (Commonly -V(C)C. Nouns can be marked for gender. PDr used masculine vs. non-masculine in the singular and human vs. non-human in the plural as follows: Sm -an/*-anre, Sn *-ay, *-i, *-e, Ph *-ar, Pn *-am/*-an. Male occupations and kin terminology use /*-anre, while female kin, animals and general neuters use *-ay and *-i.

The simplest form of the Dr noun is V-Ø, i.e. a 'cow, ox' (Tamil). The process of agglutination results in the following example: ay 'cowherd caste'; ay + an (Pn) = ayan 'female cowherd'. The basic difference between a case ending and a postposition is that: "a case ending cannot be separated from its noun by a clitic while a postposition can be " (McAlpin 1981:35). Otherwise the distinction between these items is arbitrary. Most other morphological components (augments, postpositions and clitics) are agglutinative and consist of -V, -VC, (C)CV and -VCV. They mark cases, singular and plural, gender or can be augments, as discussed above.

In addition to these elements nouns can also take a variety of pronouns, either personal or appellative. They are proforms. Personal pronouns are restricted to 1st and 2nd person and 3rd person resumptive. Dr pronouns indicate three persons and two numbers (singular and plural). Personal pronouns take the form CVC, with possession marked with C- proclitics. Third person appellative and deictic-interrogatives (except 3sm *-anre) are either -VC or -CV, with the deictics distinguished by initial *-a' glottal. Clitics also play a role in the construction of Dr nouns and can take a variety of forms (*-uN inclusion in a group etc., where N represents a glottal stop). If the Indus inscriptions are written in Dravidian then they should reflect this linguistic structure outlined above.

The PM noun

The following discussion relies heavily on Anderson (2001). In general, words in the modern Munda languages are formed as follows: monosyllabic bases + suffixes (inflectional), prefixes and infixes (formative additions). The various classes of word are not clearly distinguished, in that the same base can be used as a noun, adjective or verb. Further, inflectional (suffixes) are agglutinative. However, affixation seems to have developed only over the last few thousand years under the influence of neighboring south Asian languages. This means that the PM of the Indus period was not characterized by the heavy suffixation used in the modern languages (see below). In modern Munda languages there is no distinction of gender, nouns can be animate or inanimate, and three numbers (singular, dual and plural), but there are no real cases.

The Munda noun is normally formed in one of two ways as follows (Anderson 2001:9): 1) derivational or class prefix + monosyllabic stem form; or, 2) objective case + (pro)noun stem. Noun incorporation is an important feature of PM. It is the formal union of nominal and verbal elements into an inflectable verb, using a monosyllabic combining or stem form of nouns, but with a bi-syllabic (minimal) constraint (Anderson 2001:3, 9). Nouns are structured using various prefixes, infixes and compounding suffixes.

The Indus noun

In the discussion above regarding the syntax of Indus texts, three basic elements were identified: Verbs (initial), Noun1 (medial) and Noun2 (terminal). The two nouns were shown to consist of relatively fixed inventories of signs. This pattern is consistent at both Harappa and Mohenjo-daro.

Of course not all Indus texts contain all of these elements in every case.
The variety is great, as are the variation in the V-N1-N2 pattern. It seems
likely that N1 elements, when present, are specialized references that represent a small number of specific nouns perhaps representing Radicals
(Bonta 1995:96). N2 elements a far more varied, and are likely more representative of the entire inventory of Indus nouns. For this reason they are
the focus of the following analysis.

The most common Indus sign is 740. Although its distribution is not
completely uniform, in the vast majority of examples it is functioning as a
Terminal Marker. In Chapter 4 sign 740 was identified as a logograph.
Through the analysis of its contexts, associated sign clusters, both prefixing
and affixing can be identified. In its simplest form 740 collocates with only
an initial cluster: M-0788, SEAL:S Figure 6.f.

This texts demonstrates that 740 is a logograph and using the Dr model
should be Root + ∅, as in the example given above. A slightly more complex example, with and added affix can be seen in DK3693, SEAL:S
Figure 6.g. Here the Root (sign 740) takes an affix (sign S090). One can
speculate that this affix might be Singular masculine -an/*-anre or the
Plural human *-ar, but other explanations are possible. The addition of sign
090 could be necessitated by the replacement of sign 824 for sign 817, but
there are too few examples to verify this. In longer texts there is no correlation between sign 090 and sign 817. There is likewise no obvious pattern
for the addition of sign 090.

At the next level of complexity signs are inserted between the Initial
Cluster Terminal Marker and Terminal Marker, but without the Post
Terminal: Figure 6.h. This is the commonest pattern in the construction of
Indus nouns, and it can only be explained as the addition of adjectives to
the Root + ∅ construction. It seems likely that adjectives (and numbers)
were not a distinct form-class in PDr although numbers, color terms and a
few other forms can be reconstructed (McAlpin 1981:32). Complex inser-
tions cannot be explained in terms of PDr as we understand it: Figure 6.i.
The overall pattern in Indus text does not match the formula given above
describing the construction on Dr. nouns: ROOT (+derivational aug-
ment(s)) (+morphological augment(s)) +Case (+postpositions). The dis-
crepancy between this pattern and the reconstructed PDr morphology
effectively eliminates PDr as a candidate language.

740

6.f

6.g

090

817

824

6.h

H-012   <-insertion->   6.i

The (P)Dr verb

McAlpin (1981:41) tells us that: "The structure of the typical Dravidian verb is a complex combination of agglutination and inflection." Dr verbs tend to use two patterns: 1) the verb stem is followed by a medial and ending in an agglutinative manner, but medials tend to be unstructured; 2) the stem is followed by unitary medio-ending. But the Dr verb is not that simple, i.e. the Stem + Medial + Ending formula does not fully represent the many complex iterations of Dr verbal derivation.

The PDr verb stem consists of a syllable VC added to the root CVC. The first vowel must be a, i, or u. There are two types of augments to verbs: Primary = -VC (only Vr1, Vr2, Vl and Vz are used); and Secondary = *-C(C)-. Beyond these basic elements Dr verbs are marked for agentivity, person, gender and tense-aspect-mood (TAM). These elements as all agglutinative, and consist primarily of -V, -CV, -VC, -CVC, -VCV, but some elements are more complex.

The PM verb

The PM verb is inflected for both subject and object. Subject markers are prefixes (proclitics), while object markers are a tightly bound unit with the verb. Suffixes follow the tense marker. The normal verb takes the following form (Anderson 2001:10):

> Subject proclitic + [causative/reciprocal prefix] + verb +[incorporated monosyllabic noun] + tense/aspect/transitivity suffix + object suffix/enclitic

Note that the causative/reciprocal prefix and incorporated monosyllabic noun may have been mutually exclusive.

The Indus verb

ı	001
ıı	002
ˈ)	060

The initial clusters terminal markers are another subject of interest in the discussion of the syntax of Indus writing. There are three common Initial Cluster Terminal Markers: sign 001 (sign 1, n = 523), sign 002 (n = 119), and sign 060 (n = 157). In the case of signs 1 and 2 these frequencies are slightly inflated by polyvalent contexts that are also medial (numerals, word dividers and syllabic signs). While not present in every text, Initial Cluster Terminal Markers terminate initial clusters in many cases. If the identification of some Initial Clusters as verbs is correct, it is logical to identify Initial Cluster Terminal Markers as verbal affixes, although affixing is rare in Proto-Munda and becomes increasingly common because of the influences of adjacent languages.

Initial clusters in Indus texts often consist of two signs: the initial cluster terminal markers sign 001, sign 002, and sign 060 preceded by a variety of other signs, the most common being sign 550, sign 690, sign 817, sign 820, sign 920, and sign 861 (Figure 4.7). In some cases the Initial Cluster Terminal Marker is followed by one of sign 741, sign 742, sign 745, sign 748, and varieties of these signs. Initial clusters that normally consist of one sign, can be preceded by relatively long strings: Figure 6.j. Even in long texts Initial Clusters can be optional (M-0814), and can some times occur as texts on their own (M-1127). Initial Clusters can also occur without Initial Cluster Terminal Marker (M-0170). Cases without Initial Cluster Terminal Marker and sign 741 etc. are difficult to identify. Initial Clusters are not restricted to patterned texts (DK8254 and CH2462).

M-0355, SEAL:R: [figure of Indus script signs]   6.j

In its simplest 2 sign form Initial Clusters can be explained by an agglutinative model, as can the addition of sign 741 etc. following the Initial Cluster. Beyond the most basic level, Initial Cluster construction involves the use of prefixes, and this sort of construction is not possible within the (P)Dr system of Stem + Medial + Ending described above. The Indus verb is constructed using a series of additions, prefixing, infixing and affixing. Even if the above analysis of syntax is flawed in some way, the construction of sign clusters in the Indus script would still violate the rules of word construction in (P)Dr. In other words the Indus not likely to be Dravidian.

From the above discussion it can be seen that PDr seems a poor fit to the morphology of Indus words. While PM matches the Indus pattern better, this is not necessarily conclusive proof as the morphological patterns of PM include infixes, prefixes and affixes (most affixing is was introduced only over the last few thousand years). The degree of fit is dependent on how Indus texts are analyzed. Further, Language X cannot be included in this analysis. It is impossible to identify the Indus language with the data at hand, but the list can be narrowed to PM or X.

Conclusions

This chapter has presented arguments for and against various languages being The language of the Indus script. Some languages were eliminated from consideration based on temporal and/or spatial considerations. The short list of PDr, PM and X was examined in detail where possible. A major lacuna in the data exists in the case of Language X and Para-Munda because we only possess isolated substrate words.

The major conclusion of this chapter is that of the candidate languages considered, only Proto-Munda, Para-Munda and X cannot be eliminated from consideration. Proto-Munda and Para-Munda because the patterns of word construction are similar to those of the Indus script, and X because nothing is known about it other than words that survive in the modern Indo-Aryan languages in addition to a few words in the Ṛg Veda. The elimination of the PDr from consideration is a major step. Future research can then be focused on the reconstruction of Proto-Munda and Para-Munda and its comparison to the Indus texts, and on the analysis of the words from Para-Munda and Language X.

The structure of the Indus texts is such that the preferred language should have the following characteristics: 1) base 10 number system; 2) the numbers for 1, 2, 10, 20 and 30 should be monosyllabic or equivalent to word building elements; 3) verb initial syntax; 4) verb constructing should make sense of Initial Cluster Terminal Marker and sign 741, etc. pairings; and, 5) it must utilize prefixes, infixes and suffixes in word construction.

741

Tests of decipherment

There are two tests of any decipherment of the Indus script 1) the word for 'hare'; and, 2) the Dholavira locative.

There is a set of Indus inscriptions where signs and images replace each other - TAB:C artifacts from Mohenjo-daro. These copper wafers are engraved on both sides. The reverse bears a text and the obverse bears either an image or a text.

One subset of 16 TAB:Cs bear the inscription: Figure 6.k. Fourteen of these tablets have a picture of a hare browsing grass on the reverse, while two examples bear the sign 753. This raises the possibility that sign 753 has the meaning of 'hare'. Sign 820 occasionally functions as a Terminal Marker (n = 10), while sign 752 occurs as a separate sign in 37 inscriptions in the pair sign 740, sign 752. That is to say that sign 752 needs a Terminal Marker. Any potential decipherment must make sense of sign 753 and the occurrences of its component parts. That is, the word for hare in the proposed language should be bi-syllabic, with one component sign 820 capable of occurring initially (113), medially (23) and terminally (10) in the correct proportions.

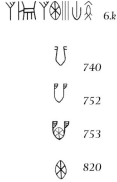

6.k

740

752

753

820

The Dholavira signboard consists of relatively long text containing 10 signs as follows: Figure 6.l. I would posit that some part of this sign sequence

798   821   001   480   850   820   388   611   820   6.l

would be the sites locative (place name). But which signs? Whatever signs form the locative might reasonably be expected to occur elsewhere in the corpus of inscriptions. Five consecutive signs from the Dholavira inscription are repeated on five artifacts from Mohenjo-daro. Three of these artifacts are bronze implements with texts given in Figure 6.9.

It seems logical that the sign sequence Figure 6.m is most likely the locative for ancient Dholavira, as it is the part of the text that is repeated. This sequence occurs again on a tag from Mohenjo-dato: Figure 6.n. It seems logical that the initial signs are what is being sent. Note too the unusual syntax of this text with the terminal number in positional notation. There is also a seal text from Mohenjo-daro whose text repeats the two initial signs 595 and 391, and the five signs of the locative Figure 6.o as follows: Figure 6.p.

Any decipherment that makes sense of these two cases and meets the five expectations listed above will be well on its way to being accepted.

391

595

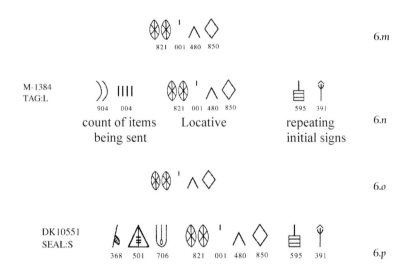

6.m

M-1384
TAG:L

904 004
count of items
being sent

821 001 480 850
Locative

595 391
repeating
initial signs

6.n

6.o

DK10551
SEAL:S

368 501 706 821 001 480 850 595 391

6.p

OTHER ITEMS OF INTEREST

In this study of Indus writing an attempt has been made to focus on some of the major issues of this script (typologies, sign list, potters' marks, numbers, morphology, and the root language). There are several interesting and important aspects of Indus writing that do not easily fit into these categories, but are significant to our understanding of the Indus script. It is the goal of this chapter to present the most relevant of this material for consideration and for further research.

Proximal association

Proximal association refers to one or more signs that are placed under the main line of text on SEAL:S artifacts. The placement of some of these signs is such that their placement cannot be explained by the continuation of the main text on a second line. Their placement suggests that they are associated with a specific signs in the main text, and are meant to be read either with the associated sign, or instead of it. There are 16 examples of a single sign being added below the main text, 13 two sign examples and 11 examples with three signs are on the second line (Table 7.1). With three signs or more it is

difficult to differentiate two line texts from signs with special placement. Indeed, the restrictions of space make the analysis of three or more signs on the second line almost impossible.

The placing of one and two signs under the main text such that their placement cannot be mistaken for boustrophedon or two line texts exists. For example DK5641 from Mohenjo-daro (Figure 7.1a), where the two signs under the main text are not adjacent. There is also a one sign example (HR2973, M-0748, Figure 7.1b) where the sign could have been placed anywhere under the last two signs of the main text. In fact there is room between the first and second sign for it to be added to the main text as well as before the initial sign, so its placement is most likely intentional. Figure 7.1c and 7.1d (M-0747 and M-0120) are both examples where the associated sign had two possible placements and the placement chosen seems to reflect a specific association with the signs in the main text. An example of the same sign being placed in various positions under the main texts is given in Figure 7.1 e-h (M-0256, M-1101, M-1005, M-0633). In these four texts sign 930 is place in the space below the

Table 7.1 Examples of proximal association tabulated by site and by number of associated signs

Site Name	1 Sign (b-h)	2 Signs (a & i-p)	3 Sign (none)	Signs 32/31 (i-l)	Total	% by Site
Mohenjo-daro	16	10	8	0	34	73.91
Harappa	0	0	0	0	0	0.00
Lothal	0	1	0	0	1	2.17
Kalibangan	0	1	1	0	2	4.35
Dholavira	0	1	0	0	1	2.17
Chanhujo-daro	0	0	2	6	8	17.39
Total	16	13	11	6	46	
% by Length	34.78	28.26	23.91	13.04		

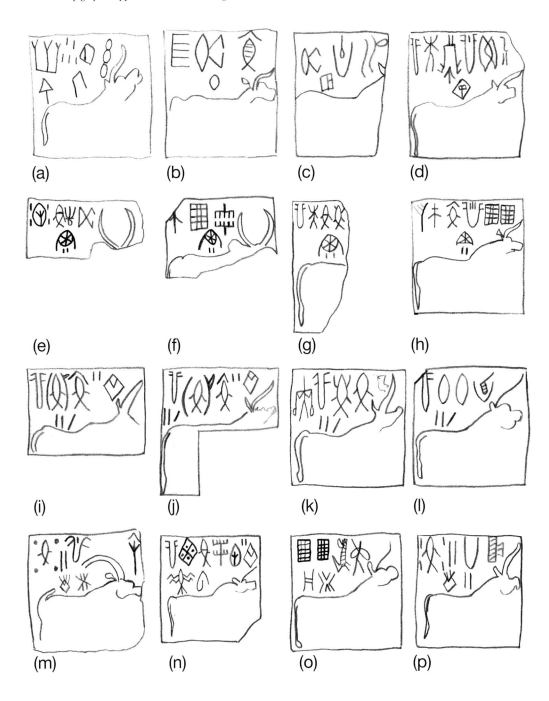

Figure 7.1 Examples of proximal association on Indus seals.

main text. Its placement varies slightly. In (e) it is placed near the middle of the available space. The same placement can be postulated for (g), but the break in the seal makes this less than certain. In the other two examples (f and h) the placement of sign 930 is as far to the right as possible. There seems to be no pattern to the signs with which it associates.

Most examples of proximal association come from Mohenjo-daro (n = 34, 74%), but there are six two-sign examples from Chanhujo-daro that form a unique set using the combination of signs 032 and 031 (Figure 7.1i-l). In these texts the placement of the associated signs seems to depend on available space. Two of these inscriptions have identical main texts (i and j), but the placement of the associated texts differs. This can only be interpreted as there being no connection between the placement of the associated signs and the signs in the main text. This raises the possibility that the Chanhujo-daro examples are a special kind of proximal association and need separate consideration.

The same pattern of placement holds for proximal associations of two and three sign clusters as was described for one sign examples. The purpose of proximal association cannot be know with certainty, but in some cases the placement of these signs seems to have some purpose beyond the utilization of available space (except the Chanhujo-daro examples). The inventory of signs and there ordering in individual examples is diverse enough to suggest that proximally associated signs come from the normal inventory of Indus signs, rather than from being a special set of signs use solely for this purpose. There are few repeated signs or sign sequences. The occurrence of proximal association deserves further study by linguists and other specialists.

A possible double enclosure

One aspect of the Indus script that presents difficulty to analysis is the occurrence of some enclosures as separate signs (i.e. signs 012, 031, 032 and 900). This makes the identification of multiple enclosures difficult. One example of a possible double enclosure is (Figure 7.a; CH 2462). One factor that makes this case more convincing is that both types of enclosures (signs 591 and 592) are found associated with the root sign (590). What makes the interpretation of the CH 2462 text difficult is that in two texts sign 592 follows sign 31, raising the possibility that this is not an example of a double enclosure, but rather simple the use of sign 031 twice in the same text. However, from the placement of the sign it seems more probable that (Figure 7.a) is intended to be read as a unit. The scarcity of double enclosures and the fact that some of the signs used to enclose signs are also independent signs make the resolution of this example difficult. For this

012

031

032

590

591

592

900

7.a

Figure 7.2 Signs of Set 55 with infixed signs

Graph	Sign No.	Total	M-d	Har	Lot	C-d	Kal	Ban	Oth	I	M	T	% Used IMT	Infixed Sign
	630	37	20	15	-	-	2	-	-	2	11	-	35.14	14
	631	2	2	-	-	-	-	-	-	-	-	-	0.00	15
	632	26	14	7	-	1	2	-	2	6	10	-	61.54	16
	633	1	1	-	-	-	-	-	-	-	-	-	0.00	17
	634	5	-	1	1	1	-	2	2	-	-	-	40.00	18
	635	1	1	-	-	-	-	-	-	-	-	-	0.00	20
	636	27	6	20	-	1	-	-	-	-	17	-	62.96	4+2h
	637	6	2	4	-	-	-	-	-	1	2	-	50.00	4+2v
	638	1	1	-	-	-	-	-	-	-	-	-	0.00	4+3h
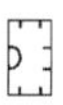	639	4	1	3	-	-	-	-	-	-	4	-	100.00	4+2+)
	640	1	-	1	-	-	-	-	-	1	-	-	100.00	4+))
	641	1	-	1	-	-	-	-	-	-	-	-	0.00	4 + sign 560
	642	1	-	1	-	-	-	-	-	-	-	-	0.00	sign 416
	Total	113	48	53	1	3	4	0	4	12	44	0		
	% of Total		42.5	46.9	0.88	2.65	3.54	0	3.54	10.6	38.9	0		

reason this sign cluster is encoded as 31-592-31 in the ICIT database. The existence of double circumfixes in terms implication of the identity of the root language

Sign Set 55

While most infixed stroke signs are easily identified there is a set of signs (Set 55) where this identification has gone unnoticed. A detailed examination of sign graphs in this set reveals the same pattern of infixed strokes as the Short Stacked numbers discussed in Chapter 5 (Table 7.1, 630-635). Of the 113 signs in this set 53 (46.9%)

come from Harappa and 48 (42.5%) from Mohenjo-daro. These proportions are somewhat unexpected in that the proportions of all signs is: Harappa = 42.77% and Mohenjo-daro = 50.27. This shift in the proportion of these signs is due to the large number of TAB artifacts from Harappa with sign 636 (the TAB effect). When this factor is controlled for, the proportions for these signs are close to the overall proportions.

These signs have 4-10 (but not 9) infixed strokes and the number of upper and lower strokes mimics the patter of strokes in Short Stacked numerals (i.e. with extra stroke in odd

Figure 7.3 Signs of Set 55 with infixed signs

Graph	Sign No.	Total	M-d	Har	Lot	C-d	Kal	Ban	Oth	I	M	T	% Used IMT
◊	490	2	-	2	-	-	-	-	-	1	-	-	50.00
◊	491	18	3	11	2	2	-	-	-	11	2	-	72.22
◊	492	2	1	-	-	-	-	-	1	-	1	-	50.00
◊	493	1	1	-	-	-	-	-	-	1	-	-	100.00
◊	494	2	1	1	-	-	-	-	-	1	-	1	100.00
◊	495	25	9	10	2	1	1	-	2	10	7	-	68.00
	Total	50	15	24	4	3	1	0	3	24	10	1	

numbers placed on top). When occurring in Indus texts these signs are found in the V1 and N2 zones only, and never occur in N1 contexts (see Chapter 6). In V1 contexts most Set 55 signs occur initially at least once. In the second position in V1 contexts there are more complex relationships, but the most common contexts for signs 630-635 are following sign 32. This association is completely lacking in signs 636-642. This raises the possibility that infixing additional signs (most commonly numerals) into the basic signs changes their values and makes the prefixing with sign 32 inappropriate. In V1 contexts none of the Set 55 signs occur right adjacent to the Initial Cluster Terminal Marker (see Chapter 4).

As stated earlier, Set 55 signs never occur in N1 contexts. They are common in N2 contexts where they serves as Bonded Clusters or components in Bonded Clusters. In these contexts Set 55 signs are often initial in the Bonded Cluster. There is no noticeable preference for specific Set 55 signs to occur in either V1 or N2 positions in Indus texts. M-0396 is an unusual context in that sign 630 occurs twice in it as follows: (Figure 7.b)

7.b

Signs 630-635 cannot be show conclusively to have infixed numbers. These internal markings may be design variations without semantic values of their own. Signs 636-642 have recognizable signs (most often numerals) infixed into signs 630, 632 and 634. Sign 642 has an unusual design and is from an eroded and fragmentary TAB:B artifact from Harappa (H-701), and for this reason its exact sign graph is in doubt. It is worth pointing out that the argument for these internal-design element being non-semantic additions is supported by the frequency of the signs. Set 55 signs with an even number of strokes are by far the most frequent, and this pattern is not evident for their counterparts in the inventory of Short Stacked numerals (Figure 5.1). This issue remains unresolved and deserves further consideration in future research.

Rhinoceros horns and Set 38 signs

The relationship between the images and signs found on Indus artifacts is difficult to define. In Chapter 1 it was pointed out that there is no definable relationship between specific signs or sign clusters and specific iconographic elements. The only exception to this fact is sign 753, which has been shown in Chapter 6 to replace for an

Figure 7.4 A human figure crouched in a tree with a tiger on the ground looking backward over its shoulder and the same scene with the human figure on the ground. Rendering by Rhonda Johnson. Used with permission.

image of a browsing hare. But there are some interesting relationships between iconographic elements and sign elements from unrelated artifacts. One such example is the similarity between some of the Set 38 signs and the design of Rhinoceros horns on Indus artifacts. There are seven examples that show internal elaboration of rhinoceros horns that resemble the Set 38 signs. Most of the other examples (20) lack the necessary details to determine their original design. There are, however, at least four examples where internal elaboration is not used and the horns are depicted with smooth surfaces. While the connection between Set 38 signs and the depiction of rhinoceros horns is not definitive, there is enough data to keep this possibility open in consideration of decipherment of the Indus script.

Human figure in a tree and the tiger

There are 17 examples depicting a human figure crouched in a tree with a tiger on the ground

looking backward over its shoulder at this figure (Figure 7.4). When the TAB effect is controlled for, the count of unique occurrences drops to twelve. It seems highly probable that this image is recounting a mythical, folk or historical story. What transpired between these two and why the human is in a tree is unknown. The interpretation of this image by specialists in the myth and mythology of this region is facilitated by the occurrence of an additional scene depicting these individuals interacting. There is a SEAL:S artifact from Chanhujo-daro (CH 926) that was published in Mackay (1943:Plate LI:18).

The iconography of this seal depicts the same iconographic elements as the other examples but with the human figure on the ground interacting directly with the tiger. The reason for pointing out this additional scene is that it has

𑀉𑀫 𑀽𑀽𑀽 𑀉 𑀩𑀽*   7.c

not been previously pointed out in the literature. The addition of this information may facilitate the interpretation of these scenes. The sequence of these scenes is not known. The scenes on Indus artifacts depict fragments of longer narratives that are unknown to modern scholars. We can only hope that some fragment of these stories will survive in human memory and that they will be recognized by modern folk scholars.

The Moneer bangle pot

Coated carinated jars (CCJs) were first identified as a result of excavations at Mohenjo-daro, Moneer southeast Area (AA.40) during the 1983-1984 field season (Halim and Vidale 1983:63-97). CCJs are part of a complex of technology applied to the manufacture of purple glazed stoneware bangles. This process needs to be executed with precision, as minor temperature changes or errors in the formula of the clay or glaze would result in defective products. From excavations of CCJs at Mohenjo-daro we know that one major problem during the cycle of production was the maintenance of proper kiln temperature. The excavation of eight discarded CCJs in 1983 has yielded detailed information regarding the process of manufacture of purple glazed stoneware bangles. All of these CCJs were over-fired and, because of post-depositional events, were in various states of preservation.

One CCJ (Jar G) in particular is of special interest here, as it has preserved as part of it closure system an impression of a SEAL:S. The iconography is the common Bull:i:I/SAN combination (Halim and Vidale 1983:82: Figures 55-56). This jar contained 82 fragments of stoneware bangles and bore the following inscription: (Figure 7.c; asterisks precede reconstructed signs). The first two signs can be reconstructed with some confidence, as they are commonly associated with sign 741 (the third sign).

Figure 7.5 A human figure is ordering the feeding or watering of livestock (M-1405). Rendering by Rhonda Johnson. Used with permission.

Halim and Vidale (1983:77; Figure 41) give a photograph of the stoneware bangle fragments found in Jar G. A crude reconstruction of the contents of Jar G can be made. No attempt is made here to match these fragments in a true reconstruction, but rather the various fragment were simple arranged to form bangles with the approximate mean internal diameter (4-5 cm). As over firing has deformed the bangles, it is likely that such a reconstruction would be impossible. In addition to the bangles being fired four or more bangle fragments were used in the closure system (Vivalde 1984:111; Figure 11). Based on this crude reconstruction we can estimate that Jar G contained 17 or 18 bangles.

The number of bangles found in this particular CCJ is important because the 017-031 sign sequence recorded on the closure sealing of this jar may be referring to its contents. The sign sequence 017-031 could be the Indus number for 17, and could be giving a count of the contents of Jar G. This association is important for several reasons:

1) it demonstrates that one of the main functions of SEAL:S artifacts is to facilitate the cycle of production;

2) it demonstrates that the text of the sealing refers to its contents;

3) the repetitive use of a seal to close near identical pots with identical contents accounts for the

Figure 7.6 Parallel inscriptions with different forms on internal elaboration used in the initial sign (M-325).

effort expended in seal manufacture, and why seal are found both exhausted and discarded; and,

4) the occurrence of 017-031 sign sequence confirms both the existence of positional notation and the function of these signs as numerals.

This is not to say there are no other uses for SEAL:S artifacts, there certainly are. Seals can be demonstrated to function as closures for doors, boxes and other packages enclosed in reeds and textiles (Toshi and Frenz 200?). Sometimes the impressions of the strings used to tie these packages are found on the reverse of the sealings. The use of seals in Indus culture was demonstrably complex, but it seems likely that in at least one instance the function of one variety of seal can be understood in terms it repetitive use to seal uniform sized CCJs.

Sign 156 and its possible meaning

It has been pointed out several times that the relationship between signs and their accompanying images is weak and poorly understood. Several exceptions have been examined earlier with interesting results. There is one artifact from Mohenjo-daro (M-1405) depicting a human figure pointing to an animal trough with a Bull:ii feeding from it, and to signaling sign 156 (Figure 7.5). One possible interpretation of this image is that the human figure is ordering the feeding or watering of the livestock. On the reverse of this artifact (TAB:B) are the images of a tiger and a rhinoceros. Sign 156 has been identified as a "bearer" based on its design (Parpola 1984). Other signs (Set 04; especially 151, 154 and 158) have been similarly identified as bearers, with variations in graph design attributed to variations in the type of bear. The image from M-1405 does not conclusively identify these signs as bearers, as this is only one example and the image is not explicit. However, the identification of these signs as bears has far stronger support considering M-1405.

Internal elaboration and M-325

The ongoing examination of the mechanics of internal elaboration focuses on whether it has two (unelaborated/elaborated) or three (unelaborated/simple elaboration/full elaboration) stages. Both states can coexist simultaneously in the Indus script. Examples of simple elaboration are

Figure 7.7 The Mohenjo-daro "procession" (M-490 and M-491).
Rendering by Rhonda Johnson. Used with permission.

rare, but the extant examples seen to indicate that simple elaboration (normally one internal hatch stroke) is used with some signs. One such example of internally elaborated signs Set 38 signs (Table 7.2). These signs are normally initial or medial in their normal contexts, and are most common at Harappa.

For Set 38 signs elaboration seems to have three stages (unelaborated/simple elaboration/full elaboration). There is one example that calls the whole case for the existence of three-stage elaboration into question - M-325 (Figure 7.6). In this example the artifact in question (SEAL:S; Bull:i:II/SAN) has parallel inscriptions on both sided. These texts are identical in every way save the use of sign 491 on one side, and sign 493 on the other. Sign 491 has one internal hatching stroke and sign 493 has two. Previously interpreted as successive stages of internal elaboration,

these demonstrate the complexity of this issue. Several explanations for this difference can be offered. Scribal error is the easiest explanation, but this is improbable as the texts were likely carved at the same time. Only 18 of 1555 SEAL:S artifacts (1.15%) are carved on both sides, and only three of these have identical texts. Of the three double-sided artifacts only M-325 has a minor variation in the text. Further, this is the only example of sign 493. What makes this issue complicated is that one could postulate that the differences in the M-325 texts result from the need to have two similar, but not identical, texts in use at once. This issue cannot be resolved with the data at hand and represents an important direction for future research.

The Mohenjo-daro procession

The point has been made in Chapter 1 that the

standards and field objects found on SEAL:S arti-facts likely had a significance beyond the decora-tive. This is born out by two mold-made (TAB:B) artifacts from Mohenjo-daro (M-490 and M-491). The scene depicted on these artifacts is of a pro-cession of four individuals each bearing a differ-ent iconographic element on a carrying pole (Figure 7.6). Unfortunately these artifacts are in very poor shape. What details remain indicate they were originally somewhat larger. The pro-cession consists of four individuals carrying (from right to left): a SAN standard, a headpiece, a Bull, a type A standard bottom. The first item is clear when both artifacts are compared. For the second item only the lower half remains. It bears a strik-ing resemblance to the headpieces worn by cer-tain individuals depicted on inscribed artifacts and in statuary. The third item in the procession is a bull. Unfortunately, the artifact is eroded and the type of bull cannot be determined with cer-tainty. The fourth item is recognizable as the bot-tom of a type A standard. Whether the top was once part of this depiction or not is unknown. In comparing the first and last item one can see that

there is a difference in scale with the first item rendered at a much smaller scale. This would seem to support the idea that only the bottom of the standard existed on the original artifact (i.e. there is not enough space to render a full sized standard at that scale).

This representation of a procession is one of a handful of depictions of Indus ritual life. The items on carrying poles are most likely symbols power and/or of specific groups within Indus culture. The distribution of these items when depicted on SEAL and TAB artifact types lead to the earlier recogni-tion of a geographic diverse but pan-Indus pattern (Chapter 1). I would postulate, based on these two lines of evidence, that these items are symbols of groups. In the case of the headpiece this may be a symbol of a specific office.

In this chapter I have presented nine sets of data that need further consideration. The analysis requires specialist knowledge in some cases and additional data in others. It is my hope that com-munity of Indus researchers will find this materi-al of interest and pursue these topics.

Appendix

Figure A1. Detail description of sign record

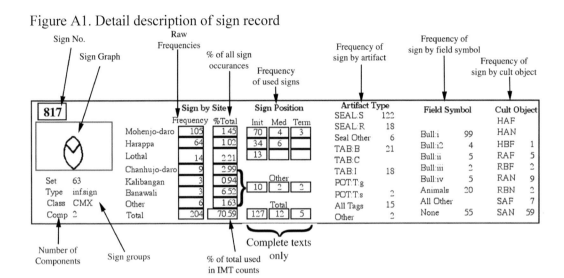

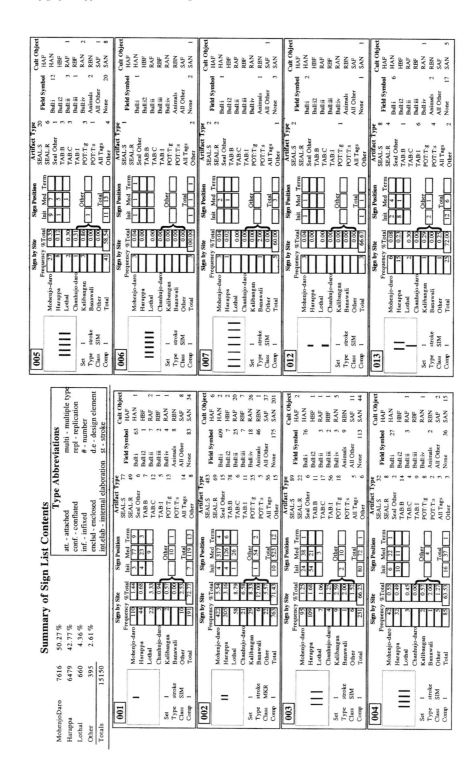

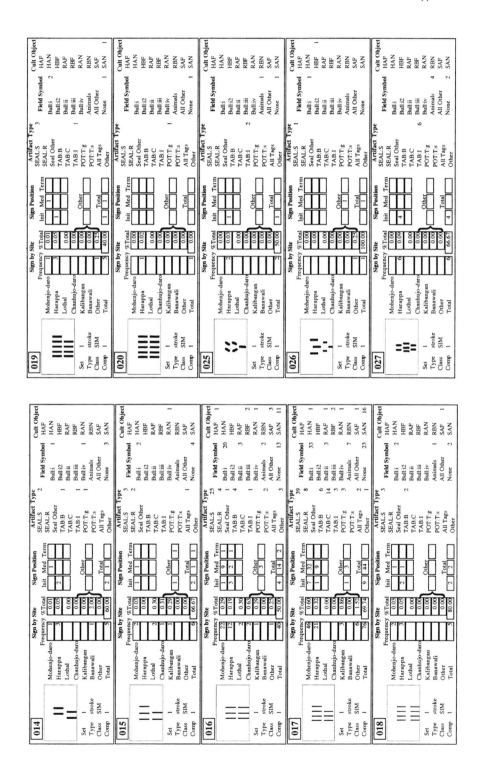

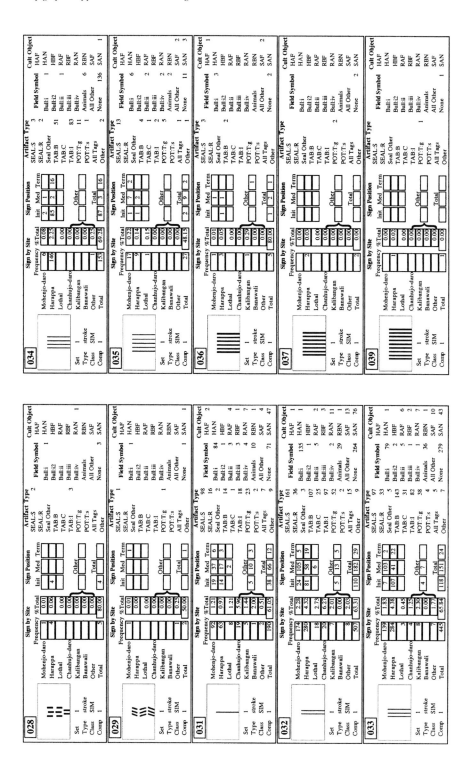

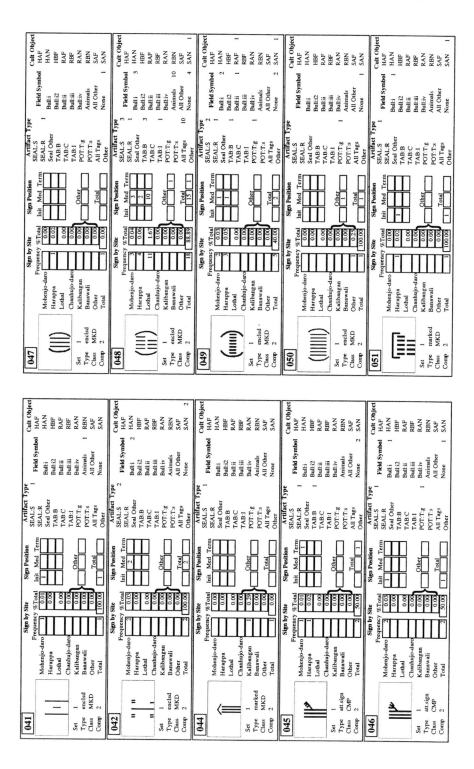

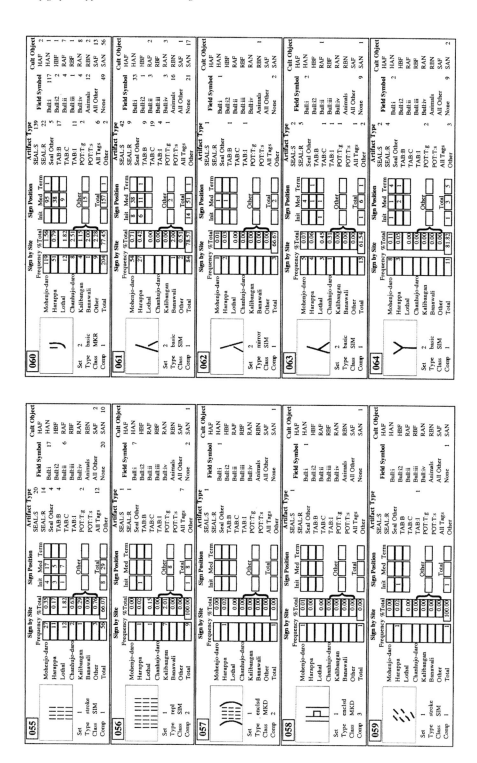

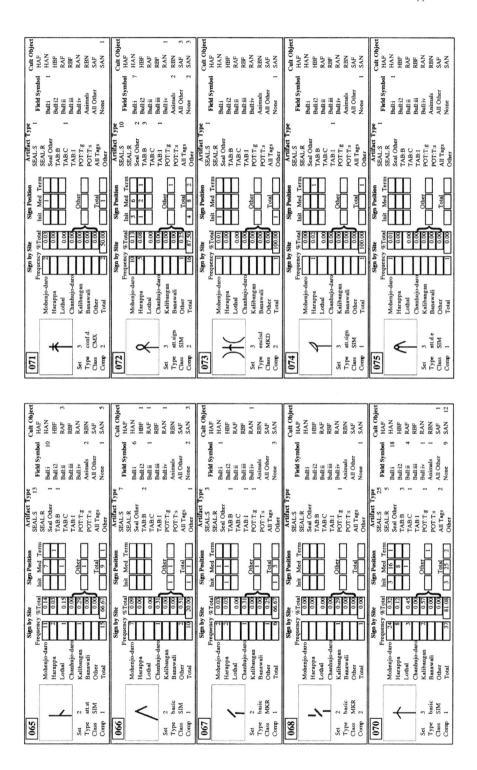

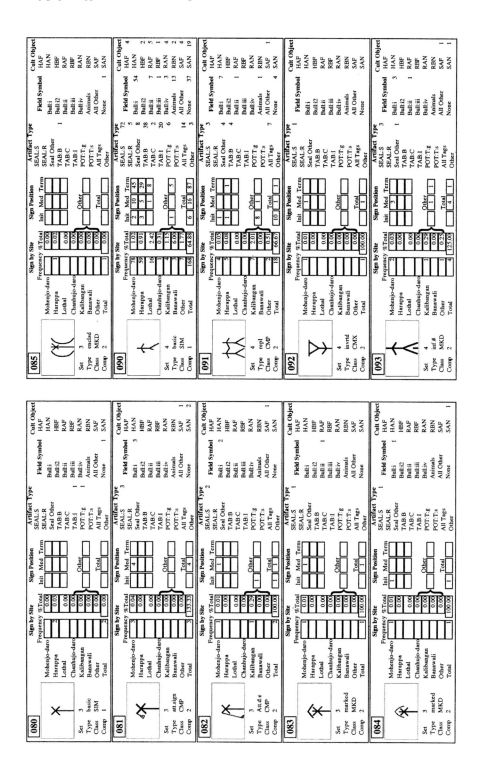

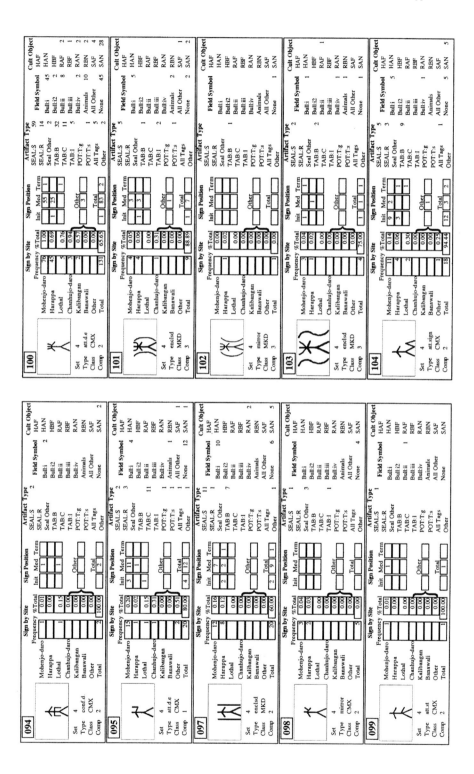

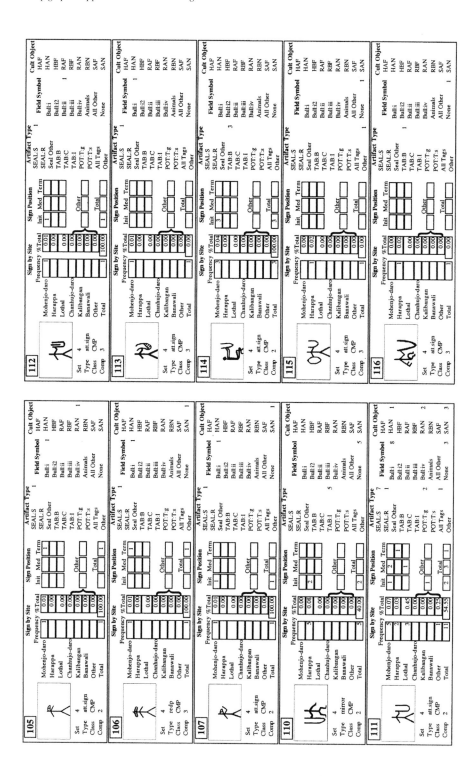

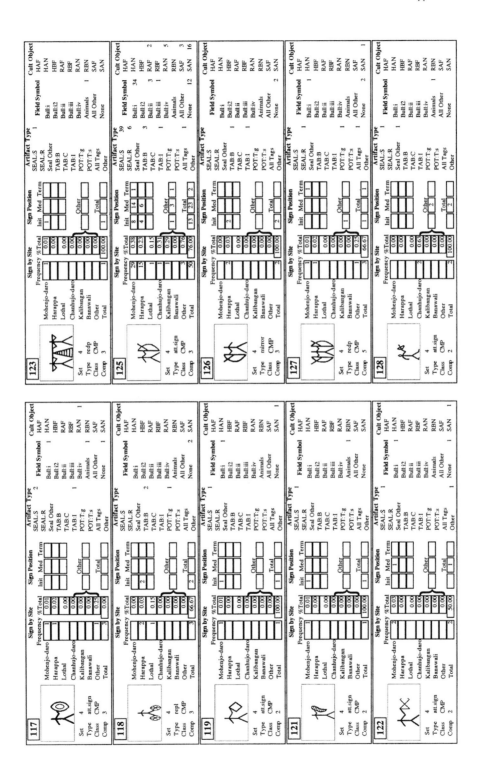

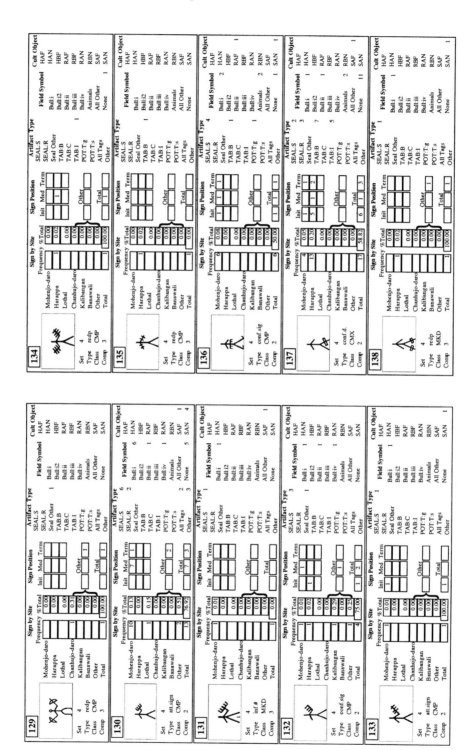

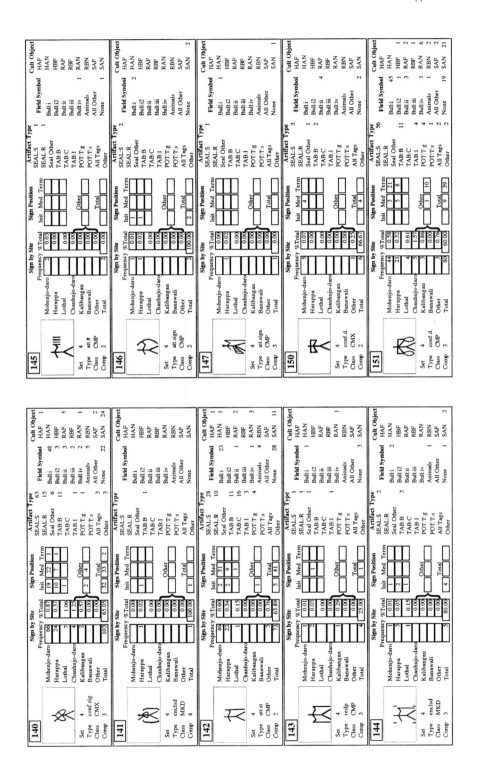

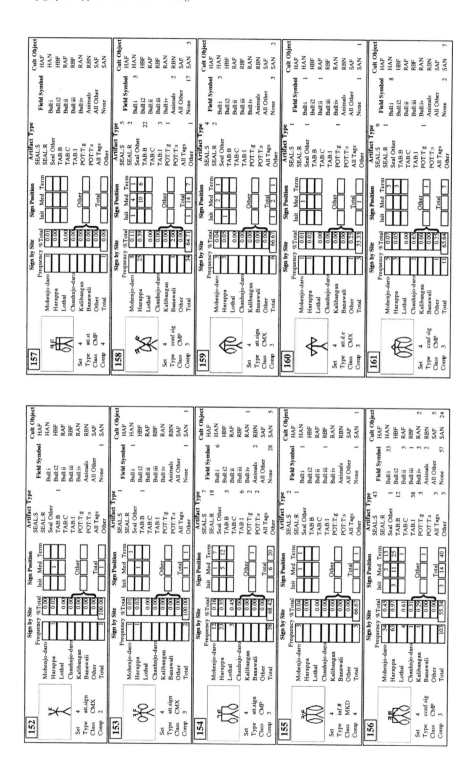

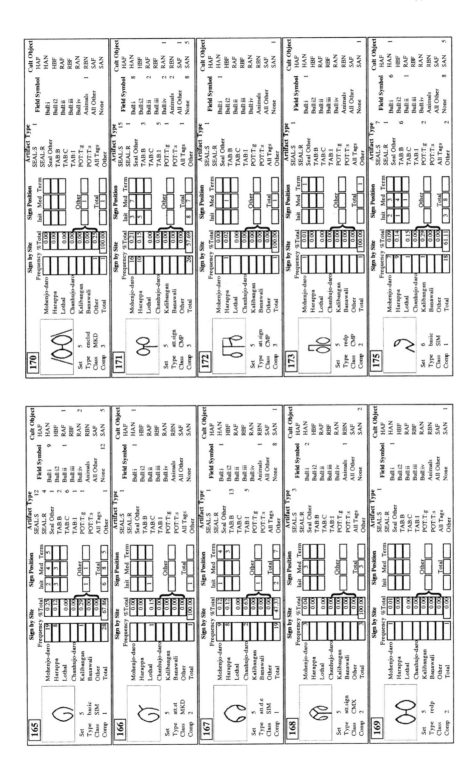

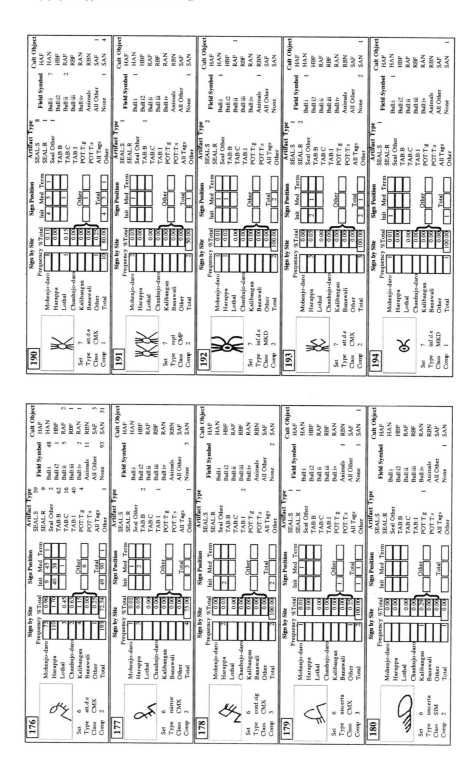

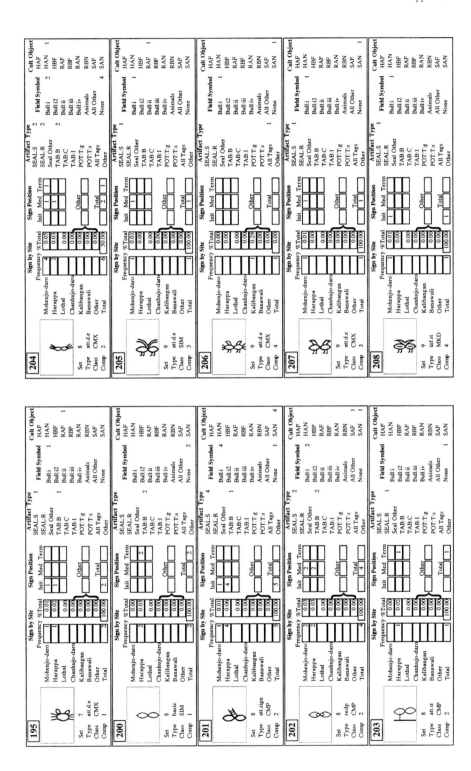

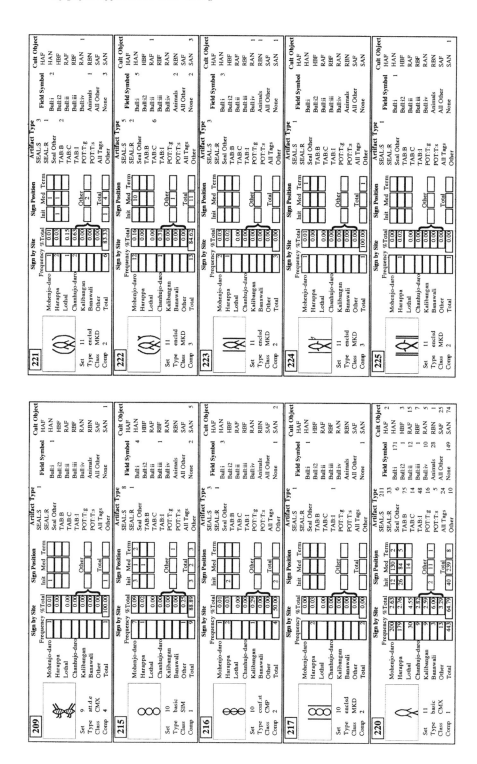

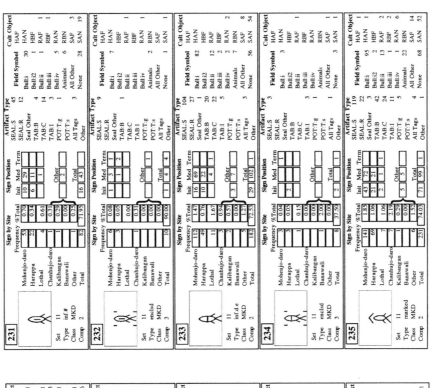

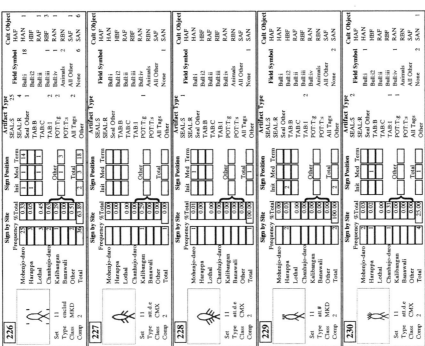

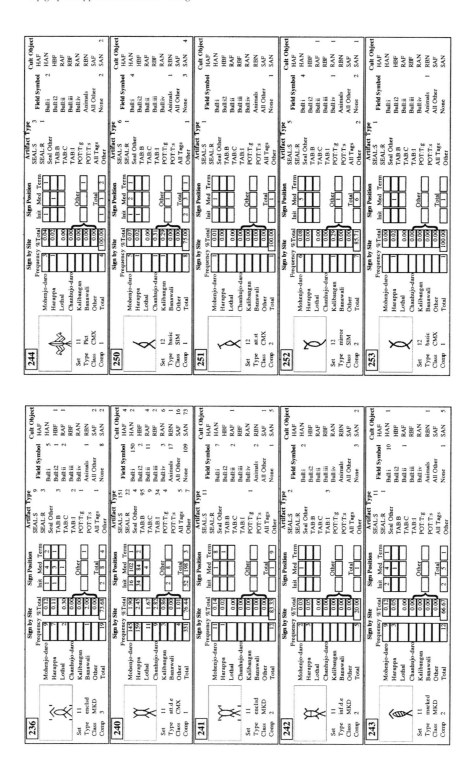

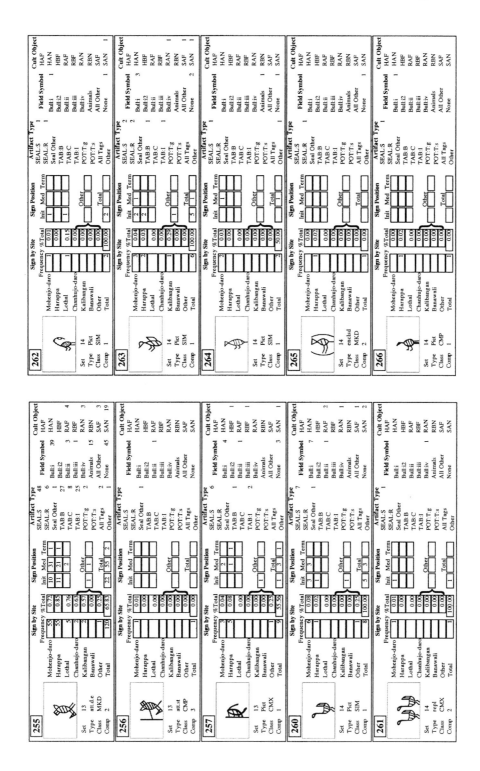

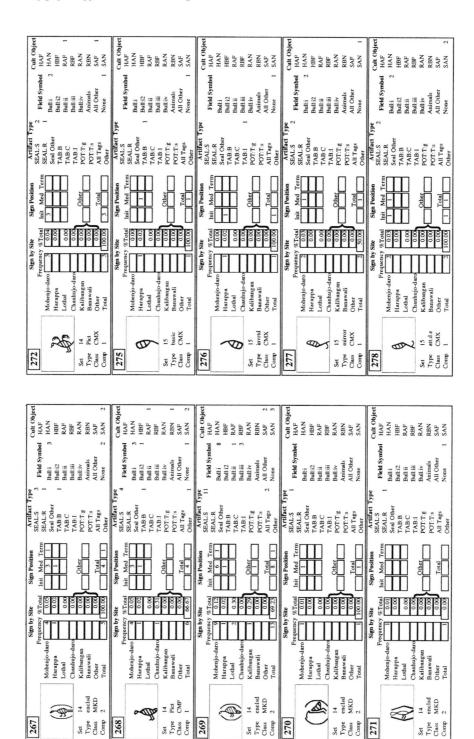

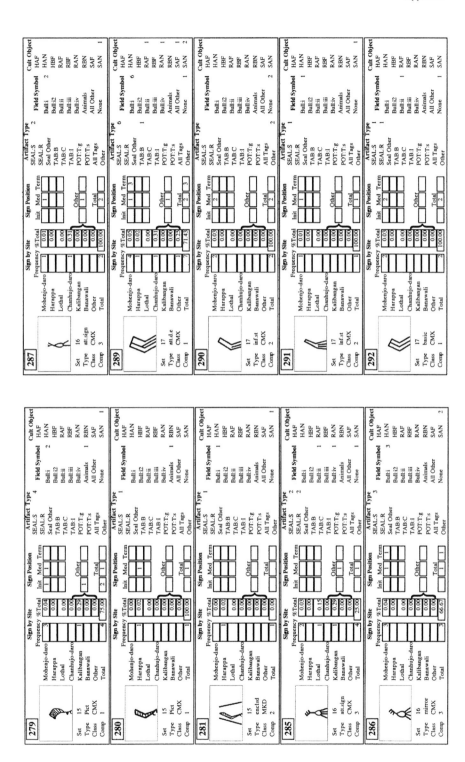

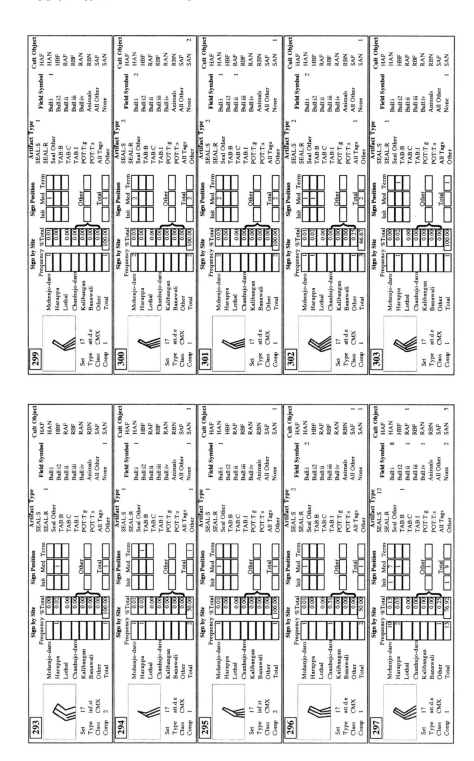

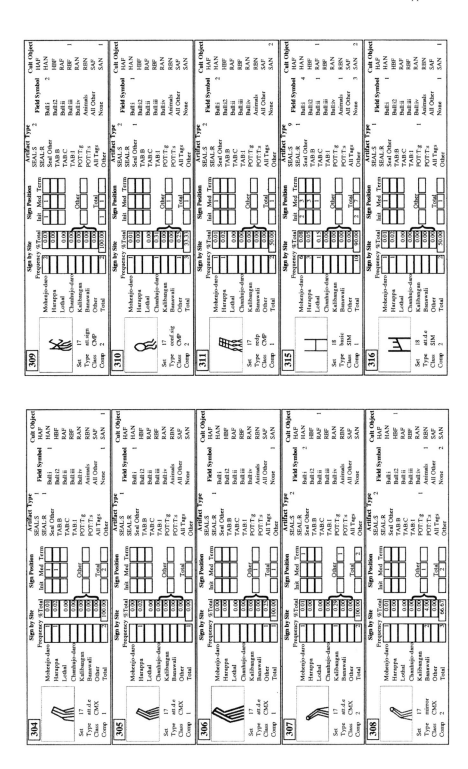

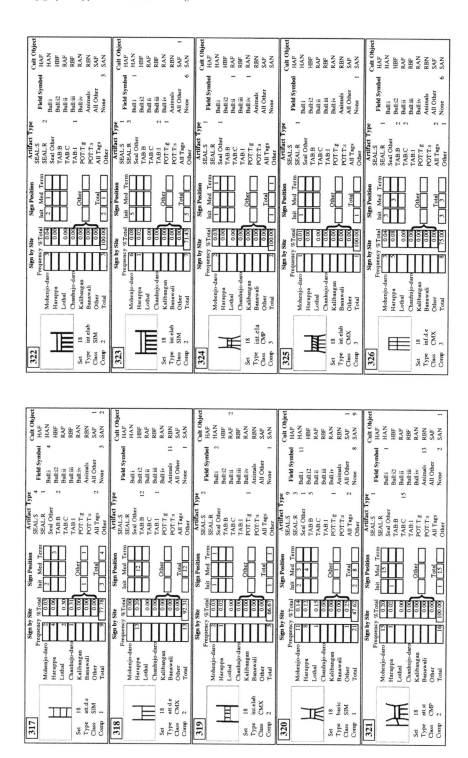

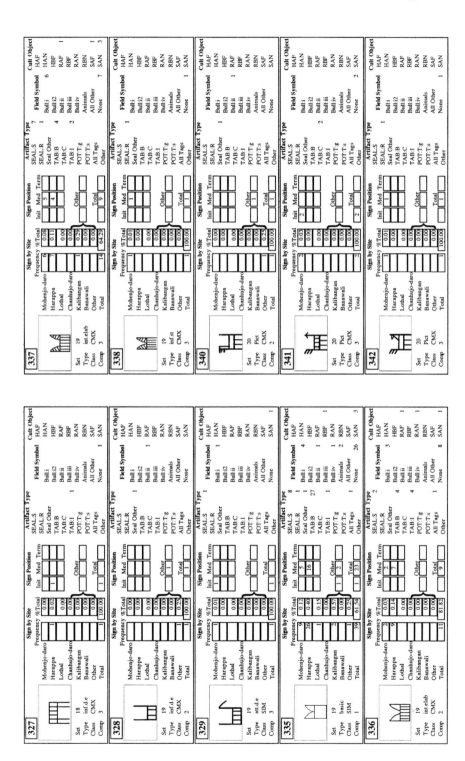

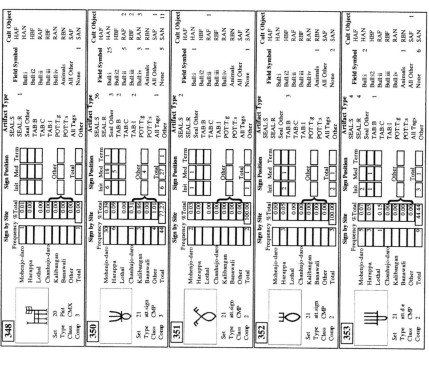

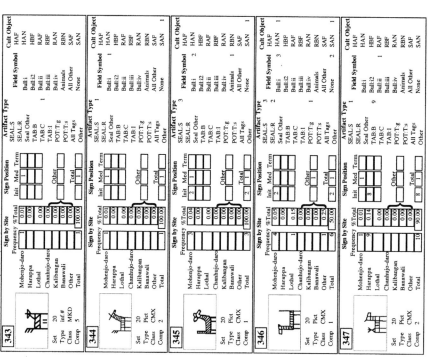

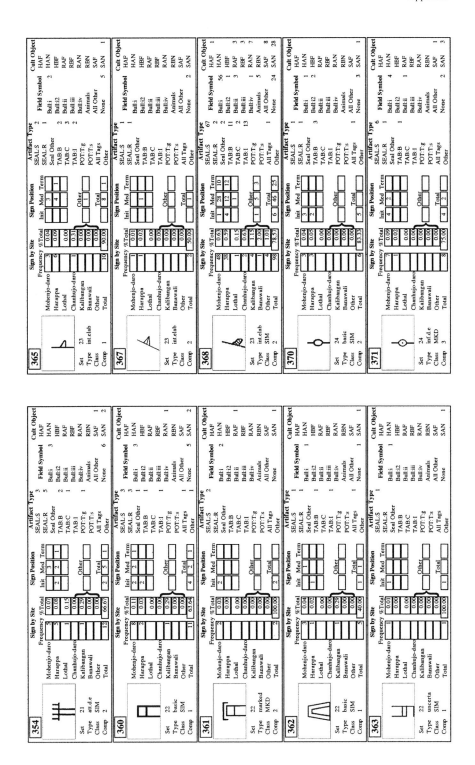

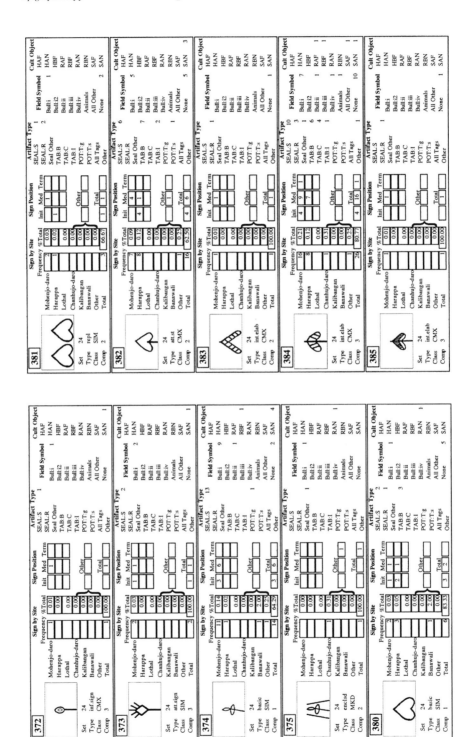

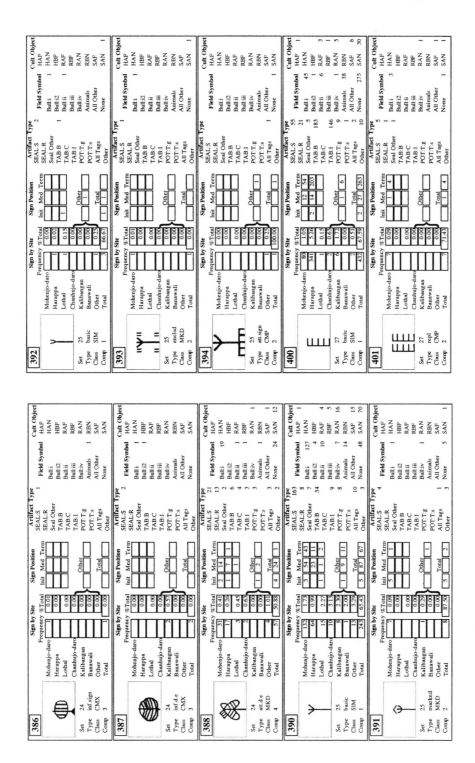

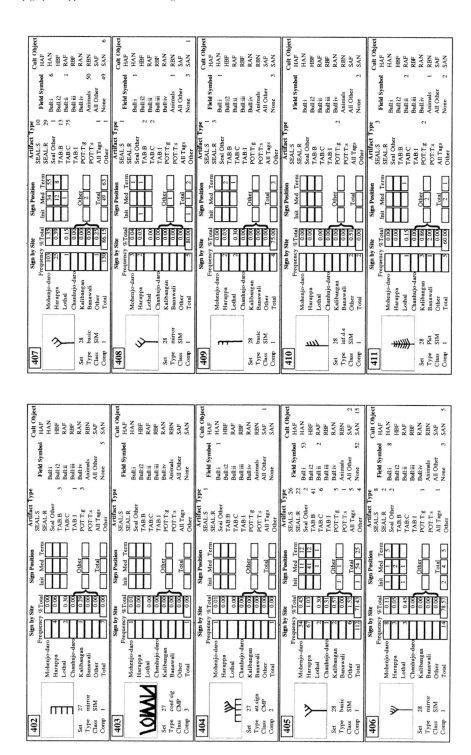

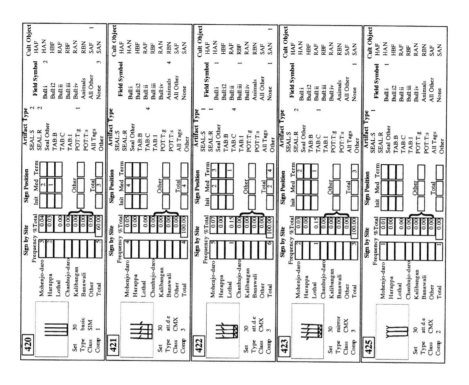

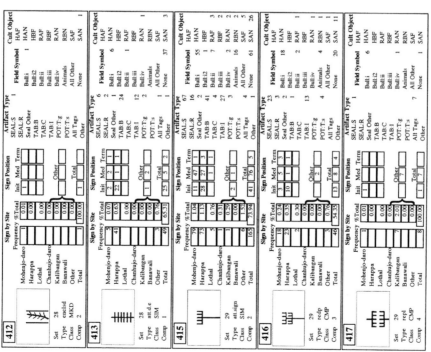

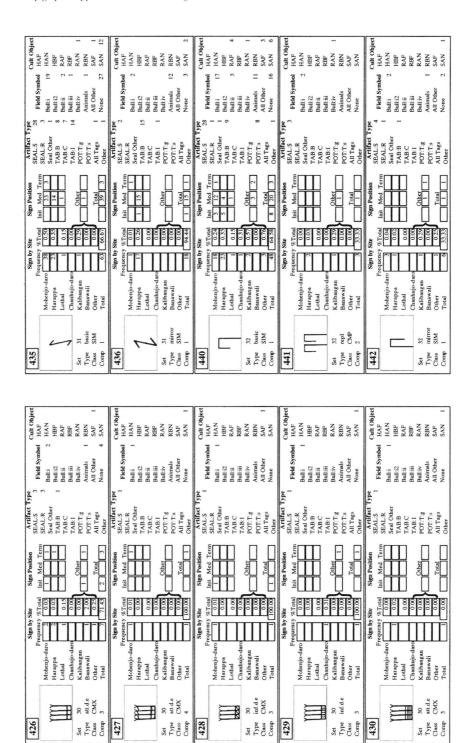

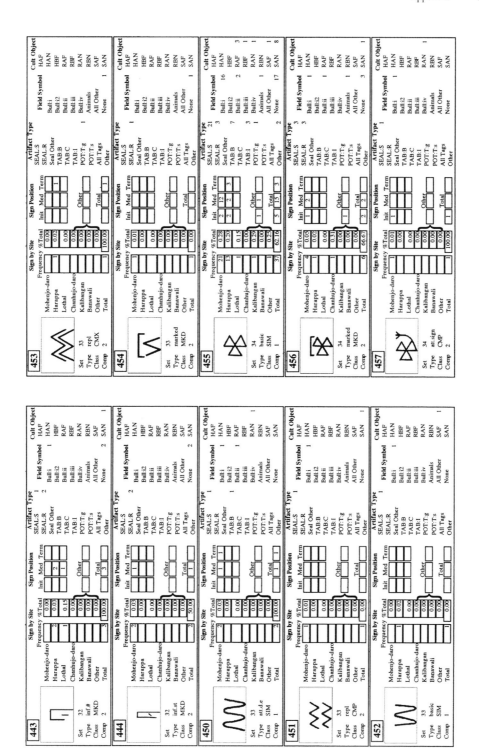

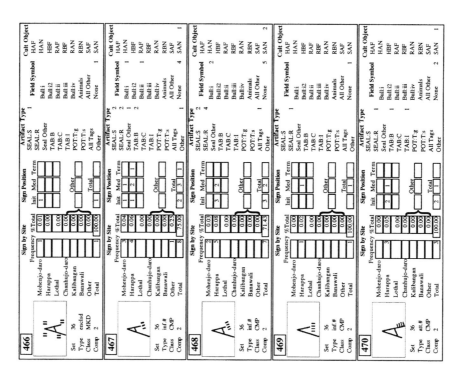

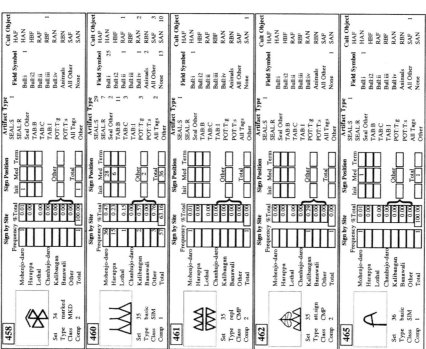

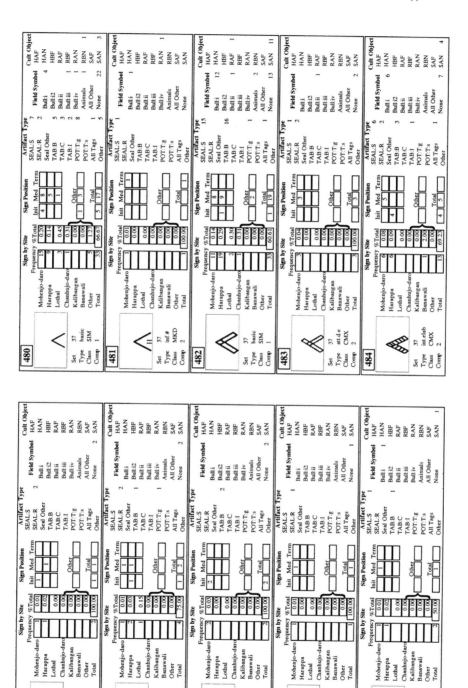

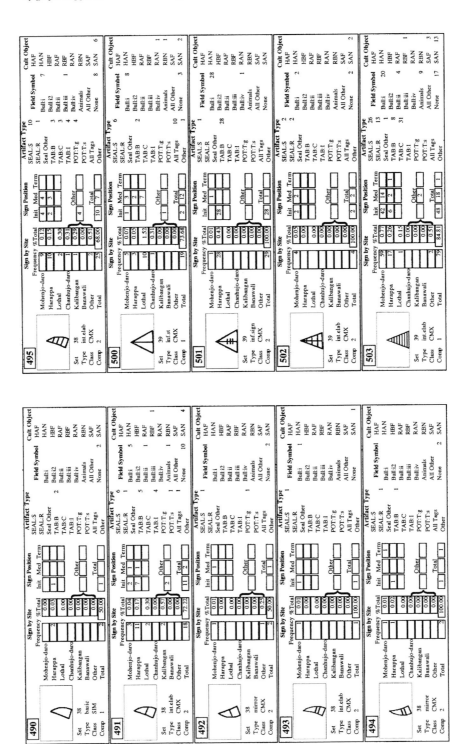

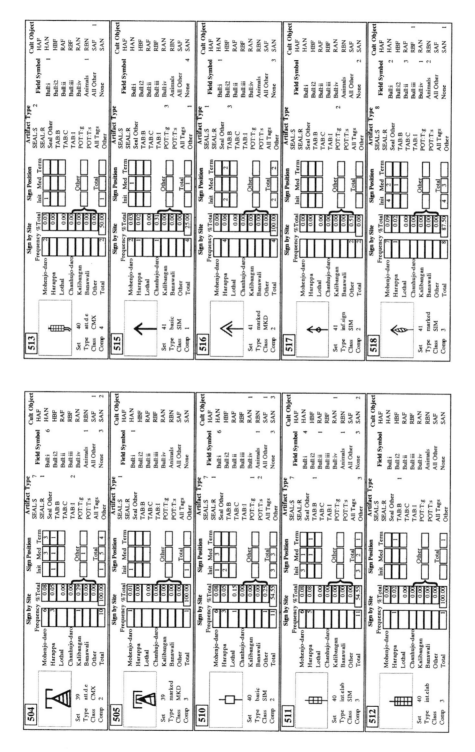

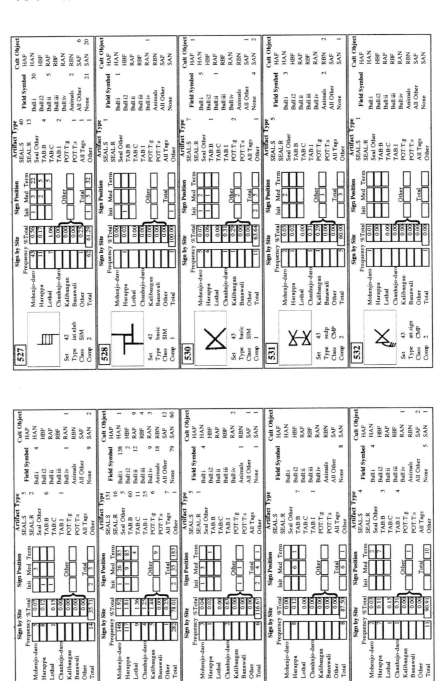

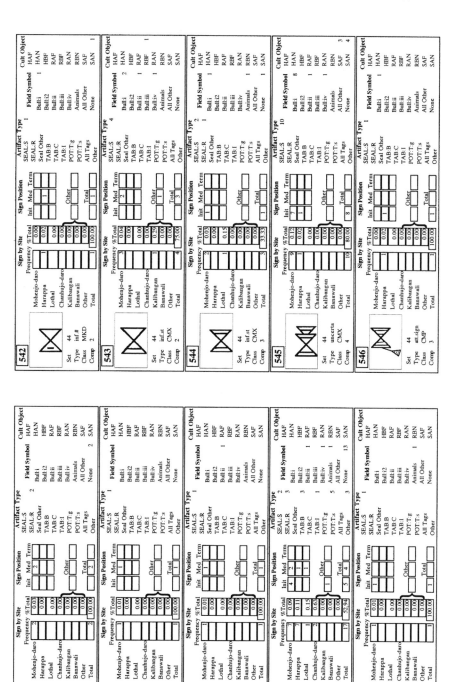

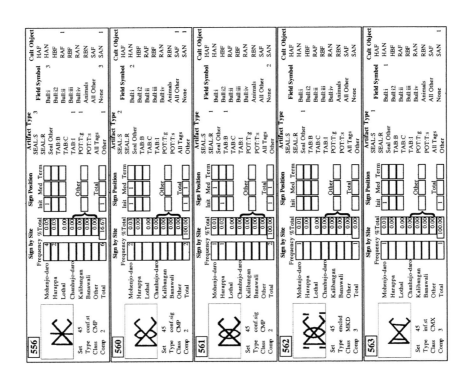

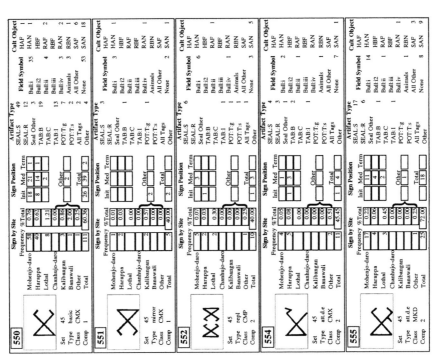

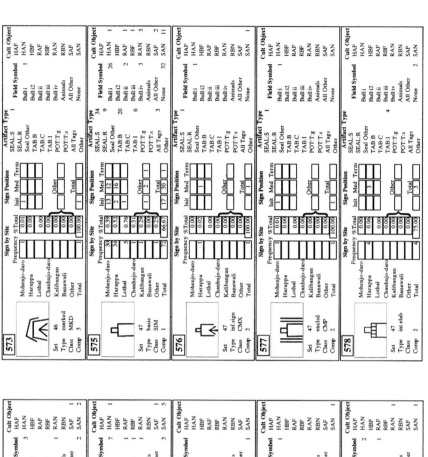

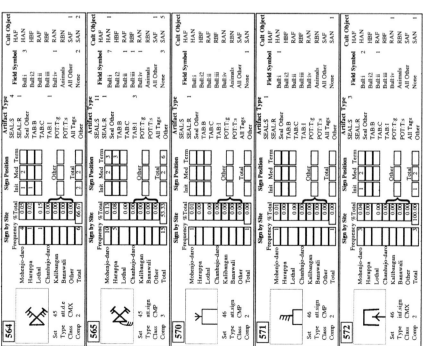

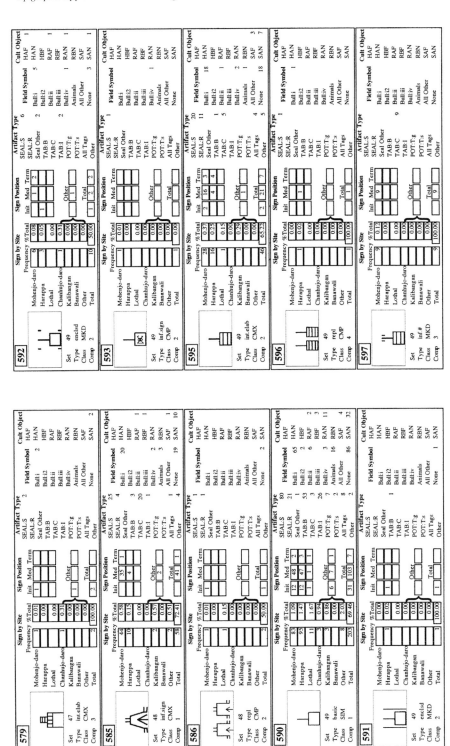

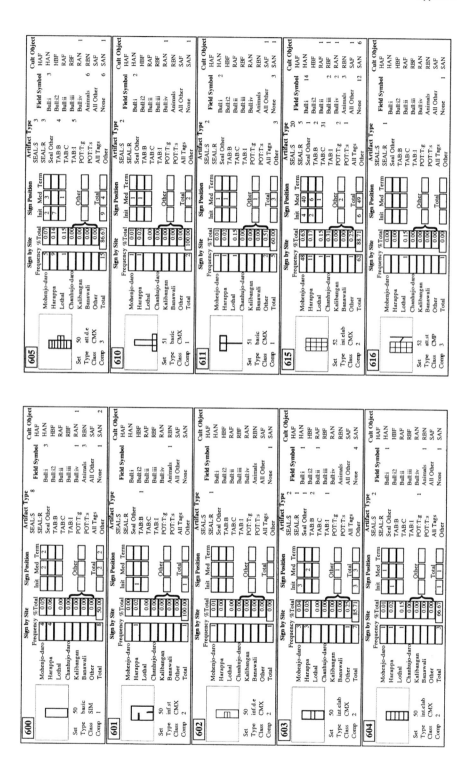

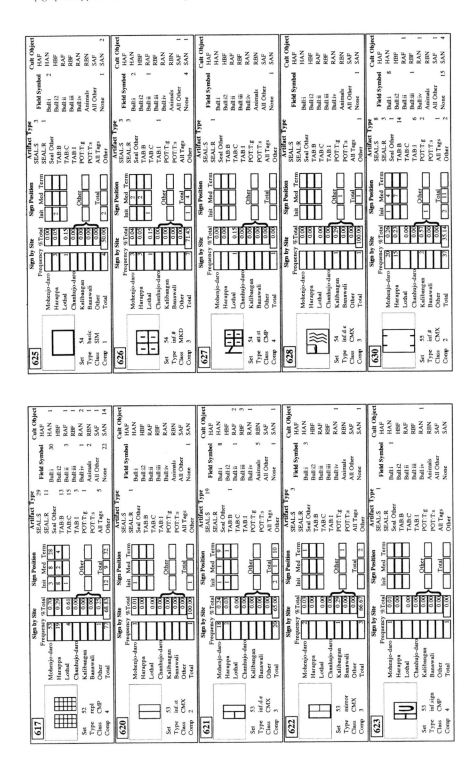

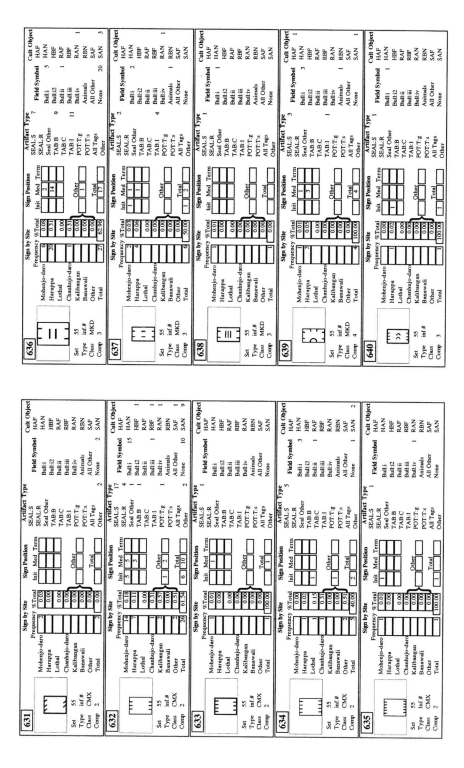

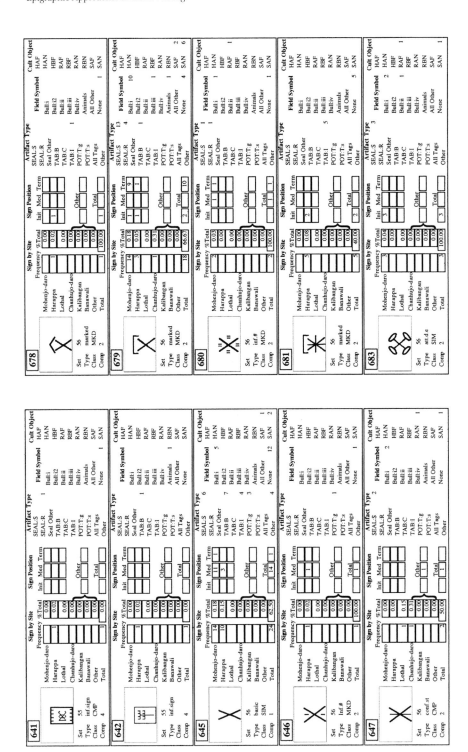

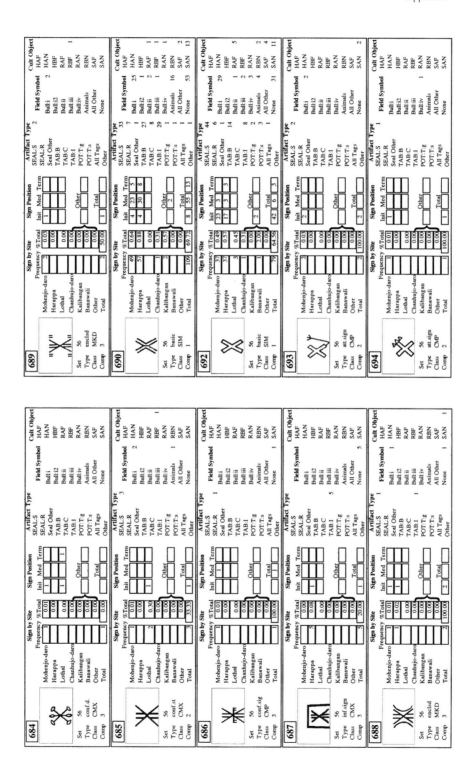

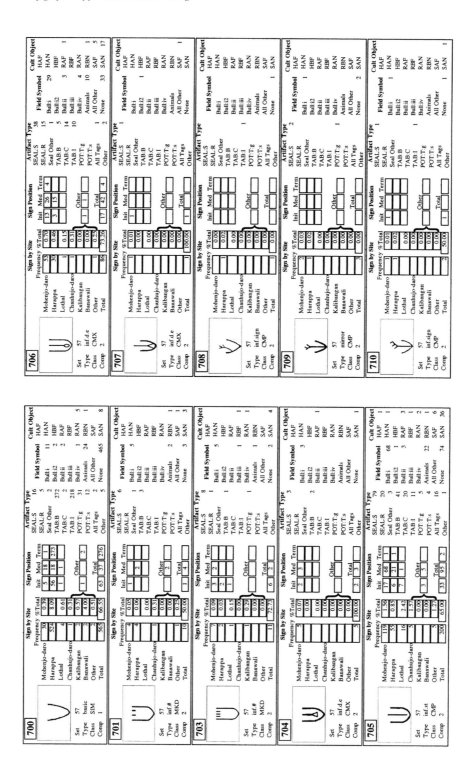

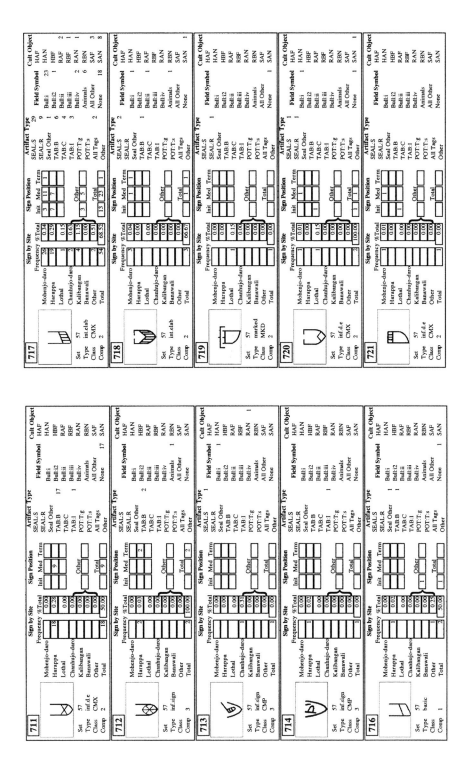

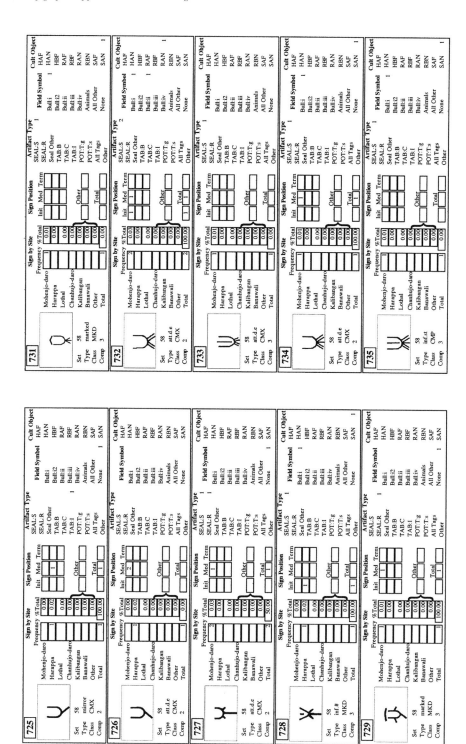

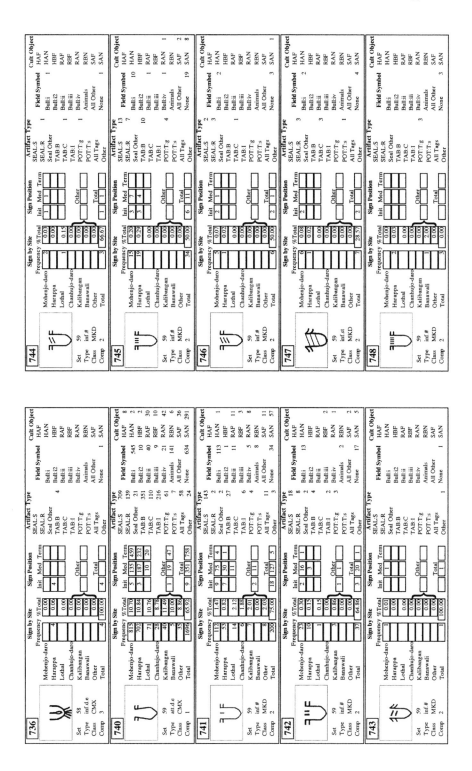

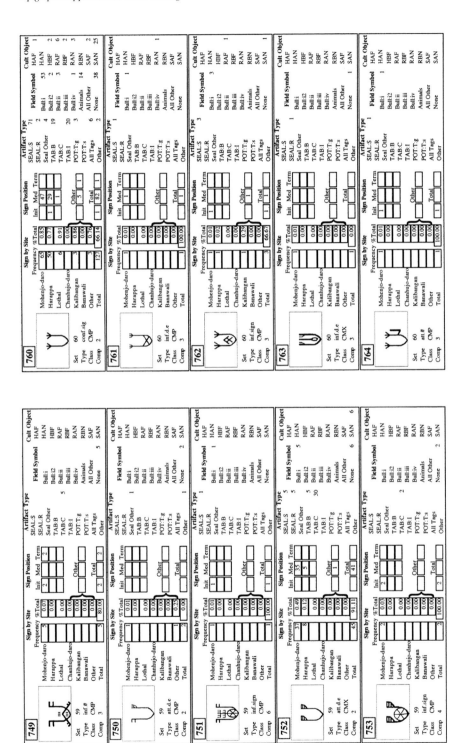

Appendix   219

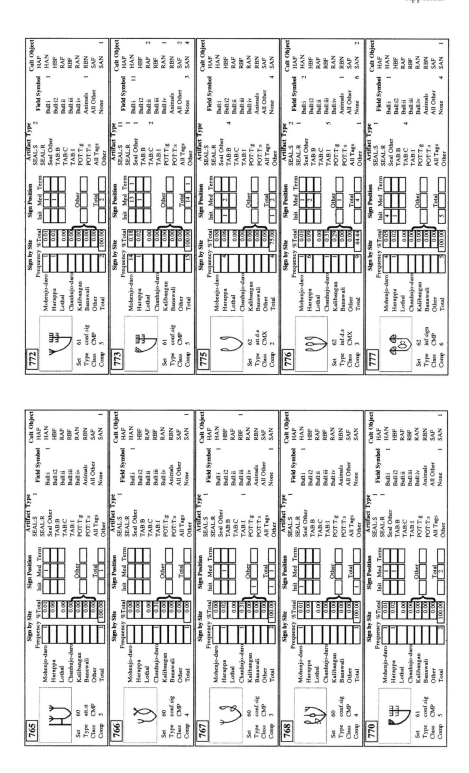

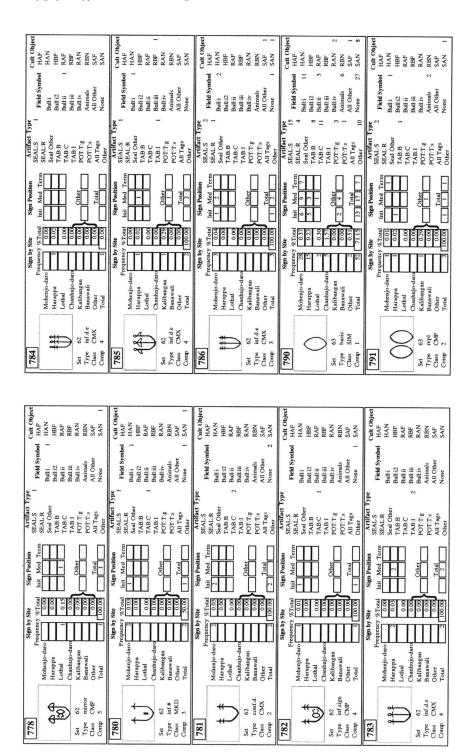

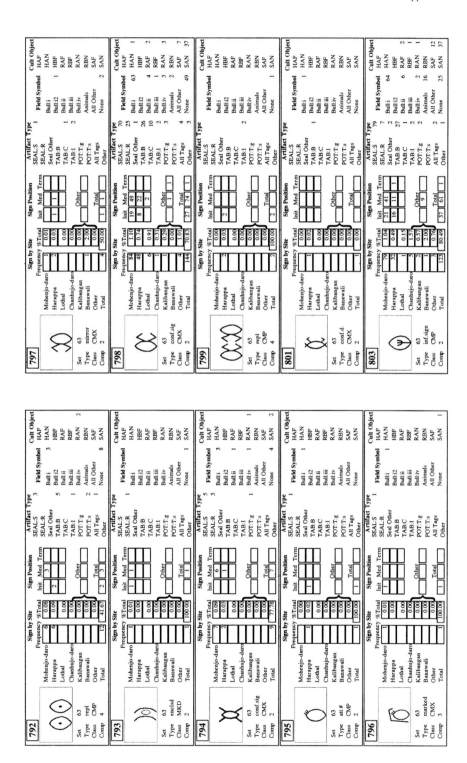

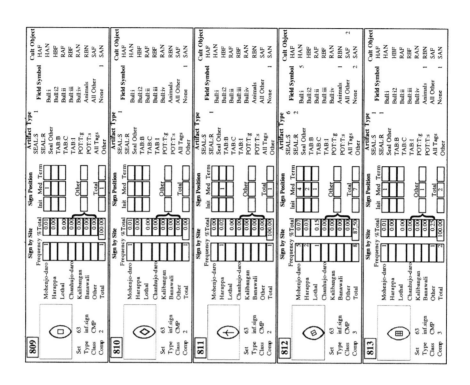

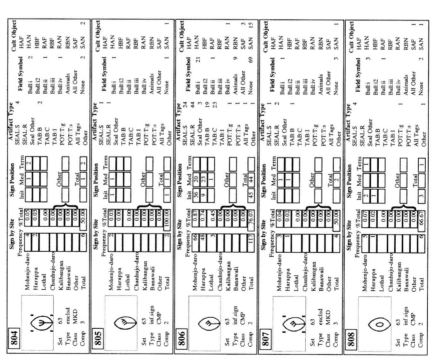

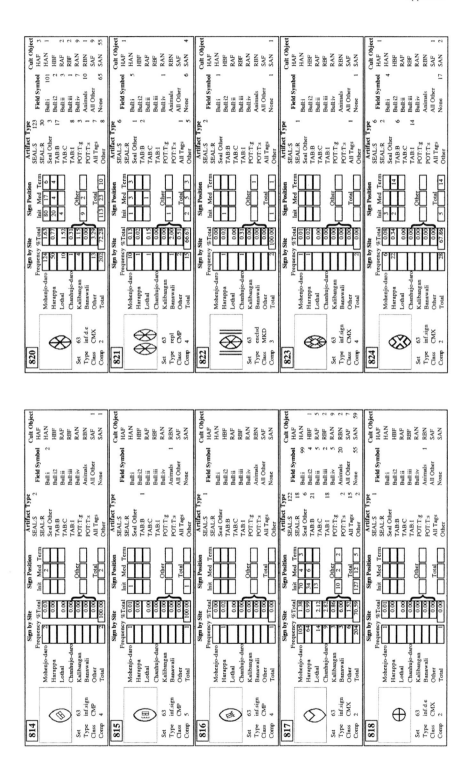

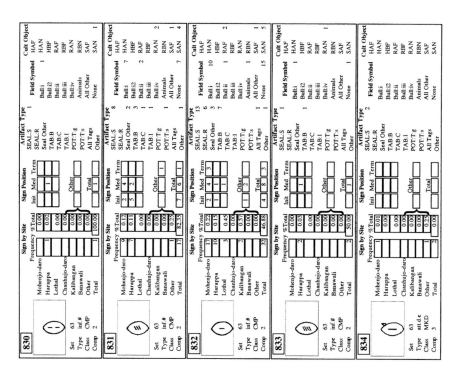

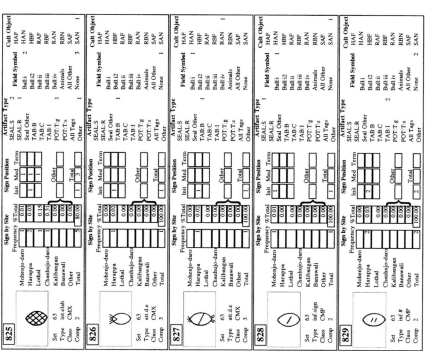

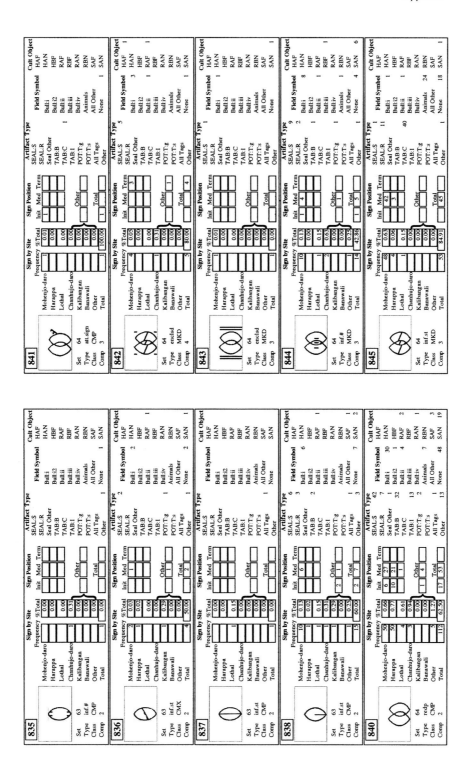

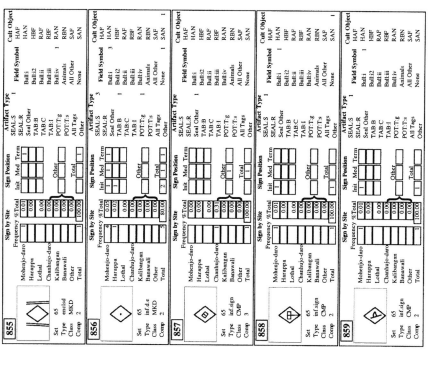

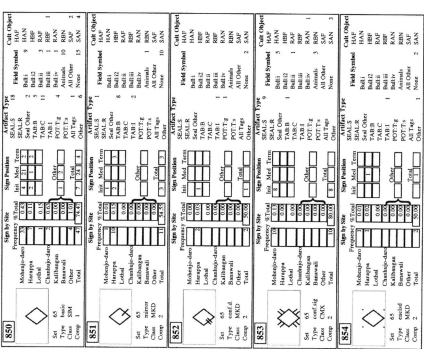

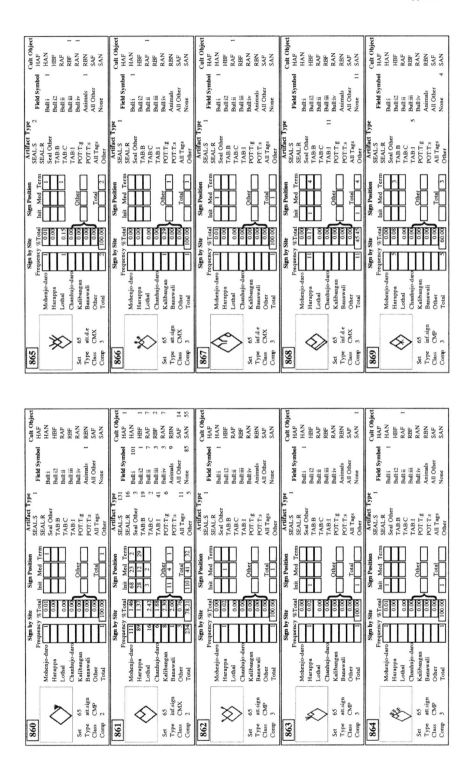

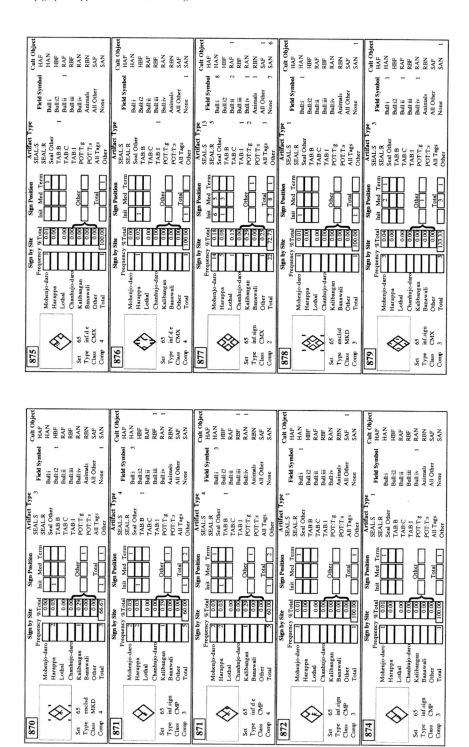

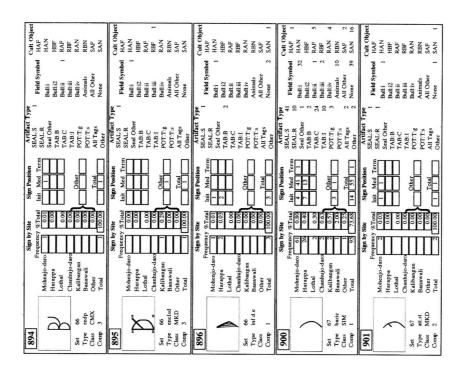

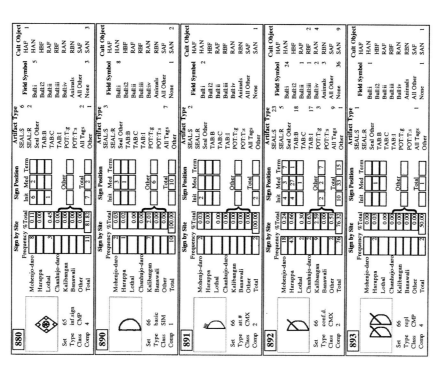

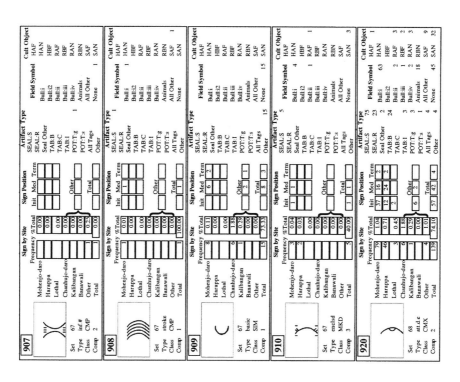

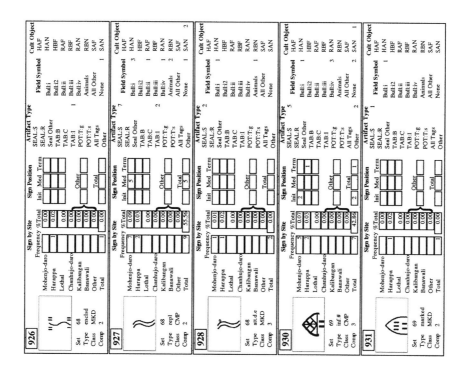

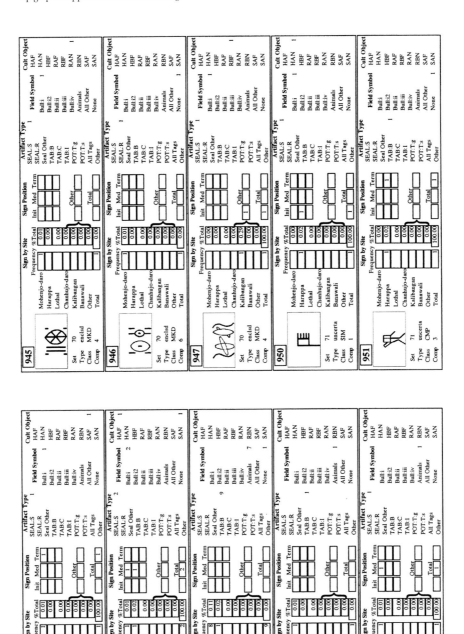

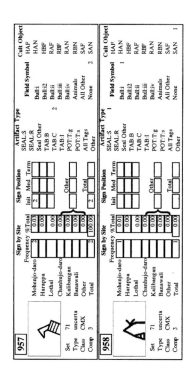

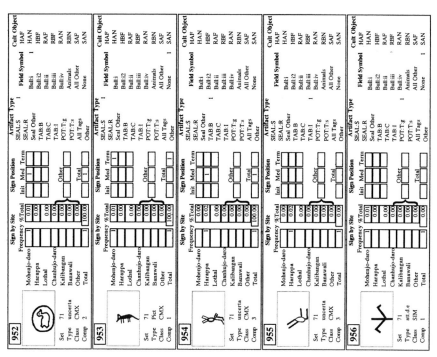

References

Anderson, G.
2001 Recent advances in Proto-Munda and Proto-Austroasiatic Reconstruction. Paper presented at the 3rd Harvard South Asia Ethnogenesis Round Table. Cambridge, MA.

Bonta, Steve
1995 Study of the Indus Valley Script. Master of Arts, Brigham Young University.

Bottéro, F.
2004 Writing on shell and bone in Shang China. In *The First Writing*, edited by S. Houston. Cambridge University Press, New York.

Brice, W. C.
1970 The Copenhagen Decipherment of the Proto-Indic Script. *Kadmos* IX:22-27.

Chadwick, John
1987 *Linear B and Related Scripts.* University of California Press, Berkeley and Los Angeles, CA.

Coe, Michael D., and Mark Van Stone
2001 *Reading The Maya Glyphs.* Thames and Hudson, London.

Coulmas, Florian
2003 *Writing Systems: An Introduction to Their Linguistic Analysis.* Cambridge University Press, Cambridge.

Dahl, J. L.
2005 *Complex Graphemes in Proto-Elamite.* Cuneiform Digital Library Journal (CDLJ).

Dales, G. F.
1979 Archaeological and radiocarbon chronologies for protohistoric south Asia. In *Ancient Cities Of The Indus*, edited by G. L. Possehl, pp. 332-338. Carolina Academic Press, Durham.

Danials, Peter D., and W. Bright
1996 *The World's Writing Systems.* Oxford University Press, New York.

Demerow, Peter, and Robert K. Englund
1989 *Proto-Elamite Texts from Tepe Yahya.* Peabody Museum of Archaeology and Ethnology, Cambridge, MA.

Fairservis, Walter A., Jr.

1956 Excavations in the Quetta Valley, West Pakistan. *Anthropology Papers of the American Museum of Natural History, New York* 45(2):169–402.

1959 Archaeological surveys in the Zhob and Loralai districts, west Pakistan. *Anthropology Papers of the American Museum of Natural History, New York* 47(2):277–448.

1971 *The Roots Of Ancient India: The Archaeology of Early Indian Civilization*. The MacMillan Company, New York.

1976 *Excavations at Allahdino*, New York.

1992 *The Harappan Civilization and Its Writing: A Model for the Decipherment of the Indus Script*. Oxford and IBH Publishing Co. PVT. Ltd., New Delhi.

Freiberg, Joran

1999 Counting and Accounting in the Proto-Literate Middle East. *Journal Cuneiform Studies* 51:106–137.

Frenez, Dennys, and Maurizio Tosi

2005 The Lothal Sealings: Records from and Indus civilization town at the eastern end of the maritime trade circuits across the Arabian Sea. In *Studi in Onore di Enrica Fiandra Studi Egei I Vicinorientali I Paris: Diffusion de Boccard*, edited by M. Perna, pp. 65–103.

Jarrige, Catherine, Jean-Francois Jarrige, Richard H. Meadow, and Gonzague Quivron (eds.)

1995 *Mehrgarh: Field Reports 1974–1985*. Department of Culture and Tourism, Government of Sindh, Pakistan, Karachi.

Gupta, S. P.

1995 *The Lost Sarasvati and the Indus Civilization*. Kusumanjali Prakashan, Jodhpur.

Hakemi, Ali

1997 *Shahdad*. Medio ed Estremo Oriente Centro Scavi E Ricerche Arceologiche, Rome.

Hall, R. N., and W. G. Neal

1902 *The Ancient Ruins of Rhodesia*. Methuen and Co., London.

Houston, Stephen D., and Michael D. Coe

2003 Has Isthmian writing been deciphered? *Mexicon* Vol. XXV:151–161

Hunter, G. R.

1934 *The Script of Harappa and Mohenjodaro and its Connection With Other Scripts*. Kegan Paul, Trench, Trubner and Co. Ltd., London.

Jansen, Michael, and G. Urban

1983 *Reports on Field Work Carried out at Mohenjo-Daro. Interim Reports Vol. 1*. IsMEO-Aachen-University.

1985 *Mohenjo-Daro: Report of the Aachen University Mission 1979–1985*. E. J. Brill, Leiden.

Jha, N., and N. S. Rajaram

2000 *The Deciphered Indus Script.* Aditya Prakashan, New Delhi.

Joshi, Jagat Pati, and Asko Parpola

1987 *Corpus of Indus Seals and Inscriptions.* Suomalainen Tiedeakatemia, Helsinki.

Kelley, David H.

1976 *Deciphering the Maya Script.* University of Texas Press, Austin.

1982 The Puuc in perspective. In *Puuc Symposium 1977*, edited by L. Mills. Central College, Pella.

Kelley, David H., and Bryan Wells

1995 Recent developments in understanding the Indus Script. *The Quarterly Review of Archaeology* 16.

Kenoyer, J. Mark

1991 The Indus Valley tradition of Pakistan and western India. *Journal of World Prehistory* 5:1-58.

1998 *Ancient Cities of the Indus Valley Civilization.* Oxford University Press, Oxford.

1996 *New Inscribed Objects from Harappa.* Lahore Museum Bulletin, IX(1). Lahore.

Knorozov, Yuri

1968 *Proto-Indica: Brief Report on the Investigation of the Proto-Indian Texts.* Academy of Sciences of the USSR, Moscow.

1970 The formal analysis of the Proto-Indian texts. *Journal of Tamil Studies* II:13-28.

Kober, Alice E.

1946 Inflection In Linear Class B: 1-Declension. *American Journal of Archaeology* 50:268-276.

1948 The Minoan scripts: Fact and theory. *American Journal of Archaeology* 52:82-103.

Koskenniemi, K.

1981 Syntactic methods in the study of the Indus script. Paper presented at Proceedings of the Nordic South Asia Conference.

Koskenniemi, K., and Asko Parpola

1979 *Corpus of Texts in the Indus Script.* Department of Asian and African Studies University of Helsinki, Helsinki.

Koskenniemi, K., Asko Parpola, and Simo Parpola

1970 A method to classify characters of unknown ancient scripts. *Linguistics* 61:65-91

Kwong-Yue, Cheung (ed.)

1983 *Recent Archaeological Evidence Relating to the Origin of Chinese Characters.* University of California Press, Berkeley.

Lal, B. B.

1962 From the megalithic to Harappa: Tracing back the graffiti on the pottery. *Ancient India: Bulletin of the Archaeological Survey of India* 2-24.

1975 The Indus Script: Some observations based on archaeology. *Journal of the Royal Asiatic Society* (2)172-177.

1979 On the most frequently used symbol in the Indus Script. *East And West* 29:27-35.

Mackay, E. J. H.

1938 *Further Excavations at Mohenjo-daro.* Munshiram Manoharlal Publishers Pvt. Ltd., Delhi.

Mahadevan, Iravatham

1970 Dravidian parallels in Proto-Indian Script. *Journal of Tamil Studies* 2:157-276.

1977 *The Indus Script, Texts Concordance and Tables.* Archaeological Survey of India, New Delhi.

1982 *Terminal Ideograms in the Indus Script.* Oxford and IBH Publishing Co, New Delhi.

1986 Dravidian Models Of Decipherment Of The Indus Script: A Case Study. *Tamil Civilization* 4:133-143.

Marshall, Sir John

1931 *Mohenjo-daro and the Indus Civilization.* Arthur Probsthian, London.

Masica, C. P.

1979 Aryan and Non-Aryan elements in north Indian agriculture. In *Aryan and Non-Aryan in India*, edited by M. Deshpande and P. E. Hook, pp. 55-151. University of Michigan, Ann Arbor.

McAlpin, David W.

1981 *Proto-Elamo-Dravidian: The Evidence and its Implications.* The American Philosophical Society, Philadelphia.

Meadow, Richard H., and J. M. Kenoyer

1993 *Harappa Archaeological Research Project: 1993 Excavations.* Director General of Archaeology and Museums.

2001 *Recent Discoveries and Highlights from Excavations at Harappa: 1998-2000.* Indo Koko Kenkyu No. 22. Indian Archaeological Society, Tokyo.

Meadow, Richard H., J. M. Kenoyer, and Rita P. Wright

1994 Harappa Excavation 1994. Director General of Archaeology and Museums.

1995 Harappa Excavation 1995. Director General of Archaeology and Museums.

1996 Harappa Excavation 1996. Director General of Archaeology and Museums.

1997 Harappa Excavation 1997. Director General of Archaeology and Museums.

1998 Harappa Excavation 1998. Director General of Archaeology and Museums.

1999 Harappa Excavation 1999. Director General of Archaeology and Museums.

2001 Harappa Excavation 2000 and 2001. Director General of Archaeology and Museums.

Mughal, M. Rafique

1997 *Ancient Cholistan: Achaeology and Architecture.* Ferozsons (pvt.) Ltd., Lahore.

Nissen, Hans J., Peter Damerow, and Robert K. Englund

1993 *Archaic Bookkeeping: Early Writing and Techniques of Economic Administration in the Ancient Near East.* The University of Chicago Press, London.

Parpola, Asko

1970 The Indus Script decipherment: The situation at the end of 1969. *Journal of Tamil Studies* II:89-110.

1994 *Deciphering the Indus Script.* Cambridge University Press, Cambridge.

Petrie, W. M. Flinders

1901 *Diospolis Parva: The Cemeteries Of Abadiyeh And Hu 1898-9.* The Offices Of The Egypt Exploration Fund, Boston.

Possehl, Gregory L.

1984 Archaeological terminology and the Harappan civilization. In *Frontiers Of The Indus Civilization,* edited by B. B. Lal and S. P. Gupta, pp. 27-36. I.M. Sharma of Books and Books, Janakpuri, New Delhi.

1996a *Indus Age: The Writing System.* University Of Pennsylvania Press, Philadelphia.

2002a *The Indus Civilization: A Contemporary Perspective.* Altamira Press, New York.

Potts, D. T.

1981 The Potter's Marks Of Tepe Yahya. *Paleorient* 7:107-122.

1982 The role of the Indo-Iranian borderland in the formation of the Harappan writing system. *dell' Istituto Universitanio Orentale d' Napoli* 42:513-519.

Quivron, Gonzague

1997 *Incised and Painted Marks on the Pottery of Mehrgarh and Nausharo-Baluchistan. South Asian Archaeology 1995,* edited by R. A. Alchin and B. Alchin. HBH, New Delhi, and Oxford.

Rao, S. R.

1973 *Lothal And The Indus Civilization.* Asia Publishing House, New York.

1984 New light on Indus script and language. In *Frontiers Of The Indus Civilization,* edited by B. B. Lal and S. P. Gupta, pp. 193-200. I. M. Sharma of Books and Books, New Delhi.

Ratnagar, Shereen

1981 *Encounters: The Westerly Trade of the Harappan Civilization.* Oxford University Press, Delhi.

Rissman, Paul

1989 *The Organization of Seal Production in the Harappan Civilization.* Wisconsin Archaeological Report No. 2s, Old Problems and New Perspectives in the Archaeological of South Asia. University of Wisconsin, Department of Anthropology, Madison.

Shah, Sayid Ghulam Mustafa, and Asko Parpola

1991 *Corpus of Indus Seals and Inscriptions.* Soumalainen Tiedeakatemia, Helsinki.

Shendge, Malati J.

1997 *The Language of the Harappans: From Akkadian to Sanskrit.* Abhinav Publications, New Delhi.

Vats, Madho Sarup

1940 *Excavations at Harappa.* Munshiram Manoharlal Publishers Pvt. Ltd., Delhi.

Ventris, Michael and John Chadwick

1953 Evidence for Greek dialect in the Mycenaean archives. *The Journal of Hellenic Studies* 73:84-103.

Wells, Bryan

1999 *An Introduction To Indus Writing.* Early Site Research Foundation, Independence.

2001 The geographic distribution of Indus signs. Paper presented at Third south Asian ethnogenesis Round Table, Harvard University.

2002 A systematic approach to defining Indus graphemes. Paper presented at Fourth south Asian ethnogenesis Round Table, Harvard University.

Winn, Shan M. M.

1981 Pre-Writing. In *Southeastern Europe: The Sign System Of The Vinca Culture ca 4000 B C.* Western Publishers, Calgary.

Witzel, Michael

1999 Early sources for south Asian substrate languages. Paper presented at the 1st South Asian Ethnogenesis Conference. Cambridge, MA.

Zauzich, Karl-Theodor

1992 *Hieroglyphics Without Mystery.* University of Texas Press.

Zvelebil, Kamil V.

1974 Dravidian and Elamite - A real break-through? *Journal of the American Oriental Society* 94:384-385.

Index